Translational Systems Sciences

Volume 17

In 1956, Kenneth Boulding explained the concept of General Systems Theory as a skeleton of science. He describes that it hopes to develop something like a "spectrum" of theories—a system of systems which may perform the function of a "gestalt" in theoretical construction. Such "gestalts" in special fields have been of great value in directing research towards the gaps which they reveal.

There were, at that time, other important conceptual frameworks and theories, such as cybernetics. Additional theories and applications developed later, including synergetics, cognitive science, complex adaptive systems, and many others. Some focused on principles within specific domains of knowledge and others crossed areas of knowledge and practice, along the spectrum described by Boulding.

Also in 1956, the Society for General Systems Research (now the International Society for the Systems Sciences) was founded. One of the concerns of the founders, even then, was the state of the human condition, and what science could do about it.

The present Translational Systems Sciences book series aims at cultivating a new frontier of systems sciences for contributing to the need for practical applications that benefit people.

The concept of translational research originally comes from medical science for enhancing human health and well-being. Translational medical research is often labeled as "Bench to Bedside." It places emphasis on translating the findings in basic research (at bench) more quickly and efficiently into medical practice (at bedside). At the same time, needs and demands from practice drive the development of new and innovative ideas and concepts. In this tightly coupled process it is essential to remove barriers to multi-disciplinary collaboration.

The present series attempts to bridge and integrate basic research founded in systems concepts, logic, theories and models with systems practices and methodologies, into a process of systems research. Since both bench and bedside involve diverse stakeholder groups, including researchers, practitioners and users, translational systems science works to create common platforms for language to activate the "bench to bedside" cycle.

In order to create a resilient and sustainable society in the twenty-first century, we unquestionably need open social innovation through which we create new social values, and realize them in society by connecting diverse ideas and developing new solutions. We assume three types of social values, namely: (1) values relevant to social infrastructure such as safety, security, and amenity; (2) values created by innovation in business, economics, and management practices; and, (3) values necessary for community sustainability brought about by conflict resolution and consensus building.

The series will first approach these social values from a systems science perspective by drawing on a range of disciplines in trans-disciplinary and cross-cultural ways. They may include social systems theory, sociology, business administration, management information science, organization science, computational mathematical organization theory, economics, evolutionary economics, international political science, jurisprudence, policy science, socioinformation studies, cognitive science, artificial intelligence, complex adaptive systems theory, philosophy of science, and other related disciplines. In addition, this series will promote translational systems science as a means of scientific research that facilitates the translation of findings from basic science to practical applications, and vice versa.

We believe that this book series should advance a new frontier in systems sciences by presenting theoretical and conceptual frameworks, as well as theories for design and application, for twenty-first-century socioeconomic systems in a translational and transdisciplinary context.

More information about this series at http://www.springer.com/series/11213

Akira Tajino
Editors

A Systems Approach to Language Pedagogy

Springer

Editor
Akira Tajino
Department of British and American Studies
Nagoya University of Foreign Studies
Aichi, Japan

Kyoto University
Kyoto, Japan

ISSN 2197-8832 ISSN 2197-8840 (electronic)
Translational Systems Sciences
ISBN 978-981-13-6271-2 ISBN 978-981-13-6272-9 (eBook)
https://doi.org/10.1007/978-981-13-6272-9

Library of Congress Control Number: 2019935852

This Springer imprint is published by the registered company Springer Nature Singapore Pte Ltd.
The registered company address is: 152 Beach Road, #21-01/04 Gateway East, Singapore 189721, Singapore

Foreword

It is with pleasure that I am able to introduce this new addition to our Translation Systems Sciences series. This volume represents the collaborative efforts of Dr. Akira Tajino and his research associates at Kyoto University, as well as distinguished scholars from other institutions in Japan, including Dr. Hajime Terauchi, President of the Japan Association of College English Teachers (JACET). All of the contributors have extensive experience in language teaching, research, and practice at various institutions and in various capacities.

This volume, unique in the field of both educational linguistics and education in general, presents a systems approach to language pedagogy, amalgamating various research areas that have traditionally been approached separately. Recognizing among practitioners and researchers a need to frame individual research disciplines in the "bigger picture" of language pedagogy as a whole, Professor Tajino achieves this adeptly in his application of principles from my field, systems science and systems thinking. His introductory chapter is supported by his colleagues' chapters, each of which may be read as a stand-alone entry or as part of a whole in this comprehensive work.

When I first met Professor Tajino on the campus of Lancaster University in the UK, about 35 years ago, we were both already grappling with the ideas and concepts that would shape our research in the years to come. Since then, we have collaborated to develop the common curriculum of English for Academic Purposes (EAP) at Kyoto University, aspects of which have been published in the journal, *Journal of English for Academic Purposes* (Elsevier, 2005), and in the volume, *The Future of University English Education* (Iwanami Shoten, 2005). Professor Tajino is a leading researcher in the field of EAP and was director of Kyoto University's International Academic Research and Resource Center for Language Education until March 2018 and is thus intimately aware of the multifaceted nature of language education.

Like any other human activity system, language education is, of course, an undertaking with various stakeholders. Concerned parties not only include students and teachers but also administrative and support staff, policymakers, and the taxpayers who fund them, each bringing with them a multitude of values and opinions.

Acutely aware of the fact that both language and pedagogy are inherently human endeavors, Professor Tajino and his research associates have come together in this project to apply systems thinking in developing a more accessible understanding of the complexities of language education which remains cognizant of the human element. They not only compile into this volume the essence of their theoretical research and practices in language education so far but also advance the enterprise.

I trust that this volume will be of benefit to a wide variety of stakeholders in language education and be a valuable resource for teachers, teacher trainers, and course coordinators. Furthermore, I sincerely hope that this work will stimulate further discussions on language pedagogy and encourage greater interdisciplinary collaboration.

Translational Systems Sciences,
Professor Emeritus,
Tokyo Institute of Technology
Daito Bunka University,
Tokyo, Japan
1 November 2018

Kyoichi Kijima

Preface

A Systems Approach to Language Pedagogy: Why This Book Now?

To create a deeper and more holistic understanding of issues that surround language pedagogy, or more specifically foreign language pedagogy, the present volume uses a systems approach to organize relevant issues in a more accessible manner for all of its stakeholders and to further develop areas of related research.

Language Pedagogy as a Human Activity System

Language pedagogy can be viewed as a complex human activity system. It involves a number of stakeholders, such as teachers, students, and administrators, in a single educational organization. In such an organization, interaction can take place among the stakeholders in different groups, and decisions may be made at different functional levels through communication for a common purpose, i.e., making language pedagogy more relevant and meaningful to everyone involved.

It seems undebatable that the roles of the stakeholders in language pedagogy are naturally interrelated. In practice, however, complexity in communication arises in human activity systems when different stakeholders follow their own individual agendas and function in separate structures. It is our belief that communication could be improved between *silos* by the adoption of a systems approach (see Chapter "Toward Managing Language Pedagogy and Language Teaching Research").

This communication may often take place in situations in which a variety of classroom factors, such as student motivation and teaching methodologies, interact with one another in a complex and sometimes unexpected manner. Furthermore, the complexity of the entire human activity system is compounded by the demands placed on all of its stakeholders to work together for a common purpose.

Arranging Language Pedagogy for Communicative Purposes

It is essential to clarify what is expected of the system's stakeholders. As Hasan (1988) suggests, human communication can be developed by the so-called five Ws and one H, i.e., who, what, where, when, why, and how. With these communication starting points, we can begin to arrange the elements of language pedagogy. Interestingly enough, these can also be organized in a simple and straightforward manner with a canonical, meaning-based clause-structure pattern of English. We discuss the applicability of this human activity system for language pedagogy that follows the English language clause-structure pattern in Chapter "Teaching English Grammar for Communicative Purposes: A Systems Approach".

We aim to arrange the complex phenomena of language pedagogy in a way which helps to clarify the relative positions of each of these and systematize the phenomena from a wider yet unified perspective. Combining the component parts of current foreign language pedagogy in different ways may create a new inter-component research area in language pedagogy which can offer an alternative to the limited communication that is endemic among stakeholders of intra-component research, also known as the silo effect (see, e.g., Tett 2015).

Viewing Language Pedagogy from a Holistic Perspective

We, practitioners and researchers, often do not recognize the relationships and relative positions of each of our individual research areas and classroom teaching experiences. We travel determinedly along on a single pathway shared by our research field colleagues and fellow teachers. The result being that we are able to go into greater depth and detail and share breakthrough insights within our separate groups.

This is crucial, of course, on its own—as research. However, true breakthroughs can only be achieved if the whole picture of language pedagogy is mutually understood, since it is a complex phenomenon. In doing so, we are able to create a common field for investigations by researchers and practitioners by combining the component parts of language pedagogy, e.g., the nature of language acquisition, pedagogical grammar, vocabulary teaching, etc.

The Outline of This Volume

Understanding the above situation, and in an attempt to bring together the somewhat disparate but nevertheless interrelated fields in language education, this volume also structures itself within the 5W1H framework (Fig. 1).

WHO	DOES	WHOM	WHAT	WHERE	WHEN	HOW	WHY
Teachers	**teach**	**language learners with L1 knowledge (Ch 2)**	**grammar (Ch 3)**	**in the classroom (Ch 5)**	**throughout life (Ch 6)**	**by instructional design (Ch 7)**	**for specific purposes. (Ch 10)**
			vocabulary (Ch 4)			**by team teaching (Ch 8)**	
						through collaboration (Ch 9)	

Fig. 1 Managing language pedagogy: An outline

Chapter "Toward Managing Language Pedagogy and Language Teaching Research" is an overview that expands upon some of the issues raised in this preface, illuminating further the reasons why it is relevant to reevaluate these issues now. Chapter "Language Acquisition: A Systemic View from Cognitive Linguistics" deals with the *whom* of teaching, our learners. It illustrates the process of language acquisition and instruction through a comparison of the similarities and differences between first and second language learning and teaching. Chapters "Teaching English Grammar for Communicative Purposes: A Systems Approach" and "Vocabulary Teaching: A Systemic Perspective" deal with the *what* (the linguistic content) of instruction, presenting a systems approach to grammar instruction and integrating soft systems methodology into vocabulary teaching, respectively. Chapter "Surveying the Landscape of Second Language Classroom Research" examines the *where*, with both the nature of the classroom and the sources of practitioner research given a thorough treatise. Chapter "A Soft Systems Approach to Lifelong Learning" revisits *when* we learn, with a particular focus on lifelong learning. A discussion of *how* to look at course design from an SSM viewpoint is addressed in Chapter "A "Softer" Instructional Systems Design for Language Pedagogy", while Chapter "Team Teaching and Team Learning: SSM Applied to the Team-Taught Classroom" utilizes a soft systems approach to teacher collaboration. Chapter "Interaction in the Language Classroom: A Systems Approach" also investigates *how,* but from the position that SSM can facilitate learner cooperation and collaboration. Finally, Chapter "Systems Thinking: An ESP Genre Approach" addresses the *why* of language learning and teaching through the lens of language for specific purposes.

Of course, the content introduced in the chapters listed above is by no means an exhaustive account of all of the fields of foreign language pedagogy. Nevertheless, it is hoped that by framing some of the key areas in this way, individual researchers may be aided in situating their own research, and communication between individual research areas might be encouraged, leading to new and more fruitful collaboration with even richer emergent properties.

I hope this book can provide an opportunity for readers to see the whole picture of foreign language pedagogy and create for themselves, by means of a systems approach, a new way of connecting its component parts.

Kyoto, Japan
10 December 2018

Akira Tajino

References

Hasan, R. (1988). The analysis of one poem: Theoretical issues in practice. In D. Birch & M. O'Tool (Eds.), *Functions and styles* (pp. 45–73). London: Edward Arnold.

Tett, G. (2015). *The silo effect: The peril of expertise and the promise of breaking down barriers.* New York: Simon & Schuster.

Contents

About the Editor and Contributors

Editor

Akira Tajino Ph.D., Professor Emeritus at Kyoto University, is currently Professor of Educational Linguistics at Nagoya University of Foreign Studies, Japan. His research interests include English for Academic Purposes (EAP), classroom research, and pedagogical grammar. He was formerly the Director of International Academic Research and Resource Center for Language Education at Kyoto University and is a Recipient of the JACET (Japan Association of College English Teachers) Award for Excellence in Teaching (2011) and the JACET Award for Excellence in Academic Publication (2014). He is the (co)author/editor of more than 20 books, including *Researching Language Teaching and Learning: An Integration of Practice and Theory* (Peter Lang, 2009), *Team Teaching and Team Learning in the Language Classroom: Collaboration for Innovation in ELT* (Routledge, 2016), and *A New Approach to English Pedagogical Grammar: The Order of Meanings* (Routledge, 2018). He has served on the editorial panel of several journals, including *ELT Journal* (Oxford University Press). e-mail: tajino@nufs.ac.jp

Contributors

David Dalsky Ph.D., is Associate Professor of Social Psychology and a founding member of the International Academic Research and Resource Center for Language Education (i-ARRC) at Kyoto University. He is interested in using EAP, Exploratory Practice, and Team Learning for e-classroom intercultural collaborative projects, which involve materials development related to indigenous psychological concepts in Japan, China, Indonesia, and Germany. e-mail: dalsky.davidjerome.8u@kyoto.u.ac.jp

Kyoko Hosogoshi Ph.D., is currently Associate Professor at the Faculty of Letters at Kyoto Prefectural University. She has taught on EAP courses at various universities in Japan. Her research interests include academic listening instruction utilizing advance organizers and textual information. She has also investigated skill-integrated tasks for task-based language teaching. e-mail: hosogoshi@kpu.ac.jp

Toshiyuki Kanamaru is Associate Professor in the International Academic Research and Resource Center for Language Education at Kyoto University. He holds a Ph.D. in Human and Environmental Studies from Kyoto University. His research interests include cognitive linguistics, natural language processing, vocabulary acquisition, and academic writing teaching. e-mail: kanamaru@hi.h.kyoto-u.ac.jp

Yoshitaka Kato Ph.D., is Lecturer in the Faculty of General Education at Chubu University, Japan. He teaches EAP classes utilizing various small group activities. His research interests include classroom research, cooperative and collaborative language learning, and task-based language education. e-mail: kato44taka@isc.chubu.ac.jp

Sayako Maswana Ph.D., is Associate Professor of Applied Linguistics at Mejiro University, Tokyo. She is currently conducting research on genre analysis. She has published articles in journals such as the *Journal of Asia TEFL*, *Ampersand*, and *Asian ESP Journal*.

Daniel Roy Pearce is Doctoral Candidate at the Graduate School of Human and Environmental Studies, Kyoto University. He has 5 years of teaching experience at the secondary level in the Yamagata Prefecture of northeast Japan and has been a summer Lecturer at Nara Women's University. His research interests include team teaching, teacher training, and pedagogical grammar. e-mail: pearce.roy.26e@st.kyoto-u.ac.jp

Yosuke Sasao Ph.D., is Associate Professor of Applied Linguistics in the Institute for Liberal Arts and Sciences at Kyoto University, Japan. His research interests include vocabulary acquisition, language assessment, pedagogical grammar, and academic writing. His articles have been published in journals such as *ITL-International Journal of Applied Linguistics*, *Language Teaching Research*, and *Language Testing*. e-mail: sasao.yosuke.8n@kyoto-u.ac.jp

Craig Smith was Professor and Director of the Community Engagement Center at Kyoto University of Foreign Studies, Japan. He received the 2011 Japan Association of College English Teachers Award for Excellence in Teaching. He authored and coauthored papers in books and international journals, including *Language Teaching Research* (SAGE, 2005) and *Team Teaching and Team Learning in the Language Classroom: Collaboration for Innovation in ELT* (Routledge, 2016).

Ryan W. Smithers is Associate Professor in the Department of Intercultural Studies at Otani University, Japan. He is also currently a Ph.D. candidate at Kyoto University and Chief Editor for the *Osaka JALT Journal*. His 20 years of TEFL experience have inspired his research interests in pedagogical grammar, reflective practice, and lifelong learning. e-mail: ryansmithers@gmail.com

Tim Stewart is Professor of TESOL at Kyoto University in Japan and a founding Faculty Member of the International Academic Research and Resource Center. He has been supervising graduate students' classroom research for over 10 years and has published on TESOL classroom research, team learning, team teaching, and professional development. He has served as an Editor for TESOL International Association journals and books since 2006. Most recently, he was the Series Editor for the six-book series TESOL Voices (TESOL Press). e-mail: stewart.timothywilliam.3m@kyoto-u.ac.jp

Akira Tajino Ph.D., Professor Emeritus at Kyoto University, is currently Professor of Educational Linguistics at Nagoya University of Foreign Studies, Japan. His research interests include English for Academic Purposes (EAP), classroom research, and pedagogical grammar. He was formerly the Director of International Academic Research and Resource Center for Language Education at Kyoto University and is a Recipient of the JACET (Japan Association of College English Teachers) Award for Excellence in Teaching (2011) and the JACET Award for Excellence in Academic Publication (2014). He is the (co)author/editor of more than 20 books, including *Researching Language Teaching and Learning: An Integration of Practice and Theory* (Peter Lang, 2009), *Team Teaching and Team Learning in the Language Classroom: Collaboration for Innovation in ELT* (Routledge, 2016), and *A New Approach to English Pedagogical Grammar: The Order of Meanings* (Routledge, 2018). He has served on the editorial panel of several journals, including *ELT Journal* (Oxford University Press). e-mail: tajino@nufs.ac.jp

Sachi Takahashi is currently Associate Professor in the International Academic Research and Resource Center for Language Education (i-ARRC) at Kyoto University, Japan. She received her M.A. and Ph.D. in International Cultural Studies from Tohoku University. Her research interests include instructional design, EAP, TBLT, materials development, and e-Learning. e-mail: takahashi.sachi.4n@kyoto-u.ac.jp

Kazumi Taniguchi Ph.D., is Professor of Cognitive Linguistics at Kyoto University. She received a doctorate from Osaka University in 2004. After teaching at the Faculty of Education at Osaka Kyoiku University for 13 years, she moved to the Graduate School of Human and Environmental Studies at Kyoto University in 2012 and there has been teaching classes of general English and cognitive linguistics. e-mail: taniguchi.kazumi.8n@kyoto-u.ac.jp

Hajime Terauchi Ph.D., is Professor of English Language and Dean of the Faculty of Commerce, Takachiho University, Tokyo. He has a B.A. in Civil Law (Keio University, Japan), an M.A. in English Language Teaching (University of Warwick, UK), and a Ph.D. in English Language Teaching (University of Warwick, UK). He is President of the Japan Association of College English Teachers (JACET). e-mail: hajime7272@gmail.com

Toward Managing Language Pedagogy and Language Teaching Research

Akira Tajino, Craig Smith, and Toshiyuki Kanamaru

Abstract This chapter provides the rationale for applying a systems approach to language pedagogy; presents a case study in which soft systems methodology (SSM), a type of soft systems approach, was applied to language curriculum development; and attempts to manage language teaching research from a communicative perspective. In doing so, it argues that language pedagogy is a complex phenomenon in which various factors affect one another in complex ways. By referring to language teaching research that investigates the nature of the factors of language pedagogy, it also argues that due to lack of communication among the research areas in the field, each of the discrete research topics has been discussed individually within the confines of those research areas, often resulting in the so-called silo effect.

Keywords Language pedagogy · Language teaching research · Soft systems methodology (SSM) · Silo effect

Introduction: Why We Need a Systems Approach

Language pedagogy involves numerous factors that interact with one another in complex ways. As such, it is important to consider "who teaches whom, what, where, when, how (in what ways), and why (for what purposes)." Furthermore, it is crucial to examine these factors systemically or from a holistic perspective.

A. Tajino (✉)
Department of British and American Studies, Nagoya University of Foreign Studies, Aichi, Japan

Kyoto University, Kyoto, Japan
e-mail: tajino@nufs.ac.jp

C. Smith
Department of Global Affairs, Kyoto University of Foreign Studies, Kyoto, Japan

T. Kanamaru
International Academic Research and Resource Center for Language Education, Kyoto University, Kyoto, Japan
e-mail: kanamaru@hi.h.kyoto-u.ac.jp

A. Tajino (ed.), *A Systems Approach to Language Pedagogy*, Translational Systems Sciences 17, https://doi.org/10.1007/978-981-13-6272-9_1

Language Pedagogy as a Human Activity System

Language pedagogy, with all of its interconnected factors, can be viewed as a system or, more specifically, a human activity system that involves a number of stakeholders, such as teachers, students, and administrators, in a single educational organization:

> A system is an interconnected set of elements that is coherently organized in a way that achieves something. … a system must consist of three kinds of things: elements, interconnections, and a function or purpose. (Meadows 2008, p. 11)

It is thus important to note that:

> [S]ystems ideas concern interaction between parts which make up a whole; also, the complexity of real situations is always to a large extent due to the many interactions between different elements in human situations. (Checkland and Poulter 2006, p. 7)

Just as a school can be viewed as a larger system that encompasses subsystems of classes and pupils, language pedagogy can be viewed as encompassing a number of subsystems such as teacher factors, learner factors, materials, and teaching environments. In other words, language pedagogy viewed as a human activity system has a layered structure as its fundamental feature, and its subsystems are expected to be interconnected and communicate with one another, so that the goal of the whole system can be achieved purposefully.

Examination of the real situation, however, reveals that language pedagogy has suffered from the so-called silo effect[1] (see Tett 2015); that is, while it seems undebatable that the roles of the stakeholders in language pedagogy are naturally interrelated, in practice, complexity in communication arises in human activity systems when different stakeholders follow their own individual agendas and function in separate structures. Furthermore, the complexity of the entire human activity system is compounded by the demands placed on all of its stakeholders to work together for a common purpose. It is our belief that the silo effect can be mitigated by the adoption of a systems approach, one that is elaborated upon in the following sections.

Soft Systems Methodology

Soft systems methodology (SSM), developed by Peter Checkland and his associates at Lancaster University in the 1970s, is an action research approach to problematical situations by means of which processes of enquiry and learning are organized

[1] The silo effect is a term used in business that describes a lack of communication between different sectors. In essence, when the effect occurs, individuals are isolated within their own *silos*, and thus cooperation is hampered.

(Connell 2001). Approaches to implementing SSM may vary widely, but the conceptual basis (e.g., Churchman 1968) remains constant.

In SSM it is recognized that different individuals have different, personally relevant, interpretations of the world. Therefore, it regards any cooperative or collaborative endeavor between individuals as human activity systems, each of which consists of a set of activities linked together in a logical structure to constitute a purposeful whole.

A human activity system is meant to be "a notional purposive system which expresses some purposeful human activity" (Checkland 1981, p. 314). It refers to a description of intellectual constructs, that is, systems thinking, a system which exists in our views or interpretations. It is therefore possible that different systems can be developed by envisaging a number of different worldviews. Intrinsic to these systems are *emergent properties*, which can be defined as:

> properties which are meaningful in relation to the whole entity, not in relation to its parts. The smell of ammonia is an emergent property of that gas which has no meaning at the level of the nitrogen and hydrogen which make up ammonia molecules. (Checkland 1983, p. 669)

SSM assumes that the unique emergent properties that any complex set of behaviors may give rise to can better be seen as characteristic of the system as a whole, rather than any particular part of it. SSM is thus viewed as a systemic (rather than systematic) methodology; i.e., its focus is on the whole, rather than on the parts.

Unlike hard systems thinking, the goal of which can be attained by hypothesis-testing experiments and thus would be appropriate for well-defined technical problems, SSM as an interpretive or *soft* systems thinking can be applied to "fuzzy ill-defined situations involving human beings and cultural considerations" (Checkland and Scholes 1990, p. 10). SSM can be helpful in exploring how we make sense of our perceived world so as to bring about manageable improvement.

From an SSM perspective, language pedagogy and language teaching research can each be regarded as a human activity system, a set of "linked activities which together could exhibit the emergent property of purposefulness" (Checkland and Scholes 1990, A7).

The traditional or classical procedure to implement SSM is a seven-stage model, which consists of two types of activities: real-world activities (Stages 1, 2, 5, 6, and 7) and systems thinking activities (Stages 3 and 4). As Fig. 1 shows, SSM first identifies problem situations (Stages 1 and 2); second, formulates from them a set of root definitions of relevant purposeful human activity systems (Stage 3); third, builds up conceptual models of the systems (Stage 4); fourth, compares the models with reality (Stage 5); fifth, makes changes that should be systematically desirable and culturally feasible (Stage 6); and finally, undertakes actions to improve the situations (Stage 7).

It should be noted, however, that not all of these stages need to be followed. SSM is characterized by flexibility in the structure of its prototype procedures. Different models may be designed for application to any group of people who are engaged in any collaborative communication situation (see Checkland 2001). This seven-stage model, for instance, can be implemented as the four-stage model shown in Fig. 2.

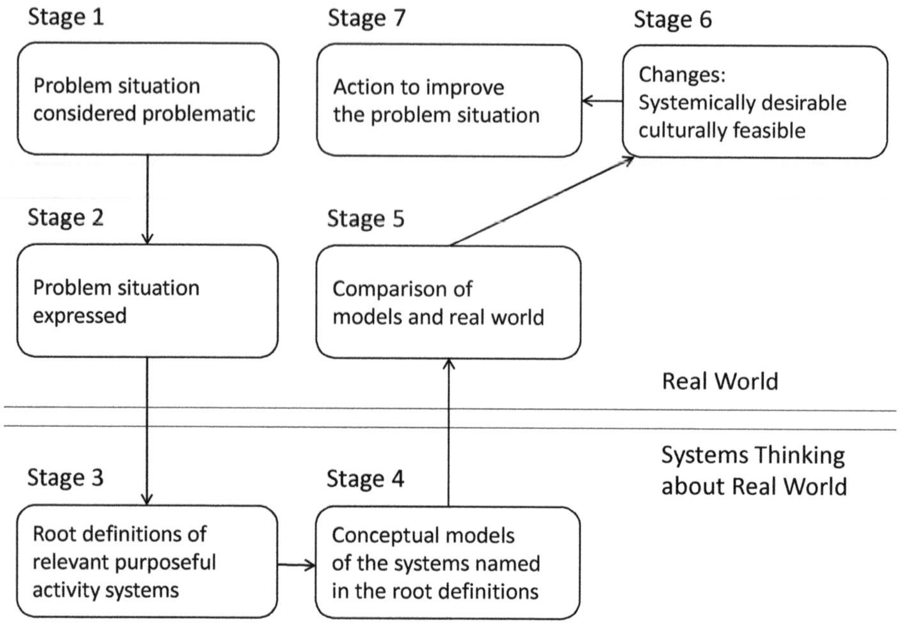

Fig. 1 The traditional seven-stage model of SSM. (Checkland and Scholes 1990, p. 27)

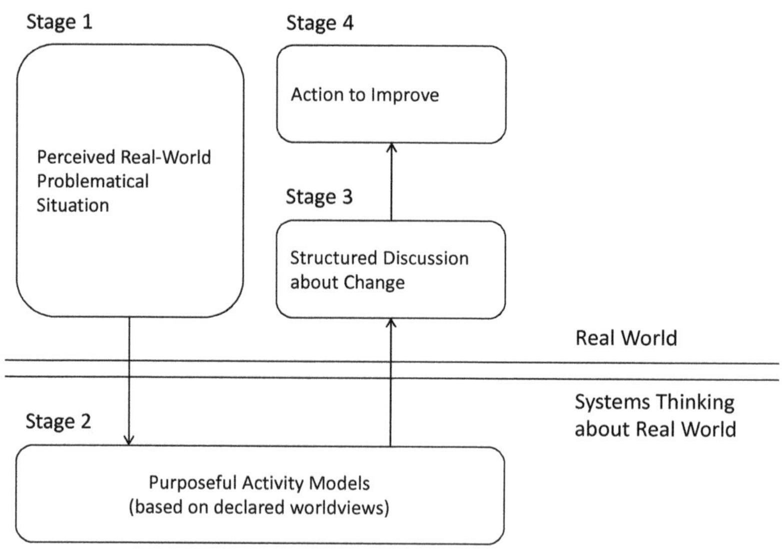

Fig. 2 The conventional four-stage model of SSM. (cf. Checkland and Poulter 2006, pp. 13–14)

Over the past four decades, there has been considerable development in the research surrounding SSM, particularly in management issues in private companies (see, e.g., Ferrari et al. 2002) but also in nonprofit organizations (e.g., Luckett et al. 2001) and healthcare services (e.g., Atkinson et al. 2002; Checkland 2001), mainly in the UK and Europe.

More recently, SSM has been applied to English language teaching contexts, and as Holliday (1990, p. 77) suggests, "SSM may provide a useful means for structuring ethnographic findings" and goes on to argue that "[t]here are clear uses for soft systems methodology (SSM) in ELT projects." The case studies include Chambers (1997), Tajino (2002), and Tajino, James, and Kijima (2005). Chambers' (1997) study is a good example of applying a systems approach to course book evaluation (although he does not specify it as SSM). It shows a way to establish and use criteria for course book selection. Tajino (2002) investigates the cause of a problematic Japanese EFL team-teaching situation by means of transformation process models from SSM. He argues that these models can help uncover the true feelings of English teachers toward their team partners.

Referring to Tajino et al. (2005) as an example, the next section describes how SSM was applied to language curriculum development at a Japanese research-oriented university.

Applying Soft Systems Methodology to Language Curriculum Development

In developing a curriculum, the educational philosophy and goals of the institution, students' needs, faculty perspectives, and practical constraints such as budgetary issues, among a plethora of other factors, must be taken into account. Under such circumstances, when a problem that needs to be addressed arises, or measures for improvement must be undertaken, it is not unusual at all to have clashes of opinions, and at the least it is usually extremely difficult to reach a consensus. This is why a systems approach becomes necessary; it can incorporate a variety of different views on language and education to provide a workable framework that encourages mutual understanding and beneficial discussion, a framework that SSM facilitates.

Curriculum Development at Kyoto University

As an example of the application of SSM to language pedagogy, the process of the EAP curriculum development at Kyoto University is introduced below.

The Problematic Situation

Kyoto University is the second-oldest university in Japan, and is well-known as a research-oriented university, with which many Japanese Nobel laureates have been associated. Operating under the principle of academic freedom, Kyoto University English education was diverse even as students were previously, in a sense expected, to learn by imitating their teachers' example. There was, previously, therefore, no solid, shared, philosophy behind the English education conducted, or it could be labelled *English for no purposes*. Because of the respect for individuality under the spirit of academic freedom and teachers' personal choice, almost all the decision-making was left to each individual teacher (under the supervision of their academic affairs committee). Thus, the objective and content of English education could hardly be explained systemically.

Developing an EAP Curriculum at the Undergraduate Level

Under the situation described above, the English department, consisting of almost 30 full-time teachers, discussed the rationale for teaching English in order to redefine the objective of English education at the university and accommodated their views and opinions with SSM procedures.

All of the teachers agreed that they had to take action to improve the situation as they had viewed it as problematic. However, it was revealed that their opinions and expectations about the knowledge and skills that students should acquire were quite different from one another. For example, regarding language skills, some teachers expected students to develop strong reading and listening skills for academic purposes; some strong writing and speaking skills for general purposes; and others yet placed emphasis on strong test-taking skills for tests such as TOEFL® or TOEIC®. In other words, their views varied at the fundamental level while simultaneously maintaining a shared purpose.

Discussion with SSM brought them to conclude that the objective of their English education was English for academic purposes or EAP (see the transformation process model shown in Fig. 3).

Kyoto University's English curriculum was therefore updated, in light of agreed-upon EAP aims, to offer Academic Reading, Academic Writing, Academic Listening, Academic Speaking, and Test-Taking courses in 2006. Due to constraints on the number of teachers and class hours, they decided to employ a flipped learning system for academic listening courses, as shown in Fig. 4.

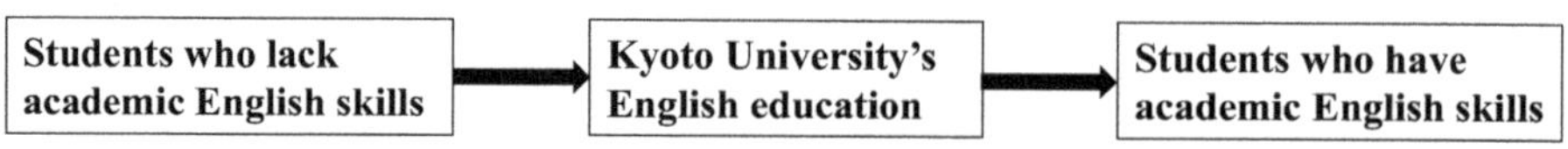

Fig. 3 Transformation process model for Kyoto University English education

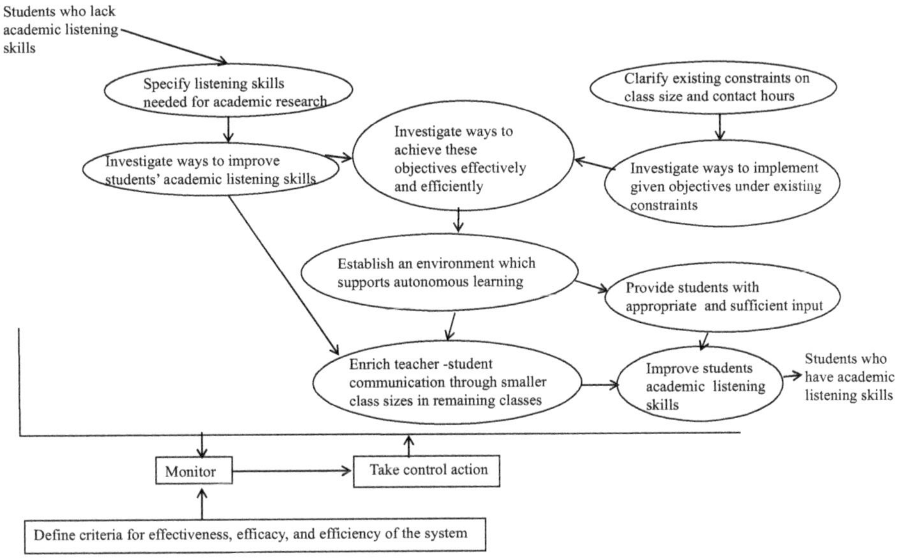

Fig. 4 A systems model for the academic listening course. (Tajino and Suiko 2005, p. 41)

The process of implementing this new curriculum included, of course, discussions between the course members mentioned above, but also a wide variety of meetings with concerned stakeholders, including faculty and the administrative staff of various departments. Such discussions were guided by an objective of desirability and cultural feasibility in change, with the result being an improvement in overall quality of teaching materials and approaches, as well as in communicability between involved parties. This was achieved through the mutual respect shown by each concerned party for the others' expertise and opinions, and the discussions for mutually acceptable accommodations were facilitated by SSM.

Of course, in the decade that has passed since the implementation of the new curriculum, changes have occurred in the environment and educational needs, and new areas for improvement have been recognized. In particular, instruction of academic listening skills was recognized as having room for improvement. In this instance, we reevaluated our listening course while maintaining an English for academic purposes (EAP) viewpoint and slightly updated the course content. E-learning materials and updated evaluation procedures were introduced, and a revised version of the curriculum was implemented in 2016, with the end result being significantly improved TOEFL® ITP scores of the learners, for example (Katsurayama et al. 2018). These updates were facilitated by the SSM process that had been undertaken a decade prior. Of course, in another decade, new changes will arise that will require new directions in the curriculum, just as in all human activity systems. SSM is aware of this, however, and does not strive for final solutions, but rather agreeable accommodations that allow for continuous improvement.

While by no means being a perfect endeavor, the SSM process conducted at Kyoto University drove the authors of this chapter to a somewhat unrelated but, nevertheless, concerning revelation. When viewing the current state of language teaching research, from the lens of the SSM principles, we can see that the individual research areas in the field suffer from a lack of communication between each other, i.e., the silo effect mentioned in the above section, "Language Pedagogy as a Human Activity System." Taking conferences as an example, the subdivision of researchers into smaller Special Interest Groups (SIGs) is an increasingly common trend, with researchers developing communities with a shared, although very narrow, focus. Of course, this is absolutely a necessary phenomenon in the deepening of academic research. However, the sharing of information between researchers with differing specialties is even more important. This is particularly relevant in language teaching research, due to the plethora of interrelated factors mentioned above, and the fact that as a research field, it covers a wide range of topics from linguistics through to education. It is impossible to further a general discussion of language teaching research from the point of view of vocabulary alone, for example.

Just as in practice, there is a need for collaboration between the individual areas of research in the field of language teaching. Drawing upon the SSM principles that drove innovation at Kyoto University, in the following sections, we outline how such collaboration might be achieved in the broader field of language teaching research (for the research areas and topics, see Johnson and Johnson 1999) (Fig. 5).

WHO	DOES	WHOM	WHAT	WHERE	WHEN	HOW	WHY
Teachers	**teach**	**learners (with L1 background)**	**grammar**	**in the classroom**	**throughout life**	**by instructional design**	**for specific purposes.**
		learners (with personality factors, attitudes, and motivation)	**vocabulary**	**outside classroom**	**at the university level**	**through homework tasks**	**for academic purposes.**
Learners	**learn**	**from their peers**	**receptive skills (listening, reading)**	**in natural settings**	**at secondary school levels**	**through collaboration**	**for occupation al/professi onal purposes.**
Teachers and learners	**learn**	**from each other**	**productive skills (speaking, writing)**	**in ESL contexts**	**at elementary school levels**	**through task-based and content-based lessons**	**for general purposes.**
...	**...**	**...**	**integrated skills**	**in EFL contexts**	**...**	**ICT, e-learning**	

Fig. 5 Arranging language teaching research with five Ws and one H

Arranging Language Teaching Research for Collaboration with Five Ws and One H

As noted in the Preface, language teaching research can be arranged and managed using the five Ws and one H aspects (see Hasan 1988). Below is a list of these aspects:

1. The WHO(M) aspect: includes teachers and students, each of whom has a variety of backgrounds and personal factors
2. The WHAT aspect: includes the four skills (i.e., listening, speaking, reading, and writing), grammar, and vocabulary
3. The WHERE aspect: includes institutions, as well as classroom settings and natural settings
4. The WHEN aspect: includes grades and periods of instruction, e.g., secondary education levels and 3 months of instruction
5. The HOW aspect: includes ways in which the target language is taught (or learned) as well as teaching (or learning) materials or tools, e.g., task-based language teaching and use of ICT
6. The WHY aspect: includes the purposes and reasons of instruction such as English for general purposes and English for specific purposes

Arranging the research areas in this way will encourage researchers and practitioners to communicate and collaborate with one another so that language pedagogy can be seen from a holistic perspective, becoming richer and more fruitful and meaningful. A combination of these aspects could help to create new research areas. For example, research on vocabulary (i.e., WHAT) in the language classroom (i.e., WHERE) through collaboration (i.e., HOW) for academic purposes (i.e., WHY) would help emergent properties take place and shed new light on language teaching research.

Conclusion

This chapter has served as an introduction to this volume, as well as a proposal for the implementation of a systems approach into language pedagogy, using an example of the Kyoto University curriculum development to examine one way how this might be achieved. It was suggested that soft systems thinking is effective in approaching the variety of worldviews and the clashes that these bring about in language education settings.

Furthermore, the necessity of this type of thinking in the broader language teaching research field was highlighted. While language teaching research has progressed and evolved alongside applied linguistics research, the compartmentalization of individual subject areas has been recognized as somewhat problematic. This chapter suggests that while this in itself is not a fatal issue, communication across the borders of the individual subject areas is desirable, and such communication may be facilitated with soft systems thinking and by approaching the field as a whole with the five Ws and one H as a framework.

The remainder of this volume addresses many of the areas that fall into the 5W1H framework and explores them in a holistic manner, often through the application of SSM. It is hoped that as a whole, this volume will contribute to an increased sharing of ideas across the broad field of language teaching research.

References

Atkinson, C., Eldabi, T., & Paul, R. (2002). Integrated approaches to health informatics research and development. *Logistics Information Management, 15*, 138–152.

Chambers, F. (1997). Seeking consensus in coursebook evaluation. *ELT Journal, 51*(1), 29–35.

Checkland, P. (1981). *Systems thinking, systems practice*. Chichester: Wiley.

Checkland, P. (1983). OR and the systems movement: Mapping and conflicts. *Journal of the Operational Research Society, 34*, 661–675.

Checkland, P. (2001). Soft systems methodology in action: Participative creation of an information strategy for an acute hospital. In J. Rosenbhead & J. Mingers (Eds.), *Rational analysis for a problematic world revisited: Problem structuring methods for complexity, uncertainty and conflict* (pp. 91–113). Chichester: Wiley.

Checkland, P., & Poulter, J. (2006). *Learning for action: A short definitive account of soft systems methodology and its use for practitioners, teachers and students*. Chichester: Wiley.

Checkland, P., & Scholes, J. (1990). *Soft systems methodology in action*. Chichester: Wiley.

Churchman, C. W. (1968). *The systems approach*. New York: Delacorte Press.

Connell, N. (2001). Evaluating soft OR: Some reflections on an apparently unsuccessful implementation using a soft systems methodology (SSM) based approach. *Journal of the Operational Research Society, 52*(2), 150–160.

Ferrari, M., Fares, B., & Martinelli, P. (2002). The systemic approach of SSM: The case of a Brazilian company. *Systemic Practice and Action Research, 15*, 51–66.

Hasan, R. (1988). The analysis of one poem: Theoretical issues in practice. In D. Birch & M. O'Tool (Eds.), *Functions and styles* (pp. 45–73). London: Edward Arnold.

Holliday, A. (1990). A role for soft systems methodology in ELT projects. *System, 18*, 77–84.

Johnson, K., & Johnson, H. (Eds.). (1999). *The encyclopedic dictionary of applied linguistics: A handbook for language teaching*. Oxford: Wiley-Blackwell.

Katsurayama, K., Takahashi, S., Kanamaru, T., Sasao, Y., Stewart, T., Dalsky, D., & Tajino, A. (2018). Kyoto daigaku ni okeru eigo kyouiku kaikaku—Eigo raiting-risuningu kousu ni shouten wo atete [English education reform at Kyoto University: A focus on the English writing–listening course]. *Kyoto University Institute for Liberal Arts and Sciences Bulletin, 1*, 111–121.

Luckett, S., Ngubane, S., & Memela, B. (2001). Designing a management system for a rural community development organization using a systemic action research process. *Systemic Practice and Action Research, 14*, 517–542.

Meadows, D. H. (2008). *Thinking in systems*. White River Junction: Chelsea Green Publishing.

Tajino, A. (2002). Transformation process models: A systemic approach to problematic team-teaching situations. *Prospect, 17*, 29–44.

Tajino, A., & Suiko, M. (2005). Daigaku eigokyoiku eno teigen—Karikyuramu kaihatsu eno sisutemu apurochi [A proposal for university English language education: A systems approach to curriculum development]. In Y. Takefuta & M. Suiko (Eds.), *Korekarano daigaku eigokyoiku* [The future of university English language education] (pp. 1–46). Tokyo: Iwanami Shoten.

Tajino, A., James, R., & Kijima, K. (2005). Beyond needs analysis: Soft systems methodology for meaningful collaboration in EAP course design. *Journal of English for Academic Purposes, 4*, 27–42.

Tett, G. (2015). *The silo effect: The peril of expertise and the promise of breaking down barriers*. New York: Simon & Schuster.

Language Acquisition: A Systemic View from Cognitive Linguistics

Kazumi Taniguchi

Abstract Among the most significant notions of systems thinking are the interaction of the whole and its parts and the emergent properties that are observable in a holistic structure which cannot be reduced to its components. Such notions are fully compatible with the theoretical views of cognitive linguistics, which assumes language as an integrated system of general cognitive abilities. In particular, the usage-based model of cognitive linguistics is a synthesis of categorization and abstraction from actual usages, involving both bottom-up and top-down organizations. The validity of the usage-based account for language acquisition will support a systemic approach to language development, which is further located appropriately in the scientific paradigm of complexity theory as suggested by Larsen-Freeman (Complexity theory: the lessons continue. In: Ortega L, Han Z (eds) *Complexity theory and language development*. John Benjamins, Amsterdam/Philadelphia, pp 11–50, 2017).

Keywords Cognitive linguistics · Constructions · Usage-based model · Complexity theory · Systems thinking

Introduction: SSM, Complexity Theory, and Language Acquisition

This chapter aims to consider how the mechanism of language acquisition can be characterized in terms of Soft Systems Methodology (SSM) and suggest its application to second language learning. Although more detailed descriptions of SSM have been given in chapters "Toward Managing Language Pedagogy and Language Teaching Research" and "Team Teaching and Team Learning: SSM Applied to the Team-Taught Classroom" in this volume, I would like to begin by briefly confirming its key notions required for the argument below.

K. Taniguchi (✉)
Graduate School of Human and Environmental Studies, Kyoto University, Kyoto, Japan
e-mail: taniguchi.kazumi.8n@kyoto-u.ac.jp

A. Tajino (ed.), *A Systems Approach to Language Pedagogy*, Translational Systems Sciences 17, https://doi.org/10.1007/978-981-13-6272-9_2

In my view, SSM is characterized as having its roots in "systems thinking" that puts importance on the "whole" as interactions of its parts, and the emergent properties of the whole as irreducible to its parts. Such features of systems thinking are reflected in SSM, as shown in the quotation below:

> Social situations are always complex due to multiple interactions between different elements in a problematical situation as a whole, and systems ideas are fundamentally concerned with the interactions between parts of a whole. (Checkland and Poulter 2006, 4)

Furthermore, if we take a broader view, the approaches and methodology aligned with systems thinking are considered to be part of a powerful scientific paradigm called "complexity theory." This metatheory originated in the physical and natural sciences (one of the most well-known representations might be "chaos theory") and has since been applied to social sciences such as sociology, anthropology, psychology, philosophy, and linguistics. Based on the concise introduction given in Larsen-Freeman (2017), the distinctive features of complexity theory are as follows:

(a) Emergence
(b) Non-reductionism; interactions of the whole and its parts
(c) Nonlinearity
(d) Dynamic
(e) Adaptive

Complexity theory emerged as an alternative to an analytic, linear, and reductive paradigm that has long been traditional in Western philosophy and science. Such analytic thinking might be elegant if it works, but faces difficulties when dealing with the complexity of human societies. Systems thinking, as opposed to analytic thinking, can offer a solution to complexity by recognizing a non-reducible, dynamic "whole" with emergent properties, as well as its interaction with the parts and with the larger whole which subsumes the system itself.

Diane Larsen-Freeman, who brought complexity theory into the field of language learning, presents significant aphorisms, applying the views of complexity theory as shown in a somewhat exhaustive quotation below:

> (a) Patterns that emerge through interaction are subsequently entrained by what preceded them, in a process of reciprocal causality, i.e., one that recognizes both local-to-global processes of construction and global-to-local processes of constraint.
> (b) L2 learning is a sociocognitive constructive process, in which learners make use of heuristics such as analogy, statistical preemption, abduction (inferencing beyond the data to which they have been exposed), recombination, relexification, co-adaptation, and alignment.
> (c) Learning is not climbing a developmental ladder; it is not unidirectional. It is nonlinear.
> (d) Language and its learning have no endpoints. Both are unbounded.
> (e) A person's history of interactions with diverse interlocutors builds up collections of experiences that contribute to the language, cognitive, affective, and ideological resources that are available to be drawn on.
> (f) These resources include physical (e.g., the use of gestures) as well as symbolic and multimodal ones.
> (g) What is important in a complex system is the interdependent relationship of the factors that comprise it. Such a focus necessitates a rejection of single-entity notions of efficient causality. (Larsen-Freeman 2017, 27)

In particular, it is worth mentioning that language acquisition, regardless of whether it is an L1 or L2, is never a linear development; children and learners are required at any time to modify the complex roadmap of language learning to adjust their current situations to valid goals. In this respect, SSM is expected to offer appropriate and efficient perspectives in improving the problematic situations that children and learners often encounter.

On the other hand, as Larsen-Freeman admits herself, such an application of complexity theory to language acquisition and learning remains theoretical and is still in need of more practical modeling. In what follows, I would like to suggest that a linguistic theory called "cognitive linguistics" offers a cognitively plausible mechanism of language acquisition that realizes systems thinking.

Systems Views of Cognitive Linguistics: Constructions as Symbolic Continuums and Language as a Cognitive System

Before discussing the issues of language acquisition, this section presents fundamental views of cognitive linguistics, especially of cognitive grammar (Langacker 1987, 1991a) and construction grammar (Goldberg 1995; Fillmore et al. 1988). One of the theoretical foundations of cognitive linguistics is the *symbolic* nature of language; the dichotomy of lexicon and syntax (or grammar) has long prevailed in linguistic theories on the basis of the argument that the former is a list of idiosyncrasies while the latter is reduced to simpler regular rules, but cognitive linguistics discards this kind of dichotomy and regards both lexicon and syntax as symbolic in nature, as will be observed in some details later.

Especially relevant to the present article is the notion of "constructions," i.e., pairings of forms and meanings in any size or kind. Linguistics knowledge is assumed to be a structured inventory of constructions; it is evident that lexical items stored in lexicon are pairings of specific phonological features and meanings, but particular syntactic patterns can also be regarded as symbolic, conveying meanings associated with those patterns.

In order to capture what constructions are really like, let us look at some typical examples in English:

(1) a. What's a nice girl like you doing in a place like this?
    b. What's this fly doing in my soup? (Kay and Fillmore 1999)
(2) a. Why don't you come over?
    b. Why don't you be seated?
(3) a. Him be a doctor?
    b. My boss raise our salary? (Lambrecht 1990)

All of the expressions above are interrogatives at a glance, but one finds some of them fairly idiosyncratic in syntactic and semantic respects. As for the construction in (1), while (1a) can be interpreted either as literally asking the content of the girl's action or as giving criticism, (1b) is no longer a literal question; it functions as accusing the hearer of being responsible for the poor quality of the soup served. In the case of (2), it is clear that these expressions do not ask for the reasons why the hearer has failed to do something; as a literal question, (2b) would rather be "why aren't you seated?" according to the rules of interrogativization. Finally, the expressions in (3), which are known as "mad magazine sentences," show syntactic properties that are by any means inexplicable in English grammar: the noun phrase with accusative case actually functions as sentential subject, followed by a bare infinitive verb (no agreement with the number/person of the subject noun). What is also characteristic of this construction is that it conveys the speaker's incredulous attitude toward a proposition; in the case of (3a), the speaker doubts the fact that he is a doctor (cf. Lambrecht 1990; Fillmore et al. 1988). Thus, it is impossible to reduce the expressions (1)–(3) to general grammatical rules of English; instead, they are regarded as instantiations of "constructions" listed in (4), all of which are pairing of forms (on the left-hand side) and meanings (on the right-hand side):

(4) a. [*What's* X *doing* Y?]: criticism
  b. [*Why don't you* Vinf?]: suggestion, invitation
  c. [NPacc Vinf X?]: incredibility

The forms of constructions can be of varying degrees of specificity; for example, [*What's* X *doing* Y?] construction in (4a) contains fixed words (*What's, doing*) together with variables X and Y to be filled with particular lexical items. On the other hand, the mad magazine construction in (4c) is highly schematic in that it does not comprise any specific words; it only designates the syntactic status (such as accusative case and bare infinitives) of the elements comprising the overall configuration.

Note that the meanings associated with the constructions (henceforth "constructional meanings") shown in (4) are pragmatic and expressive rather than propositional, and therefore these constructions are used for an interactive purpose of the speaker and the hearer. In the case of (4a), Bybee (2010) shows that a central instance "What's a nice girl like you doing in a place like this?", which first appeared in a movie, came to be used so frequently that it brought about the appearance of similar expressions which modify the subject and the locative phrase as in (1b). Then, the productive pattern [*What's* X *doing* Y?] was extracted, with the critical connotation left.

What is also significant is that such semantic (or pragmatic) aspects of constructions are never derived from the meanings of the words themselves. In this regard, Fillmore et al. (1988) call them "formal idioms," claiming that conventional associations of forms and meanings can be observed not only in the lexicon but in the morphosyntactic phenomena. This also leads us to reject the idea of "full compositionality," which assumes that the whole meaning of a sentence equates with the sum of the meanings of the lexical items that compose the sentence. The constructions like (1)–(3) explicitly show that the whole bears some "emergent" properties that are not reducible to its parts. This is also consistent with the "Language as Gestalt" view generally adopted by cognitive linguistics.

Fig. 1 Spectrum of form-meaning pairings

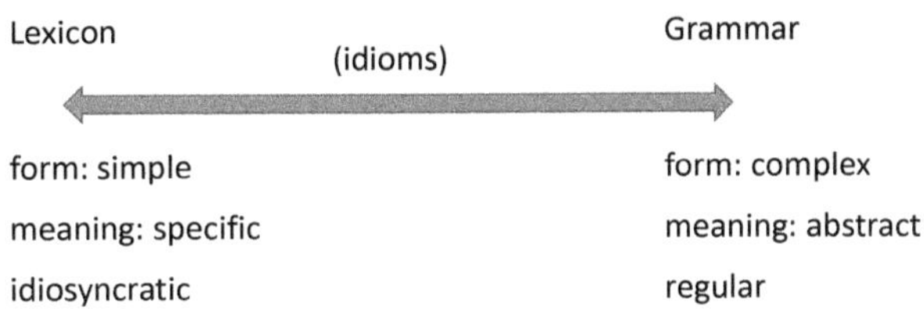

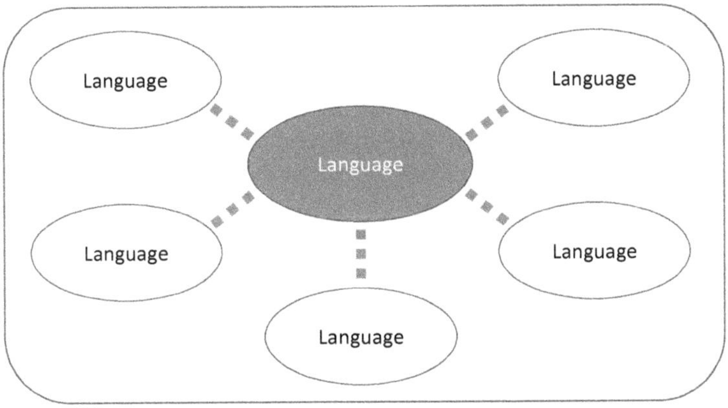

Fig. 2 Language and the human cognitive system

Viewed this way, the whole system of a particular language cannot be described just by decomposing it into discrete and autonomous components such as lexicon, syntax, semantics, and pragmatics, as has been supposed by generative grammar. Instead, cognitive linguistics regard lexicon and syntax as the two extremes of a symbolic continuum, i.e., a spectrum of form-meaning pairings, which only differ in specificity and size, as shown in Fig. 1. Furthermore, cognitive linguistics does not make a clear distinction between semantics and pragmatics as interpretations of linguistic expressions inevitably evoke some specific contexts as well as the encyclopedic knowledge concerning them. Traditional linguistic theories have distinguished semantics from pragmatics since, according to theory, semantics deals with the propositions denoted by sentences derived through syntactic operations, while pragmatics is just "outside" the core realm of syntax and therefore a peripheral issue. However, if constructions are associated with pragmatic meanings as in (4) and constitute our grammatical knowledge, it does not make sense to preserve such a distinction of semantics and pragmatics according to whether it is relevant to grammar or not.

Another important tenet of cognitive linguistics is to situate language in the intersections of general cognitive and psychological faculties, including memory, categorization, perceptual processing, inference, and so on, as depicted in Fig. 2.

This indicates that cognitive linguistics locates language within a larger system of human cognition. The functional interplay of language and cognitive abilities will be more evident in the model introduced in the following section.

Language Acquisition and Usage-Based Model

If constructions-pairings of forms and meanings constitute our linguistic knowledge, the question is: how do individuals acquire such constructions? Whereas Chomskyan generative grammar posits "Universal Grammar (UG)"as an innately hardwired device that enables us to acquire any language, cognitive linguistics accounts for the mechanism of language acquisition without resorting to UG since it rather regards language as emerging as a result of associations of domain-general cognitive abilities, as shown in Fig. 2. In addition, cognitive linguistics assumes that grammatical "rules" do not explain the whole picture; as demonstrated by the constructions in (1)–(3), syntactic phenomena are not reduced to derivations by means of rules that regulate how to align the components of a sentence. Thus, it would be insufficient to assume that UG generates syntactic expressions, functioning in a top-down fashion.

In contrast to UG theory, cognitive linguistics broadly adopts the "usage-based model" (cf. Langacker 2000; Tomasello 2003; Bybee 2010) for an appropriate characterization of dynamic aspects of language, including language acquisition, diachronic change, and so on. The usage-based model functions in a bottom-up fashion: starting from actual usages, and later some commonalities and regularities emerging among them.

Usage-Based Acquisition of Word Meanings

As an illustration of how the usage-based model actually works, let us consider the case of acquiring meanings of a noun, for example, *ring*.[1] Suppose that a child first encounters the noun *ring* as designating a piece if circular jewelry to put on a finger; this will become a "prototype" of the child's knowledge of what a ring is. On the other hand, designations of *ring* in reality are not limited to the child's prototype; it can also refer to other pieces of jewelry such as arm rings, earrings, and so on. She may find it from these usages that what a ring commonly denotes a circular accessory, no matter where it is put. Then, she will extract from these usages a perceptual commonality of [CIRCULAR JEWELRY], which functions as the "schema" of *ring* (see Fig. 3).

Then, suppose she goes on to encounter another usage of *ring* as designating her toys of quoits. This is no longer a jewelry sort of thing and therefore deviates from the schema she has established. However, it will not be difficult for her to notice that both the pieces of jewelry and the quoits are circular physical objects with hollows in the middle. Thus, she will create a new schema that accommodates both the pre-established schema and the novel instance of *ring*: [CIRCULAR PHYSICAL OBJECT] (Fig. 4).

---

[1] The usage-based model representation of *ring* is partly based on the network analysis in Langacker (1991b: 3).

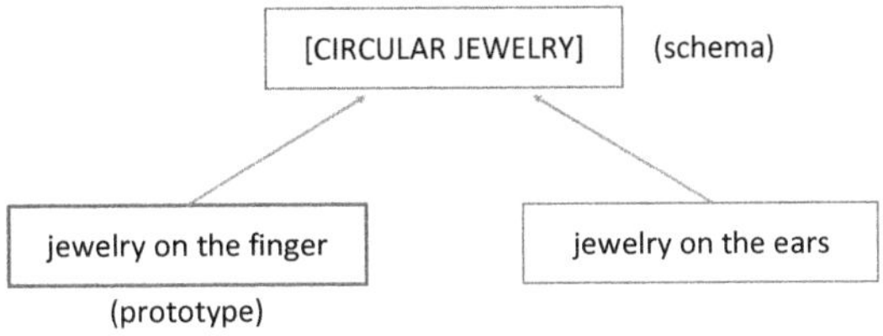

Fig. 3 Schema for "ring"

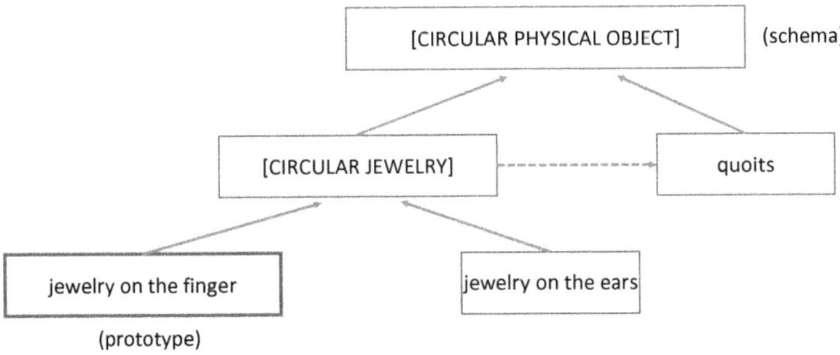

Fig. 4 New schema for "ring"

Of course, her learning of the meanings of *ring* will not end here. When she eats a *ring* of pineapple or a cinnamon *ring* doughnut, they will be accepted as straightforward instances of the schema [CIRCULAR PHYSICAL OBJECT]. However, if she goes to the station and finds that a signal indicating a loop line is called *ring*, or if she hears someone say that a tree stump has multiple growing *rings*, these usages of *ring* do not instantiate the schema [CIRCULAR PHYSICAL OBJECT] as they are rather two-dimensional marks and lines. Here, again, she will further derive a novel, higher-level schema to accommodate them, as [CIRCULAR PHYSICAL ENTITY] (Fig. 5).

Furthermore, as she gets older, she will encounter an array of other usages which conflict with the schemas she has established so far. For example, a *ring* of thieves refers to a group of people sharing the same purpose, and a boxing *ring* to a square arena. It might be difficult to find any relevance of these usages to the higher-level schema [CIRCULAR ENTITY], but they can be accommodated in the network of ring to the extent that one recognizes some correlations between a group of people and a circular shape (perhaps because such closely related people often discuss matters sitting in a circle), and the historical origin of arenas such as the Roman Colosseum. Such usages of *ring* are just located as "extensions" from the schema as they can be related back to the schema in indirect ways.

As has been indicated above, the usage-based model synthesizes basic cognitive abilities of categorization and abstraction (i.e., schematization). Here, it is important to confirm the nature of schemas in the following two respects. First, while a schema functions as categorical judgment of whether a novel instance is sanctioned or not, it is also flexible enough to allow for a new, deviant instance appearing fre-

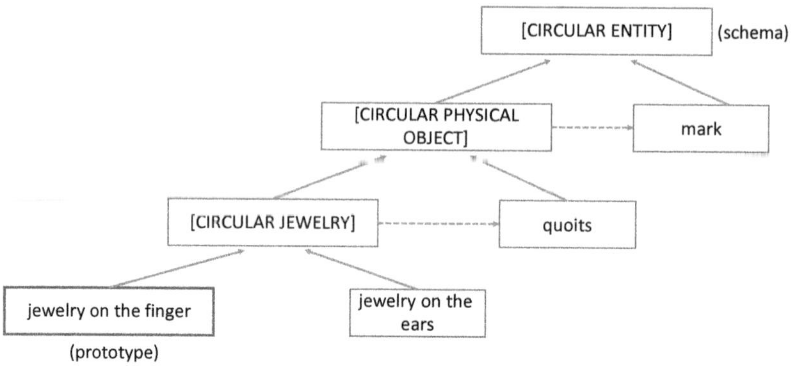

Fig. 5 Higher-level schema for "ring"

quently in our usage events. Second, the higher-level, more abstract schemas (the upper schemas in the above figures) do not negate the low-level schemas that have been extracted earlier, but rather add the detailed information involved in actual usages. This means that our linguistic knowledge is multilayered, developing over time while preserving the traces of development. This is exactly where systems thinking and the usage-based model converge, as we will observe in the following sections.

Usage-Based Acquisition of Constructions

The usage-based account for language acquisition also holds for the case of clausal expressions, where regular patterns emerging among actual usages are labelled "constructional schemas" that capture the formal and semantic commonalities among instances. Figure 6 is a representation of the bottom-up development of the double object construction in English.[2]

In the case of the double object construction, for example, the schema [(Subj) V Obj_1 Obj_2] combined with the constructional meaning CAUSE-RECEIVE can be extracted from instances such as "gimme chocolate" and "send him money"; such verb-specific usages are called "verb islands," in the sense that they are acquired independently (Tomasello 2003). Of course, children are not innately capable of learning constructions. The extraction of the constructional schema presupposes their cognitive development, since abstraction at the relational level is much more complex than abstraction at the lower level of physical objects, which can utilize perceptual clues such as shape as we have seen in the case of *ring* in 3.1. In fact, according to Tomasello (2003), children start to generalize over specific instances around at the age of 3.

[2]The description of the double object constructions reflects the construction grammar analysis by Goldberg (1995).

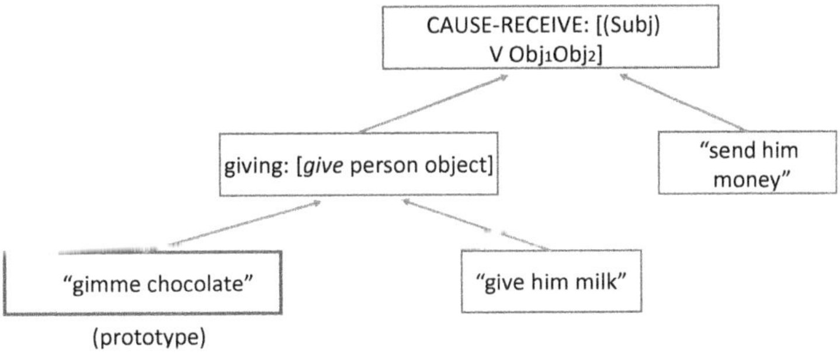

Fig. 6 Constructional schema for double object construction

> Up until age 2:6—for many children until 3;0 or older-syntactic component is best characterized as simply an inventory of independent verb island constructions that pair a scene of experience and an item-based construction, with no structural relationship among these constructional islands. (Tomasello 2003, p. 121)

In addition, it is important to note that children acquire a construction in relation to the setting in which it is used. That may lead to children's sensitivity to the pragmatic functions of constructions embedded in physical and social experiences. As an illustration, let us look at the following excerpt of interesting conversations where both of the two children are pleased to hear their mother suggest going to McDonald's, but their verbal responses are opposite:

(5) Mother: Do you mind eating at McDonald's?
Child (younger): Yes!
Child (older): No! (Shiotani 2004:100)

It is clear that the younger child strongly reacted to the constructional meaning of [*Do you mind* Ving?], which is roughly equivalent to "Let's V." This occurs precisely because the holistic, constructional meaning is accessed prior to its parts including the literal meaning of *mind*. This example indicates that, as Tomasello points out above, the setting of the utterance and its interpersonal function are learned in association with the construction.

Compatibility of Usage-Based Model and Systems Thinking

If language is learned and constructed in usage-based manners, it is quite reasonable to assume that adults' linguistic knowledge is a product of continuous interactions of bottom-up and top-down processing and of specific instances and abstract schemas, respectively. The constructions (or some kinds of regularities) emerge from the actual usages, with syntactic or semantic properties irreducible to their parts. Such a view of language acquisition is fully compatible with SSM as well as complexity theory. Although cognitive linguists do not refer explicitly to the relevance to complexity theory or systems thinking, their theoretical stances are apparently of the same vein. In fact, Larsen-Freeman (2017) also enumerates usage-based linguists (Ronald W. Langacker, Adele E. Goldberg, Michael Tomasello, among others) as those working in the paradigm of complexity theory.

As for the usage-based model of language acquisition, it involves interactions between the whole and the parts at multiple dimensions:

(a) Actual usages (instances) and schema
(b) Lower schema and higher schema
(c) Linguistic expressions and context
(d) Language users and their environment
(e) Language and cognitive system

Of course, each item listed above does not function independently, and the interaction itself is subject to further interaction with its higher or lower layer. Moreover, the interaction of the whole and the parts plays an important part not only in language development of individuals but in adaptive changes of a given language community. One of the most outstanding phenomena is the appearance of novel instances observed in SNSs, including Twitter, where users often modify the rules established in the language and share newly invented usages among their followers in a memetic fashion (possibly to enhance their solidarity), further spreading them by means of retweets. If such a novel usage is entrenched enough in the community and starts to appear outside the SNS, it might have an impact on the language system as a whole, forcing it to revise the current rules.

Concluding Remarks

This chapter has shown that cognitive-linguistic views, especially the usage-based model, may present a plausible mechanism of language acquisition, in ways fully compatible with systems thinking regarding its emphasis on the interaction of the whole and the parts. As a final remark, I would like to observe some perspectives on further applications of SSM to the learning and teaching of L1 and L2.

In the case of L1, a child acquires her native languages through fairly local communication with her caregivers, from whom she receives few corrections of her errors. In this regard, the acquisition of L1 is more *autopoietic* in the sense that constructions or rule-like regularities emerge in self-organizing manners, with properties unpredictable from mere examination of the parts. In addition, the goal of L1 acquisition is not presented explicitly at any stage of development; though the caregivers can be linguistic mentors of a child, she is not directed as to what to learn next. She therefore needs to construct "children's grammar" in the interim, which approximates adults' grammar through continuous updates and modifications over time. As a result, it can be presumed that the acquisition of L1 involves heuristic utilization of systems thinking.

On the other hand, it can be assumed that many learners of L2 are more explicitly aware of their ultimate goal: being fluent speakers of the language they are learning.

The philosophy behind SSM may be more feasible for second language acquisition, as it is a methodology aimed at improving problematic states in a purposeful action, and the increased understandings that it promotes may also encourage increased linguistic hypothesizing. As for further applications of SSM, it is possible to take the following issues into consideration: first, the interaction of individual students and the classroom as a whole can be treated as a soft system. Unlike the L1 which develops in local and natural conversations, L2 is generally taught and learned within the peculiar environment of classrooms. The goals of the classes therefore will be modified according to the students' achievements. Second, the integration of language skills such as reading, listening, writing, and speaking is also important for L2 learning. Instead of handling them as separate tasks, one must recognize that a combination of these skills will give rise to another difficulty for learners which would not emerge in isolation. SSM is thus expected to provide learners and teachers with new, larger perspectives by which they can manage the course of development in a flexible and efficient way.[3]

References

Bybee, J. (2010). *Language, usage and cognition.* Cambridge: Cambridge University Press.

Checkland, P., & Poulter, J. (2006). *Learning for action: A short definitive account of soft systems methodology and its use for practitioners, teachers and students.* West Sussex: Wiley.

Fillmore, C. J., Kay, P., & O'Connor, M. C. (1988). Regularity and idiomaticity in grammatical constructions: The case of *let alone*. *Language, 64*(3), 501–538.

Goldberg, A. E. (1995). *Constructions: A construction grammar approach to argument structure.* Chicago: University of Chicago Press.

Kay, P., & Fillmore, C. J. (1999). Grammatical constructions and linguistic generalizations: The 'What's X doing Y?' construction. *Language, 75*(1), 1–33.

Lambrecht, K. (1990). "What, me worry?": 'Mad magazine sentences' revisited. *BLS, 16*, 215–228.

Langacker, R. W. (1987). *Foundations of cognitive grammar vol.1: Theoretical prerequisites.* Stanford: Stanford University Press.

Langacker, R. W. (1991a). *Foundations of cognitive grammar vol.2: Descriptive application.* Stanford: Stanford University Press.

Langacker, R. W. (1991b). *Concept, image and symbol: The cognitive basis of grammar.* Berlin/New York: Mouton de Gruyter.

Langacker, R. W. (2000). A dynamic usage-based model. In M. Barlow & S. Kemmer (Eds.), *Usage-based models of language* (pp. 1–63). Stanford: CSLI Publications.

Larsen-Freeman, D. (2017). Complexity theory: The lessons continue. In L. Ortega & Z. Han (Eds.), *Complexity theory and language development* (pp. 11–50). Amsterdam/Philadelphia: John Benjamins.

Shiotani, S. H. (2004). *How do American children learn English?* Tokyo: Shodensha.

Tomasello, M. (2003). *Constructing a language: A usage-based theory of language acquisition.* Cambridge, MA: Harvard University Press.

Verspoor, M. (2017). Complex dynamic systems theory and L2 pedagogy: Lessons to be learned. In L. Ortega & Z. Han (Eds.), *Complexity theory and language development* (pp. 143–162). Amsterdam/Philadelphia: John Benjamins.

[3] In this regard, see Verspoor (2017) who offers some practical suggestions on second language learning in terms of usage-based model and complexity theory.

Teaching English Grammar for Communicative Purposes: A Systems Approach

Akira Tajino

Abstract This chapter addresses issues considered to be problematic in grammar instruction, first by presenting a discussion of the nature of English grammar instruction for communicative purposes and then proposing a grammar teaching model that can be used dynamically to improve pedagogy. This chapter follows the procedure of soft systems methodology, which is often used to improve situations judged to be problematic: in this case, the instruction of grammar in EFL/ESL contexts. To this end, the chapter first attempts to identify the situation that is seen as problematic in grammar instruction; second, to make a purposeful activity model judged to be relevant to this situation; third, to discuss the desirability and the cultural feasibility of the model when applying it to the real-world situation in the EFL context; and, finally, to take action to improve the situation and revise the model. In other words, the outline of this chapter reflects that of the soft systems methodology procedure itself. In this way, it is possible to see how English grammar might be arranged so that it may be taught systematically and dynamically for communicative purposes. This should bring about systemic change in grammar instruction, shifting the focus from grammar-for-explaining to grammar-for-use.

Keywords Imijun · MAP Grammar · Soft systems methodology (SSM) · Two dimensions

Introduction: Grammar Instruction Viewed as Problematic

It is generally agreed upon in the literature of language education that grammar or grammatical knowledge plays a significant role in facilitating language production and comprehension. Moreover, grammar competence plays a fundamental role in improving each of the four macro skills: listening, speaking, reading, and writing (Crystal 2004a). In fact, without grammatical knowledge or grammatical

A. Tajino (✉)
Department of British and American Studies, Nagoya University of Foreign Studies, Aichi, Japan

Kyoto University, Kyoto, Japan
e-mail: tajino@nufs.ac.jp

A. Tajino (ed.), *A Systems Approach to Language Pedagogy*, Translational Systems Sciences 17, https://doi.org/10.1007/978-981-13-6272-9_3

competence, it would be nearly impossible for us to communicate with one another. Grammatical competence is widely understood to be a key factor in communicative competence (Canale 1983; Canale and Swain 1980), with many studies demonstrating the necessity of grammar instruction to improve learners' language abilities (see Smithers and Gray 2018). While acknowledging the significance of grammar, however, it seems that learners often find it difficult to learn grammar. Why is this the case? If we consider English grammar as it is, David Crystal is right in claiming that English grammar is unfortunately not a neat regular phenomenon:

> The grammar of a language is not a neat, logical, regular phenomenon. There are always exceptions to rules, and sometimes there are so many exceptions that is awkward deciding what the rule should be. Often a single sentence can be analysed in more than one way. (Crystal 2004b, p. 15)

This is indeed a problematic situation, which seems difficult to approach, as we of course cannot willfully change the rules of grammar to make it easier for learners. While it cannot easily be altered by teachers, it is possible for grammar to be arranged in a user-friendly, meaningful way so that it can be made to look simpler, neater, and thus easier to teach and learn (Tajino 2018).

Learners Struggling with Grammar

While the approach to be outlined in this chapter is applicable to both English as a second language (ESL) and English as a foreign language (EFL) contexts, given the often-greater demand for and struggles with grammar that occur in EFL contexts, it is perhaps worth beginning this chapter by turning our lens to learners in these contexts. A survey conducted nationwide in Japan, for example, shows that grammar instruction was ranked first by high school students as a cause of negative attitudes toward English (Benesse Educational Research and Development Institute 2014). A great number of secondary school students struggle with the study of English grammar, and there are some students who despair that they do not even know what it is they do not know (see Watari et al. 2012). Unfortunately, it seems that Japan does not have a reputation for producing proficient English users. Perhaps this (at least perceived) weakness of productive skills in Japanese learners of English can be attributed to their lack of grammatical knowledge for use. A relatively recent nationwide survey conducted in high schools in Japan showed that almost a fifth of high school students had left the writing section on an English test blank, obtaining a score of zero (MEXT 2016). This may serve as evidence to show that many learners are unable to use grammar to even begin making a sentence.

This situation is not necessarily limited to the Japanese EFL context, and it seems this is also the case with other EFL or ESL contexts. For example, Dr. Christine Sinclair, who teaches ESL at a British university, states:

> I have seen so many students who have problems with grammar and use of language. … the students who come to see me often tell me that they don't know *where to start* … . There are *too many technical terms to learn* and *rules that seem to be broken all the time*. (Sinclair 2010, p. 2) [*Italics* mine.]

Many teachers would probably agree with her. For instance, anecdotal evidence is available to claim that learners often do not know where they should start to study grammar because no *road map* of grammar has yet been made available to them and they may have to learn many technical terms (such as subject, object, and complement) which we often feel obligated to use in *explain*ing grammar (see Tajino 2018). These issues may be the primary causes of difficulty in learning English grammar.

Another potential cause of learner struggles may lie in how grammatical items are presented to them. One way to see how grammar has been taught would be to examine grammar course books that have been widely used. A review of some English grammar course books commonly used worldwide shows that each grammatical item tends to be dealt with independently, and as such, there is no demonstration of interconnections among the items, as represented in Fig. 1.

Given this situation, it is not surprising that learners do not know where to start studying English grammar. In fact, the whole picture of English grammar, or even a general road map of grammar, has not been made available yet. This chapter aims to introduce that road map in the following sections, but let us first consider the purposes of grammar instruction.

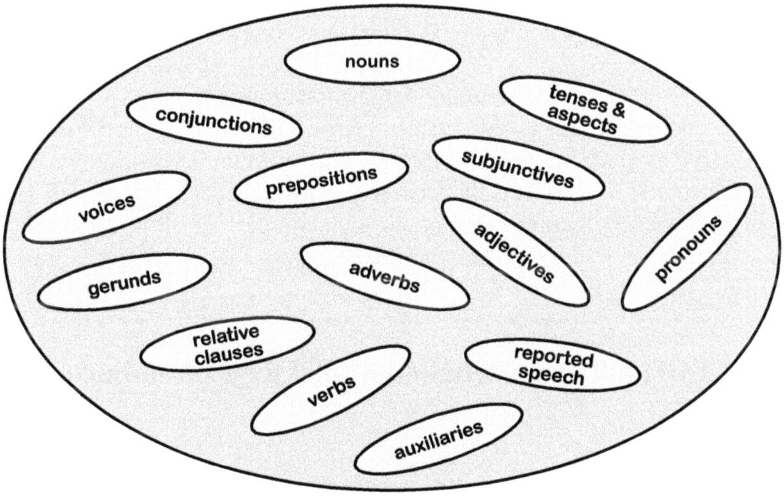

Fig. 1 A lack of interconnections among English grammatical items

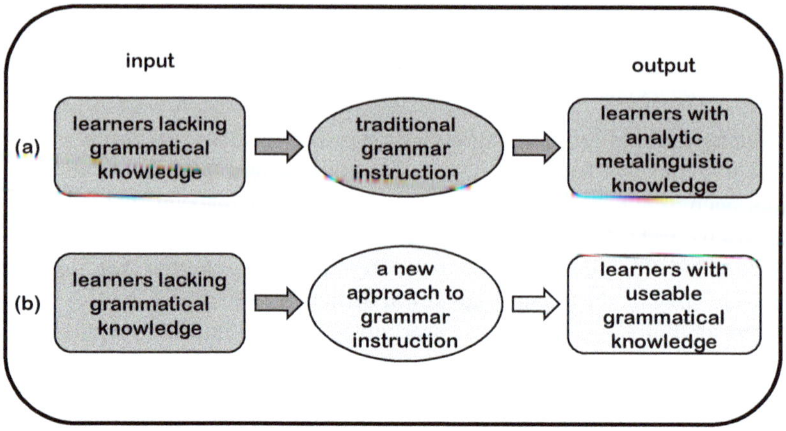

Fig. 2 Transformation process models for grammar instruction

Purposes of Grammar Instruction: Transformation Process Models

It is possible to describe the way grammar has been taught by means of transformation process models. Figure 2 describes the transformational processes for grammar instruction and shows that grammar instruction helps "learners who lack grammatical knowledge" to be transformed into "learners who have analytic metalinguistic knowledge," or knowing the *what* of grammar (Fig. 2a), and to be transformed into "learners who have usable grammatical knowledge" or knowing the *how to* of grammar use (Fig. 2b).

As noted above, the MEXT survey demonstrated almost 30% of the third-year high school students in Japan were unable to write anything at all on the written test. This may serve as evidence to claim that the type of grammar instruction they had received was that of Fig. 2a. It is the situation shown in Fig. 2a that we see as problematical for fostering learners' communicative competence. It is, then, the model of Fig. 2b that we should focus on.

Building a Grammar-Instruction Model for Communicative Purposes

Given the problematic situation above, how can we build a grammar teaching model? In attempting to answer this question, as Crystal (2004a) points out neatly, it is important to appreciate how grammar relates to *meaning*, which is of course why we communicate. Thus, instruction to provide learners with useable grammatical knowledge must provide opportunities in which learners can grasp how grammar and meaning relate to each other. For many of our learners, the connection between grammatical items and meaning has thus far not been so clear. Taking meaning as the core of communication, we can start with the following assumptions:

1. Every learner makes errors, and the errors can be divided into two from a communicative perspective: *global errors* that impede communication and *local errors* that are still understandable (e.g., Burt 1975).
2. English is a fixed-word-order language (Pinker 1994). If the learners can master the structure of an English clause, they can avoid global errors, which would make them successfully communicate with others.
3. The English clause structure can be viewed as consisting of *meaning units* (see Halliday 1994; de Oliveira and Schleppegrell 2015).

All of this suggests, given that the purpose of grammar instruction involves a communicative aspect, that it is important to take a meaning-based approach to English grammar.

Starting with the English Clause Structure

Beginning with the understanding that English is a fixed-word-order language (Pinker 1994), we can see that errors with the clause structure (i.e., global errors) may impede communication. Clause structure is perhaps, then, the basic foundation upon which grammar instruction should be built. If so, it would be appropriate to first focus on the instruction of clause structure and reconsider the way it might be approached and taught.

Various Worldviews in Approaching English Clauses

Multiple approaches may be taken to characterize English clause elements, for example, according to their function, grammatical category, or semantic role (e.g., Imai et al. 1995). Accordingly, there are multiple ways in which the clause may be viewed. Table 1 summarizes these views with the sentence "Christina planted a flower in the garden" as an example.

Table 1 Multiple approaches to the English clause

	Christina	*planted*	*a flower*	*in the garden.*
(1)	Subject	Verb	Object	Adverbial
(2)	Noun	Verb	Noun Phrase	Prep. Phrase
(3)	Agent	Action	Goal	Location
(4)	Who	Does	What	Where

Fig. 3 The order of meanings (cf. Tajino 2018) (Notes: (1) Conjunctions and interrogatives, etc. fall under "α"; (2) WHOM/WHAT(HOW) = WHOM and/or WHAT(HOW); and (3) "HOW" and "WHY" as options)

Which of these four ways is more accessible and comprehensible for learning useable grammar, in terms of the different labels given above? The first approach (1) has been predominantly used in grammar instruction and is widely known as the five (or sometimes seven) clause patterns. This has been useful for analyzing and explaining grammar. The labels in (2), just as in (1), would be helpful for explaining English clauses. For instruction from a communicative perspective, however, (3) should receive attention since it is based on semantic roles; that is, it is meaning-based. One critical issue with (3), however, may be the technical terms used (e.g., Will learners easily understand the term "agent?"). To solve this, the fourth approach (4) employs everyday language that should be user-friendly. Since our main purpose is to build a grammar-instruction model for communicative purposes, it is this fourth approach that is focused on in this chapter; it is called "the order of meanings."[1]

The Order of Meanings: Five Ws and One H

Human communication involves the so-called Five Ws and One H (5Ws and 1H) meaning units: who(m), what, where, when, why, and how. Germaine to this discussion, Hasan (1988, p. 63) suggests that the transitivity structure in a clause "is concerned with a coding of the goings on: *who does what in relation to whom/what, where, when, how and why*" [emphasis added]. Accordingly, we should examine how the set of these meaning units can be applied to the teaching of English clauses.

Related to the above, Fig. 3 shows a model of the teaching of English structure that has been developed by Akira Tajino (e.g., Tajino 2011, 2014, 2018). The *order of meanings* refers to "*Who> Does (Is) >Who(m) / What (How) > Where > When.*" Figure 4 outlines the referents that fall into each of the order of meanings categories.

---

[1] Known as *Imijun* (*imi* = meanings, *jun* = the order) in Japan, where it was first proposed by the author. *Imijun* has been included in a wide variety of publications, from academic journals to learner materials (e.g., Tajino, 1995, 1999, 2011, 2012, 2014, 2018). It has also received acclaim at institutions, where it has been adopted as a method of instruction (see Fukumasu 2017).

Fig. 4 The referents of the meaning units

Meaning Units	*Referents*
Who	persons, things, etc.
Does(Is)	the doing, the being, etc.
Who(m)	persons, things, etc.
What	things, etc.
(How)	attributes of persons, things, etc.
Where	places, locations, directions, etc.
When	times, durations, frequencies, etc.
Options	
α	conjunctions, subordinate clauses, etc.
How	manner, means, instruments, etc.
Why	reasons, causes, purpose, etc.

The Desirability and the Cultural Feasibility of Applying the Order of Meanings

From the perspective of both desirability and cultural feasibility, it would be important to see how *the order of meanings* can be compatible with the seven clause patterns and metalanguage, such as *subject* and *object*, that have thus far been dominant in the teaching of English clause structures.

The Order of Meanings and the Seven Clause Types

Figure 5 shows how both the order of meanings and the seven clause types are compatible with each other. This would make the order of meanings potentially easier to grasp by replacing the seven patterns with a more user-friendly model.

The Order of Meanings and English Clauses

Let us examine how to use the order of meanings for producing and understanding English clauses. Figure 6 is a Matryoshka doll or Russian nesting doll. It represents the idea that the order of meanings has a hierarchical structure, with each meaning

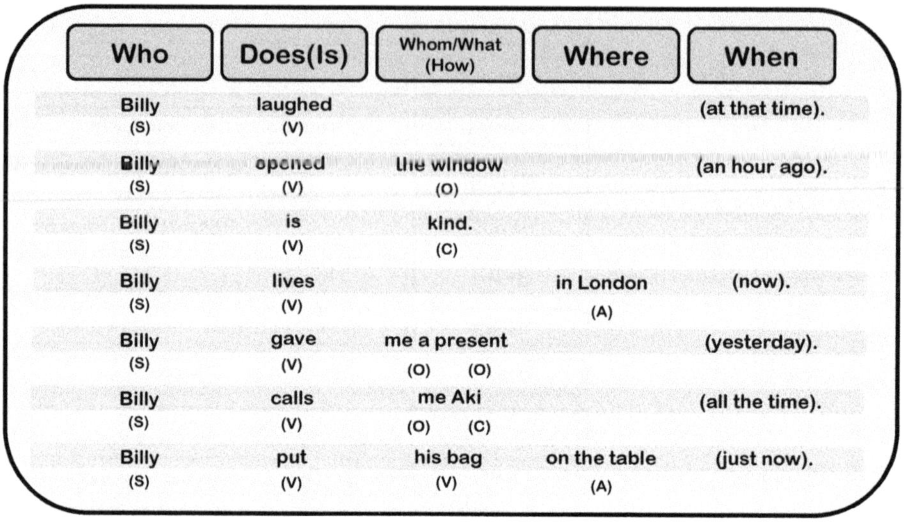

Fig. 5 The order of meanings and the seven clause types

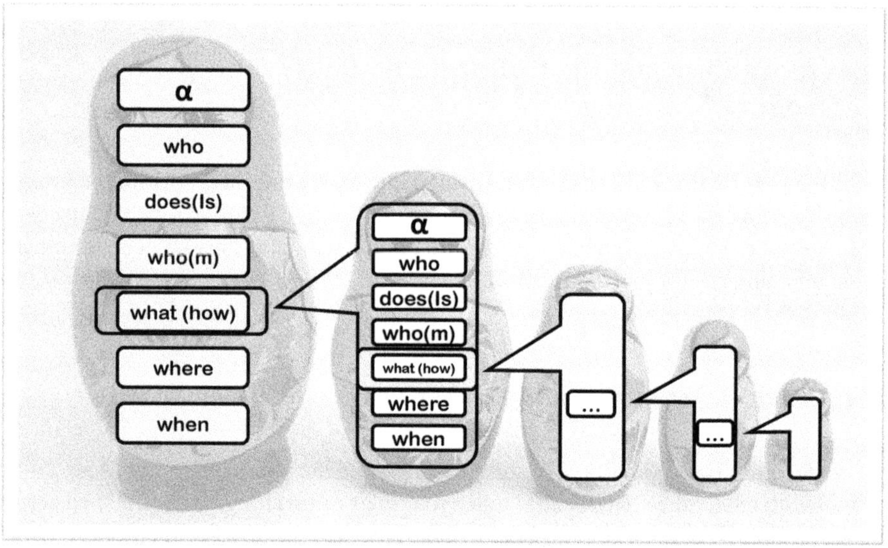

Fig. 6 The hierarchal nature of the order of meanings

unit, including its own suborder of meanings – in this way, even grammatically complicated sentences/clauses such as complex sentences and relative clauses can be visualized, which may help learners understand the sentence/clause structures more easily.

Tables 2, 3, and 4 show how this hierarchal nature of the order of meanings might be expressed using two layers.

Table 2 That clauses: "I think that he is a pilot"

α	WHO	DOES(IS)	WHOM/WHAT(HOW)	WHERE	WHEN
	I	think	*that*		
	he	*is*	*a pilot.*		

Table 3 Relative pronouns: "I have a colleague who works in New York"

α	WHO	DOES(IS)	WHOM/WHAT(HOW)	WHERE	WHEN
	I	have	*a colleague*		
	who *(that person)*	*works*		*in New York.*	

Table 4 Adverbial clauses (when): "She was cooking in the kitchen when I came home"

α	WHO	DOES(IS)	WHOM/WHAT(HOW)	WHERE	WHEN
	She	was cooking		in the kitchen	*when*
	I	*came*		*home.*	

As shown above, the order of meanings can help us produce and understand English clauses or sentences visually and in a way that is easy for learners to grasp.

Taking Action: Utilizing the Order of Meanings to Teach Grammar

There have been an increasing number of studies to investigate the effectiveness of the order of meanings. Research includes Bolstad et al. (2010), Watari et al. (2012), Smithers and Gray (2018), and a complete volume that discusses the order of meanings as a viable alternative to traditional grammar teaching (Tajino 2018). More specifically, the studies highlight how students at junior high school made fewer errors during direct translation of sentences (Okuzumi 2016) and were able to improve sentence cohesion after 12 months of study (Jojima et al. 2018). Furthermore, high school students found the order of meanings to be highly motivating (Kanamaru and Pearce 2018), while university students reported parsing during listening tasks to be facilitated (Hosogoshi et al. 2018). Lastly, in a study on lifelong learners studying EFL in Japan, Smithers and Gray (2018), examining the order of meanings under the Japanese label *Imijun*, concluded that meaning-order instruction was able to enhance the lives of older learners. The teacher's voice (Smithers and Gray 2018, p. 15) in their study revealed that:

> [*Imijun*] was just what the doctor ordered. It was medicine that tasted good. It gave students a renewed sense of confidence in themselves, and that led to motivated learning that enabled some students to overcome physical and mental issues,

while student voices (Smithers and Gray 2018, p. 14) validated these sentiments during their 6-week study:

- "I was so excited to study *Imijun*. I could sort out my head by *Imijun*" (Week 1, S10).
- "*Imijun* is useful for my brain to arrange my learning English" (Week 2, S7).
- "Before, I studied S + V + O, but I couldn't understand [the 5 sentence patterns] well, but now I can understand English easily because I have a picture in my head" (Week 4, S1).
- "I feel like I have reduced my mistakes because of *Imijun*" (Week 4, S5).
- "I felt *Imijun* is worth learning" (Week 5, S6).
- "Since I have been studying *Imijun*, I was motivated by it a little" (Week 6, S3).
- "I thought even a complicated sentence was applicable to *Imijun*" (Week 6, S8).
- "Learning English is complicated, but learning English with *Imijun* is fun" (Week 6, S2).

To summarize the results from these studies, *Imijun* (the order of meanings) motivated both teachers and students and led to improved practice. Moreover, students gained more confidence and were better able to produce coherent and grammatically correct sentences. Despite the fact that these studies seem to depict the order of meanings as a sort of panacea, we would be remiss if we did not acknowledge that grammar is far more complicated than what has been described here. Nevertheless, it is thought that the order of meanings can provide a solid foundation for learners from which they can build their grammatical competence.

Toward Designing the Whole Picture of English Grammar

We have so far discussed the order of meanings, which may replace or supplement the five or seven clause patterns that have been dominant in English language teaching for a long time. However, we have not yet touched upon other grammatical items such as auxiliaries, tense, and aspect. How might the order of meanings contribute to the teaching of these items?

A Two-Dimensional Approach to Grammar: MAP Grammar

In this section, and the remainder of the chapter, we will integrate the order of meanings with the abovementioned grammatical items to create a *meaning-order approach to pedagogical grammar*, or MAP Grammar, for short. Referring to Saussure's syntagmatic and paradigmatic relations, Culler (1976, p. 104) adopts a food system metaphor. He states that in the food system, one can define on the horizontal (or syntagmatic) axis the combinations of courses which can make up meals of various sorts and each course or slot can be filled by one of a number of dishes which are in paradigmatic contrast with one another, that is, forming a vertical axis.

Beginning a meal with an entrée, then moving on to the main dish, and concluding with a dessert is a typical flow in Western food culture (Fig. 7). This kind of progression can be used to represent the horizontal axis, while the contents or choices at each stage are on the vertical axis and can be seen as food selection options (e.g., beef, chicken, or fish as the main dish). In this way, English grammar can be similarly represented (see Fig. 8).

Fig. 7 A food system metaphor (Culler 1976)

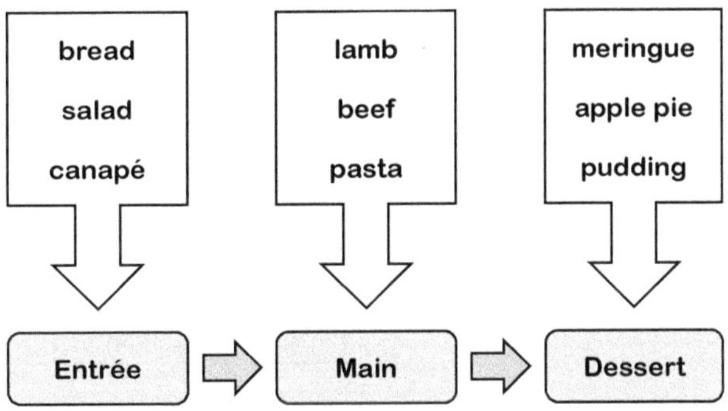

Fig. 8 The food system metaphor as clause structure

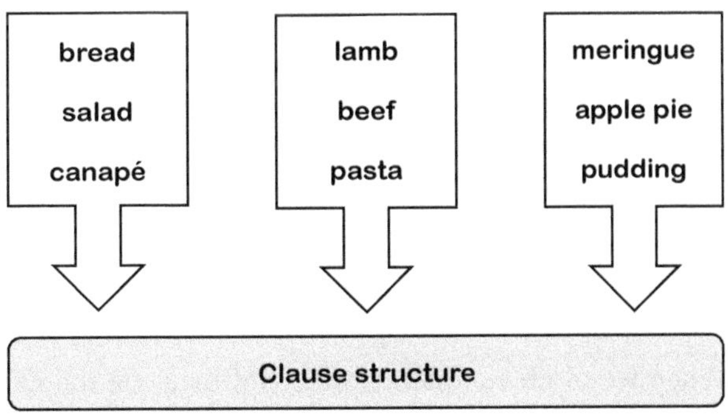

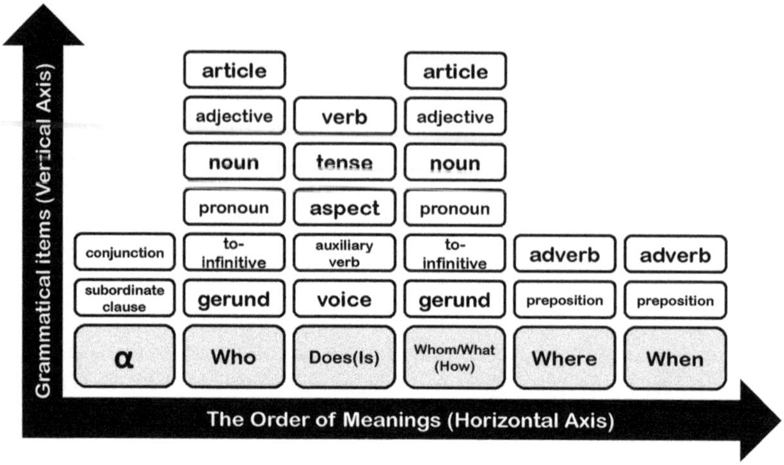

Fig. 9 A two-dimensional approach to English grammar: horizontal and vertical axes

Fig. 10 A vertical axis: teaching auxiliaries

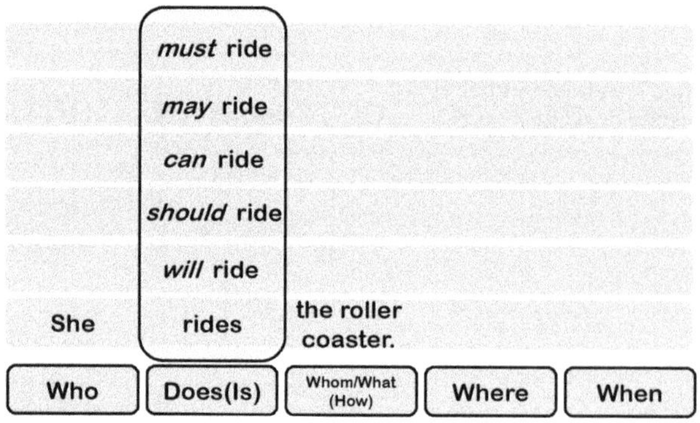

English Grammar Viewed in Two Dimensions

This food system metaphor makes it possible to view English grammar in two dimensions: the order of meanings (a clause or sentence) on the horizontal axis and each of the grammatical items (each of which can be associated with a particular part of the clause, that is, one of the meaning units) on a vertical axis (see Fig. 9).

Teaching Auxiliaries, Tense, and Aspect

When we teach auxiliaries, we could focus on the DOES (IS) unit and treat these items vertically, as is shown in Fig. 10.

When we teach tense and aspect, currently listed out in an unmeaningful order in grammar course books, we can examine another aspect of the usefulness of the

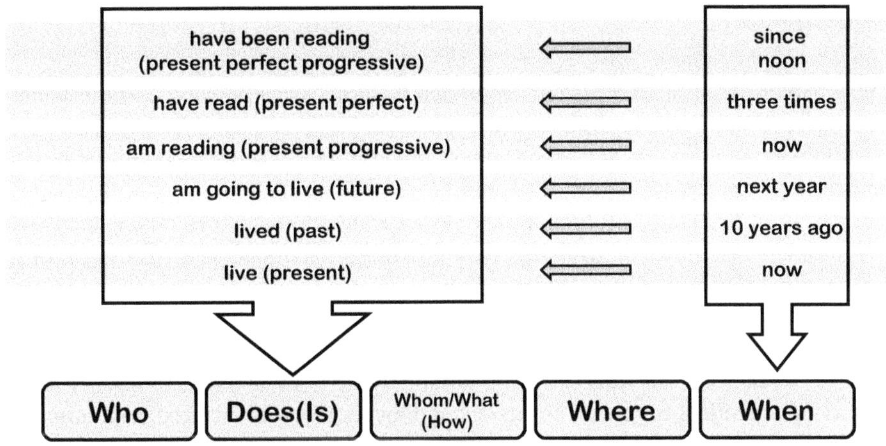

Fig. 11 A vertical axis: teaching tense and aspect

vertical axis in MAP Grammar. By taking these sentences below, for example, we can see how easy it is to draw learner attention to how the WHEN unit influences the use of tense in the DOES unit. For example, in the sentence "I live in Kyoto now," the "now" determines the choice of tense for "live." If the "now" were 10 years ago, the "live" becomes "lived" and so on.

(1) I *live* in Kyoto *now*.
(2) I *lived* in Hiroshima *10 years ago*.
(3) I *am going to live* in Tokyo *next year*.
(4) I *am reading* a book *now*.
(5) I *have read* this book *three times*.
(6) I *have been reading* this book *since noon*.

These six sentences can be represented visually with MAP Grammar, as seen in Fig. 11.

In this way, English grammar can be described by (1) the axis which is a combination of words or phrases on the horizontal axis and (2) the axis of selection of grammatical items, each of which can be associated with a particular meaning unit. By separating discrete grammatical aspects and the basic clause structure into these two axes, learners are provided with a visual model in which they can locate what they are learning, and the teacher can also employ the model to diagnose learner errors and provide appropriate instruction. Lastly, by labelling each unit with everyday language, it should be easier for teachers to draw learner attention to connections between grammatical function and meaning and, for the learner, to grasp those connections.

Conclusion

This chapter has applied a systems approach to address problematic areas in grammar instruction. We have discussed the nature of English grammar instruction for communicative purposes and then suggested a grammar teaching model that might be used to improve pedagogy. The building of this model followed soft systems methodology, firstly by outlining the problematic situation and then raising the issue of multiple worldviews of grammar, before building the model and showing how it has been put into action to desirable effect.

This model, just as the soft systems procedure itself, is not a self-contained whole that solves all of the problems with grammar teaching. Rather, as particular hurdles in grammar teaching are often unique to the individual teaching context, it is part of a cyclical approach to understanding those problems and beginning to solve them. The MAP Grammar model presented here does this by presenting a road map for teachers and learners. It functions in such a way that when the next problem arises, both teachers and learners can return to this road map to find out where they are, where they are having their problem, and thereby how to address it and where to move to next.

The actual implementation of MAP Grammar in the classroom, for example, will therefore also necessarily be slightly different for each individual that employs it. In this way, the MAP Grammar model itself is a *soft* system – one that helps to shed new light on grammar instruction as a whole, to the benefit of all of those involved in the human activity system.

References

Benesse Educational Research and Development Institute. (2014). *Chukosei no eigo gakushu ni kansuru jittai chosa 2014* [A survey on secondary school students' English language learning 2014]. Retrieved from http://berd.benesse.jp/up_images/research/Teenagers_English_learning_Survey-2014_ALL.pdf

Bolstad, F., Kanamaru, T., & Tajino, A. (2010). Laying the groundwork for ongoing learning: A scaffolded approach to language education in Japanese elementary schools and beyond. In *Proceedings of INTERSPEECH 2010 satellite workshop on "Second language studies: Acquisition, learning, education and technology"* (pp. 1–4).

Burt, M. K. (1975). Error analysis in the adult EFL classroom. *TESOL Quarterly, 9*(1), 53–63. https://doi.org/10.2307/3586012.

Canale, M. (1983). From communicative competence to communicative language pedagogy. In J. C. Richards & R. W. Schmidt (Eds.), *Language and communication* (pp. 2–27). London: Longman.

Canale, M., & Swain, M. (1980). Theoretical bases of communicative approaches to second language teaching and testing. *Applied Linguistics, 1*(1), 1–47. https://doi.org/10.1093/applin/I.1.1.

Crystal, D. (2004a). *Making sense of grammar*. Harlow: Pearson Education.

Crystal, D. (2004b). *Rediscover grammar* (3rd ed.). Harlow: Pearson Education.

Culler, J. (1976). *Saussure*. London: Fontana.

de Oliveira, L. C., & Schleppegrell, M. J. (2015). *Focus on grammar and meaning*. Oxford: Oxford University Press.

Fukumasu, H. (2017, June 23). *Imijun eisakubun jugyo ni* [Using the order of meanings in English composition classes]. Yomiuri Shimbun.

Hasan, R. (1988). The analysis of one poem: Theoretical issues in practice. In D. Birch & M. O'Tool (Eds.), *Functions and styles* (pp. 45–73). London: Edward Arnold.

Halliday, M. A. K. (1994). *An introduction to functional grammar* (2nd ed.). London: Edward Arnold.

Hosogoshi, K., Hidaka, Y., & Pearce, D. (2018). MAP Grammar and listening. In A. Tajino (Ed.), *A new approach to English pedagogical grammar: The order of meanings* (pp. 137–147). Abingdon: Routledge.

Imai, K., Nakajima, H., Tonoike, S., & Tancredi, C. (1995). *Essentials of modern English grammar*. Tokyo: Kenkyusha.

Jojima, T., Oyabu, H., & Jinnouchi, Y. (2018). Developing a base of English expressions using MAP Grammar. In A. Tajino (Ed.), *A new approach to English pedagogical grammar: The order of meanings* (pp. 175–184). Abingdon: Routledge.

Kanamaru, T., & Pearce, D. R. (2018). MAP Grammar and ICT applications. In A. Tajino (Ed.), *A new approach to English pedagogical grammar: The order of meanings* (pp. 83–93). Abingdon: Routledge.

MEXT. (2016). *Eigo kyoiku kaizen no tame no eigo ryoku chosa jigyo hokokusho* [Report on English proficiency survey for the English education reform]. Retrieved from http://www.mext.go.jp/component/a_menu/education/detail/__icsFiles/afieldfile/2016/12/16/1375533_1.pdf

Okuzumi, K. (2016). Imijun eigo shidoho: Komyunikeishon ni tsunagaru gakushueibunposhido. [Teaching English with the order of meanings: Language pedagogy for communicative purposes] *Bulletin of Saitama English Educational Research Association,* 102–110.

Pinker, S. (1994). *Language instinct*. New York: W. Morrow and Co.

Sinclair, C. (2010). *Grammar: A friendly approach* (2nd ed.). Maidenhead: McGraw-Hill Education.

Smithers, R., & Gray, J. (2018). Enhancing the quality of life in lifelong learners: The influence of a meaning-order approach to pedagogical grammar on motivation and self-efficacy. *Applied Linguistics Review*, *0*(0), 1–21. Retrieved 23 Nov 2018. https://doi.org/10.1515/applirev-2017-0095.

Tajino, A. (1995). *Eikaiwa eno saitankyori* [Shortcut to English conversation]. Tokyo: Kodansha.

Tajino, A. (1999). *Tsukuru eigo o tanoshimu* [Fun with creative English]. Tokyo: Maruzen.

Tajino, A. (2011). *Imijun eisakubun no susume* [The order of meanings: The key to English composition]. Tokyo: Iwanami Shoten.

Tajino, A. (2012). *Gakushusha nitotte yoriyoibunpo towa nanika: Imijun no teian.* [MAP Grammar as a learner-friendly grammar]. In Y. Ohtsu (Ed.), *Gakushu eibunpou o minaoshitai* [A review of learners' English grammar] (pp. 157–175). Tokyo: Kenkyusha.

Tajino, A. (2014). *NHK kisoeigo: Imijun kakikomi renshuchou* [NHK English Basics: *Imijun* writing workbook]. Tokyo: NHK Publishing.

Tajino, A. (2018). MAP Grammar: A systemic approach to ELT. In A. Tajino (Ed.), *A new approach to English pedagogical grammar: The order of meanings* (pp. 9–25). Abingdon: Routledge.

Watari, H., Hosogoshi, K., Kato, Y., Kanamaru, T., Takahashi, S., & Tajino, A. (2012). Teaching English through L1: Effects of IMIJUN on Japanese high school students' writing. *Studies in English Teaching and Learning in East Asia, 4*, 33–49.

Vocabulary Teaching: A Systemic Perspective

Yosuke Sasao

Abstract The purpose of this chapter is to discuss ways in which soft systems methodology (SSM) may be applied to the field of vocabulary learning and teaching. It begins by addressing the current problematic situation in this field and then attempts to approach the problem by borrowing the transformation processing model from SSM. In this chapter, I argue that teachers may benefit from focusing on fostering students' vocabulary learning ability which contributes to effective vocabulary learning, rather than their vocabulary knowledge per se, because teachers typically do not have enough time to deal with vocabulary in class. I also suggest that vocabulary instruction should be seen as part of a broader language education system. More specifically, I propose that vocabulary and grammar instruction may be interconnected with each other within the framework of Meaning-order Approach to Pedagogical (MAP) Grammar, and explore ways in which vocabulary is learned effectively for communicative purposes using the MAP Grammar model.

Keywords Vocabulary · Soft systems methodology · MAP Grammar · Vocabulary learning ability

Introduction

Vocabulary knowledge plays a critical role in language use because no verbal communication is possible without words. In the last couple of decades, there has been a growing interest in vocabulary learning as a key aspect in the field of second-language acquisition. The recognition of the importance of increasing vocabulary knowledge has led researchers to investigate effective methods of vocabulary learning and teaching (e.g., Webb and Nation 2017). One approach is to create vocabulary learning materials such as word lists complied from useful words for a certain group of students. Another approach is to identify the most effective vocabulary learning activities to help students increase their vocabulary knowledge efficiently.

Y. Sasao (✉)
Institute for Liberal Arts and Sciences, Kyoto University, Kyoto, Japan
e-mail: sasao.yosuke.8n@kyoto-u.ac.jp

A. Tajino (ed.), *A Systems Approach to Language Pedagogy*, Translational Systems Sciences 17, https://doi.org/10.1007/978-981-13-6272-9_4

The last couple of decades have seen an abundance of vocabulary-related research, but it is still unclear how we can teach vocabulary effectively. As Webb and Nation (2017, p. 1) put it, “there are many approaches to learning words, a great deal of variation in how vocabulary is presented in materials, and large differences in the lexical development of learners. This suggests a lack of clarity on how vocabulary might best be learned.”

In this chapter, I propose that SSM may be useful for improving the problematic situation where effective methods of vocabulary teaching are still unclear. SSM focuses on the whole rather than the parts and assumes emergent properties which are inherent to purposive human activities (Checkland 1983). Vocabulary teaching is a complex human activity because different learners have different worldviews on it. Some may believe that words should be learned in context through reading or listening, while others learn words through deliberate repetitions. Furthermore, suppose a teacher deals with a new word in class, some students forget it soon after class, while others may remember the word for a long period of time. The success of vocabulary learning is not the simple sum of the teacher’s teaching skill and the student’s intelligence, but it is affected by many other factors such as students’ attention, motivation, personal experience, or degree of preparation for the learning activity. This indicates that seeing vocabulary teaching as a systemic whole may provide a new insight to it.

A Systemic Approach to Vocabulary Teaching

Vocabulary learning is one of the most challenging tasks for second-language learners, and thus there is a need to improve vocabulary instruction. Research indicates that children in an English-speaking country learn 1000 words a year (Biemiller and Slonim 2001) and adult English native speakers have knowledge of more than 20,000 words (Goulden et al. 1990; Zechmeister et al. 1995). For second-language learners, however, learning the same amount of vocabulary as native speakers is a daunting task. Research suggests that, in theory, knowledge of 8000–9000 words allows pleasurable reading (Laufer and Ravenhorst-Kalovski 2010; Nation 2006). This learning goal for vocabulary is still challenging for students. For example, research shows that Japanese university students who have learned English for at least 6 years have knowledge of 3000 words on average (Barrow et al. 1999; Mochizuki and Aizawa 2000; Schmitt and Meara 1997). Nurweni and Read (1999) estimated that Indonesian university students knew an average of 1226 words after receiving 6 years of English language instruction. Webb and Chang (2012) tracked Taiwanese high school and university students’ vocabulary growth for 5 years and found that they gained knowledge of 18–430 words annually. Their findings also showed that after 5 years of instruction, 53% of the participants were not able to master the 1000-word level, and 84% did not arrive at the mastery level for the 2000-word level. This indicates that many learners are still far behind the desirable

Table 1 Aspects of vocabulary knowledge

Form	Spoken form
	Written form
	Word parts
Meaning	Form and meaning
	Concepts and references
	Associations
Use	Grammatical functions
	Collocations
	Constraints on use

Nation (2001, 2013)

vocabulary level (i.e., 8000 words), and more effective methods of vocabulary instruction are needed.

In addition to the quantitative aspect of vocabulary knowledge (i.e., how many words are needed), how well a word is known is another important issue. Knowing a word involves more than knowing its meaning. For example, Nation (2001, 2013) argues that vocabulary knowledge has at least three aspects, each of which may be subdivided into three (Table 1). In relation to actual language use, vocabulary knowledge is often divided as receptive and productive knowledge, referring to the knowledge of vocabulary essential for receptive language skills (reading and listening) and knowledge of how to use the words productively (writing and speaking), respectively. Fluency (the speed at which words are processed) is also an important part of vocabulary knowledge.

While learners need to expand their vocabulary to around 8000 words to achieve a sufficient understanding of most general texts, and meet words repeatedly in a variety of contexts to enrich their vocabulary knowledge, teachers cannot teach all of those words directly in class due to limited class hours. Research shows that the 1000 most frequent words account for 65–85% of the words used in written and spoken texts (Dang and Webb 2016), and the 3000 most frequent words cover 95% of the words in the spoken discourse (Schmitt and Schmitt 2014). This relative importance of high-frequency words may lead teachers to focus on these frequent words in class; however, the learning of many other relatively low-frequency words is often left to learners as an extracurricular activity. By borrowing the transformation process model (TPM)[1] from SSM, the current situation may be expressed as illustrated in Fig. 1. In the present situation, instruction attempts directly to deal with vocabulary, but this does not seem desirable or feasible, because instruction cannot cover all the necessary words and learners still need to learn many words on their own.

This situation may be improved by enhancing learners' vocabulary learning ability (VLA) instead of focusing on direct teaching of vocabulary. VLA is the ability

[1]The transformation process is one of Checkland and Scholes' (1999) CATWOE elements (C, customers; A, actors; T, transformation process; W, weltanschauung; O, owner(s); E, environmental constraints). The transformation process plays a critical role in SSM, because it conceptualizes the change that SSM attempts to make (see Tajino (2002) for further discussion).

that facilitates vocabulary learning and is believed to consist of a variety of components such as guessing from context, deliberate word-pair learning, dictionary use, knowledge of word parts, knowledge of a sound system, and knowledge of sound-spelling relationships (Sasao 2013, in press). As shown in Fig. 2, instruction may focus on enhancing students' VLA which will in turn help them expand their vocabulary knowledge effectively. Teachers may spend time increasing learners' VLA as part of vocabulary instruction, which will lead to efficient self-study of words.

The TPM illustrated in Fig. 2 may be elaborated as shown in Fig. 3. This model is an input-output transformation for vocabulary instruction based on Tajino et al.'s (2005, p. 37) transformation model for EAP course design. An arrow from one activity to anther indicates that the latter is dependent on the former.

Figure 3 involves the function of monitoring and control to clarify "the operations and take control action to change and/or improve [the activities]" (Checkland 1989, p. 90). For monitoring students' vocabulary learning and taking action for improving the learning activities, diagnostic VLA tests may be of great value. Currently, two of the VLA tests (Word Part Levels Test and Guessing from Context Test) are available (Sasao and Webb 2017, 2018). These tests are beneficial to teachers because they diagnose their students' vocabulary learning strengths and weaknesses in these skills and indicate weak areas to improve in teaching. Future research may create and validate diagnostic tests measuring other VLA components.

We have looked at how SSM may be applied to vocabulary instruction. The subsequent section will discuss how vocabulary instruction may be situated in a broader system, that is, language education in general.

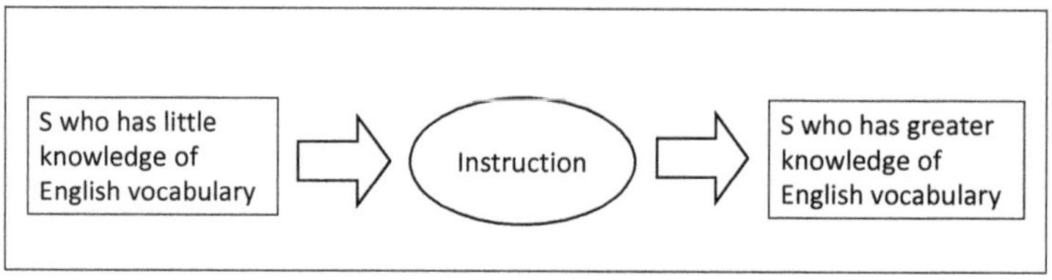

Fig. 1 Transformation process model (present situation)

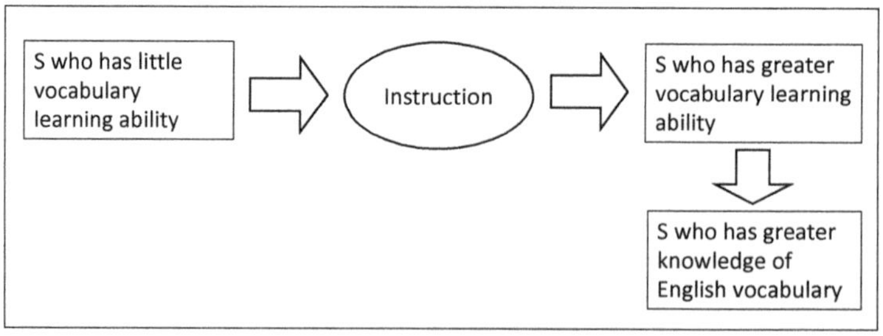

Fig. 2 Transformation process model (suggested future direction)

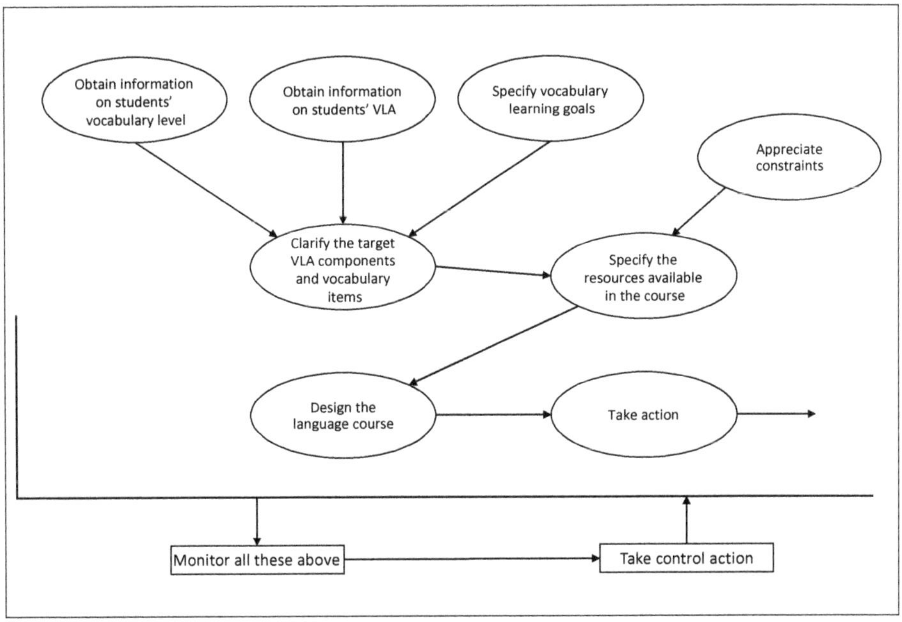

Fig. 3 Model building for vocabulary instruction

Vocabulary Teaching in a Broader System

Chapter "Toward Managing Language Pedagogy and Language Teaching Research" of this book provides an overall picture of language education from a systemic perspective using the 5W1H framework. The model assumes interrelationships among the components which exhibit emergent properties. Vocabulary teaching is categorized in the *What* slot together with grammar instruction. This indicates that vocabulary and grammar are not mutually exclusive modules, but rather these should be seen as interrelated to each other.

One big problem in the vocabulary learning literature is that it seems to have limited its scope only to vocabulary, and very few attempts have been made to synthesize vocabulary and grammar instruction. In order to effectively achieve a vocabulary learning goal, various types of word lists have been developed. Well-known word lists include West's (1953) General Service List of English Words which contains roughly 2000 words that are believed to be used frequently in general language use, Nation's (2012) British National Corpus/Corpus of Contemporary American English word family lists which contain the 25,000 most frequently and widely used words, and Coxhead's (2000) Academic Word List for students learning English for academic purposes. These word lists are of great use because they help raise learners' awareness of useful words which appear frequently in general or specific contexts and efficiently arrive at the learning goals. However, in many cases, words are listed in an alphabetical or frequency order, and it is hard to find connections

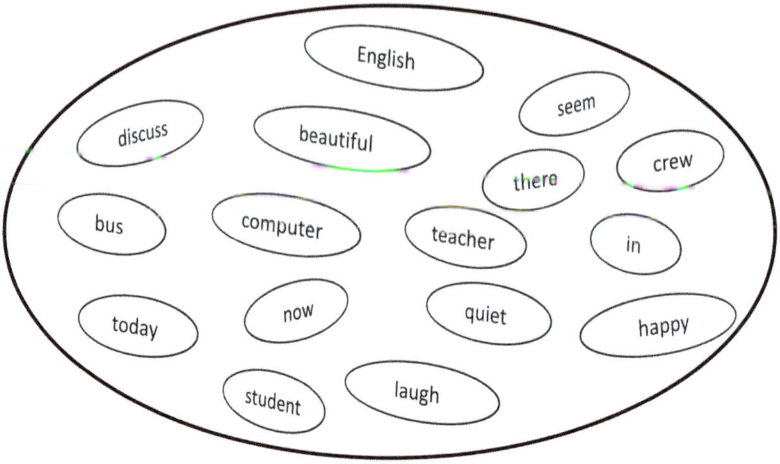

Fig. 4 Words in a typical word list: no interrelations among them

between words. This situation may be conceptualized in Fig. 4 which shows there is no connection among words. Learners may often feel list learning boring or uninteresting and find it difficult to bring the gained knowledge into productive use.

For communicative purposes, words need to be presented so that they will facilitate comprehension and production of a sentence. This need may be addressed by providing words in the framework of Meaning-order Approach to Pedagogical Grammar (MAP Grammar). MAP Grammar is a pedagogical English grammar that proposes only one pattern for English sentences in terms of the order of meanings: *Who/Does (is)/Who(m) What (How)/Where/When* (see chapter "Teaching English Grammar for Communicative Purposes: A Systems Approach" for detailed explanation of MAP Grammar). There are at least five advantages in MAP Grammar for communicative purposes (see Sasao (2017) for further discussion).

1. It uses *wh-* words which may be easy to understand even to novice learners.
2. It is directly related to meaning (semantic roles) in a sentence. It avoids the use of conventional grammatical terminologies (e.g., *subject*, *object*, *agent*, and *goal*).
3. It may help avoid global (word order) errors which lead to the breakdown of communication. Local errors such as singular/plural and tense do not usually seriously affect communication.
4. It may promote active reading and listening. When you process the *Who* and *Does (is)* components, you will be able to infer the information that follows. For example, when you hear someone say "Mary gave …," you can predict that something she gave and someone she gave it will come next.
5. Research (Tajino et al. 2015) indicates that the explicit knowledge of MAP Grammar increases the speed and the accuracy of sentence processing.

A communicative word list may be created by categorizing words according to semantic roles in the MAP Grammar model (Fig. 5). This word list is of great value because vocabulary learning and its use are directly connected; in other words, words are learned with the indication of how to use them based on the MAP Grammar model. This may encourage learners to use the newly learned words, which helps them strengthen the knowledge as well as sees the relationship between vocabulary learning and its use.

Another advantage of the MAP Grammar model is that it can present learners with both single- and multi-word expressions effectively, because it sees the semantic roles (rather than individual words) as a meaningful component of a sentence. Table 2 shows example expressions for single- and multi-word items. These words and expressions may be introduced to learners as items that can fill the *Does(is)* slot. Knowledge of multi-word expressions (or often called *formulaic sequences*) is important because they seem to contribute to fluent, accurate, and natural language use (Boers et al. 2006). Its importance can also be seen in corpus-based studies. Erman and Warren (2000) showed that more than half of the words used in their spoken and written corpora would be regarded as formulaic sequences. Foster (2001) found that formulaic sequences accounted for 32.3% of the speech by English native speakers.

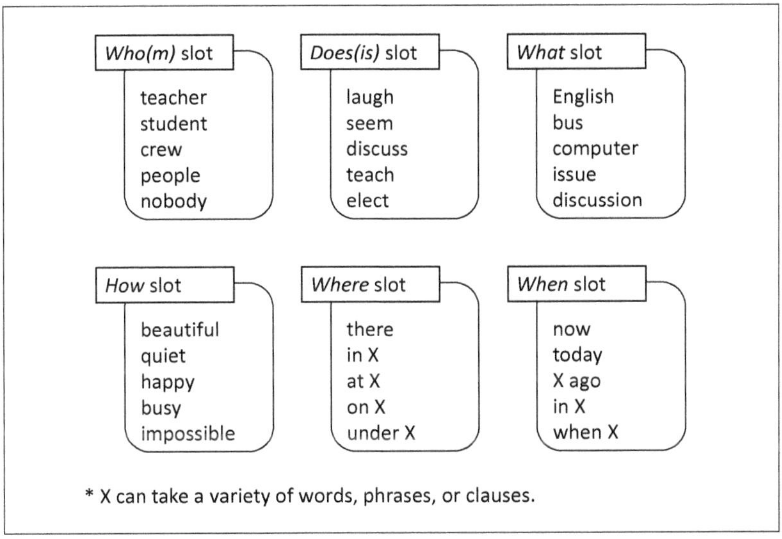

Fig. 5 Words grouped in the MAP Grammar meaning units

Table 2 Example single- and multi-word expressions for the *Does*(*Is*) unit

Single-word		Multi-word	
laugh	teach	get up	look forward to
become	call	put off	come up with
play	live	carry out	take care of

Conclusion

This chapter has argued that SSM may be a useful model to deal with the current problematic situation in the field of vocabulary teaching. English learners need to learn a large number of words to arrive at the mastery level, however, teachers have little time to deal with vocabulary during class hours, and vocabulary learning is often left to students. A new TPM was proposed to better cope with the current situation. The model suggests that instruction should include fostering students' VLA which will facilitate their future vocabulary learning. The TPM involves the monitoring process which may be put into practice through diagnostic VLA tests such as the Word Part Levels Test and the Guessing from Context Test.

This chapter has also proposed that vocabulary instruction may be situated in a broader system. Given the framework of language education discussed in the chapter "Toward Managing Language Pedagogy and Language Teaching Research," vocabulary instruction can be seen as one of the *What* components together with grammar instruction. Seeing the interrelationships between vocabulary and grammar instruction may yield a new approach to vocabulary learning. Specifically, this chapter has argued that MAP Grammar may be a useful model for connecting vocabulary and grammar systemically and learning words for communicative purposes. While the present work aims to propose a possible way of applying SSM to vocabulary instruction, future research may provide empirical data through interviews and anthropological fieldwork with teachers using this model in class. It should also be of great value to create word lists as shown in Fig. 5.

References

Barrow, J., Nakanishi, Y., & Ishino, H. (1999). Assessing Japanese college students' vocabulary knowledge with a self-checking familiarity survey. *System, 27*, 223–247. https://doi.org/10.1016/S0346-251X(99)00018-4.

Biemiller, A., & Slonim, N. (2001). Estimating root word vocabulary growth in normative and advantaged populations: Evidence for a common sequence of vocabulary acquisition. *Journal of Educational Psychology, 93*(3), 498–520. https://doi.org/10.1037/0022-0663.93.3.498.

Boers, F., Eyckmans, J., Kappel, J., Stengers, H., & Demecheleer, M. (2006). Formulaic sequences and perceived oral proficiency: Putting the Lexical Approach to the test. *Language Teaching Research, 10*(3), 245–261. https://doi.org/10.1191/1362168806lr195oa.

Checkland, P. (1983). O.R. and the systems movement: Mapping and conflicts. *Journal of the Operational Research Society, 34*(8), 661–675. https://doi.org/10.1057/jors.1983.160.

Checkland, P. (1989). An application of soft systems methodology. In L. Rosenhead (Ed.), *Rational analysis for a problematical world*. Chichester: Wiley.

Checkland, P., & Scholes, J. (1999). *Soft systems methodology in action*. Chichester: Wiley.

Coxhead, A. (2000). A new academic word list. *TESOL Quarterly, 34*(2), 213–238. https://doi.org/10.2307/3587951.

Dang, T. N. Y., & Webb, S. (2016). Evaluating lists of high-frequency words. *ITL – International Journal of Applied Linguistics, 167*(2), 132–158. https://doi.org/10.1075/itl.00009.sas.

Erman, B., & Warren, B. (2000). The idiom principle and the open choice principle. *Text, 20*(1), 29–62. https://doi.org/10.1075/itl.167.2.02dan.

Foster, P. (2001). Rules and routines: A consideration of their role in the task-based language production of native and non-native speakers. In M. Bygate, P. Skehan, & M. Swain (Eds.), *Researching pedagogic tasks: Second language learning, teaching, and testing* (pp. 75–93). Harlow: Longman.

Goulden, R., Nation, P., & Read, J. (1990). How large can a receptive vocabulary be? *Applied Linguistics, 11*(4), 341–363. https://doi.org/10.1093/applin/11.4.341.

Laufer, B., & Ravenhorst-Kalovski, G. C. (2010). Lexical threshold revisited: Lexical text coverage, learners' vocabulary size and reading comprehension. *Reading in a Foreign Language, 22*(1), 15–30.

Mochizuki, M., & Aizawa, K. (2000). An affix acquisition order for EFL learners: An exploratory study. *System, 28*(2), 291–304. https://doi.org/10.1016/S0346-251X(00)00013-0.

Nation, I. S. P. (2001). *Learning vocabulary in another language*. Cambridge, UK: Cambridge University Press.

Nation, I. S. P. (2006). How large a vocabulary is needed for reading and listening? *Canadian Modern Language Review, 63*(1), 59–82. https://doi.org/10.3138/cmlr.63.1.59.

Nation, I. S. P. (2012). *The BNC/COCA word family lists*. Retrieved May 17, 2018, from http://www.victoria.ac.nz/lals/about/staff/paul-nation

Nation, I. S. P. (2013). *Learning vocabulary in another language* (2nd ed.). Cambridge: Cambridge University Press.

Nurweni, A., & Read, J. (1999). The English vocabulary knowledge of Indonesian university students. *English for Specific Purposes, 18*(2), 161–175. https://doi.org/10.1016/S0889-4906(98)00005-2.

Sasao, Y. (2013). *Diagnostic tests of English vocabulary learning proficiency: Guessing from context and knowledge of word parts*. Unpublished doctoral dissertation. Victoria University of Wellington, New Zealand.

Sasao, Y. (2017). MAP Grammar and vocabulary. In A. Tajino (Ed.), *A new approach to English pedagogical grammar: The order of meanings* (pp. 128–136). Oxford: Routledge.

Sasao, Y. (in press). Measuring the ability to learn words. In S. A. Webb (Ed.), *The Routledge handbook of vocabulary studies*. Oxford: Routledge.

Sasao, Y., & Webb, S. (2017). The word part levels test. *Language Teaching Research, 21*(1), 12–30. https://doi.org/10.1177/1362168815586083.

Sasao, Y., & Webb, S. (2018). The guessing from context test. *ITL – International Journal of Applied Linguistics, 169*(1), 114–140. https://doi.org/10.1075/itl.00009.sas.

Schmitt, N., & Meara, P. (1997). Researching vocabulary through a word knowledge framework: Word associations and verbal suffixes. *Studies in Second Language Acquisition, 19*(1), 17–36. https://doi.org/10.1017/S0272263197001022.

Schmitt, N., & Schmitt, D. (2014). A reassessment of frequency and vocabulary size in L2 vocabulary teaching. *Language Teaching, 46*(4), 484–503. https://doi.org/10.1017/S0261444812000018.

Tajino, A., James, R., & Kijima, K. (2005). Beyond needs analysis: Soft systems methodology for meaningful collaboration in EAP course design. *Journal of English for Academic Purposes, 4*(1), 27–42. https://doi.org/10.1016/j.jeap.2004.01.001.

Tajino, A. (2002). Transformation process models: A systemic approach to problematic team-teaching situation. *Prospect, 17*(3), 29–33.

Tajino, A., Kanamaru, T., & Sasao, Y. (2015). *Bunpousei handan no seikakusa to ryuuchousa eno "Imijun" chishiki no kouka* [The effects of the "MAP Grammar" knowledge on accuracy and fluency in grammaticality judgement]. Paper presented at the 159th Higashi Asia Eigo Kyouiku Kenkyukai [English Education in East Asia Research Project], Seinan Gakuin University.

Webb, S. A., & Chang, A. C.-S. (2012). Second language vocabulary growth. *RELC Journal, 43*(1), 113–126. https://doi.org/10.1177/0033688212439367.

Webb, S., & Nation, P. (2017). *How vocabulary is learned*. Oxford: Oxford University Press.

West, M. (1953). *A general service list of English words*. London: Longman, Green & Co..

Zechmeister, E. B., Chronis, A. M., Cull, W. L., D'Anna, C. A., & Healy, N. A. (1995). Growth of a functionally important lexicon. *Journal of Reading Behavior, 27*(2), 201–212. https://doi.org/10.1080/10862969509547878.

Surveying the Landscape of Second Language Classroom Research

Tim Stewart

Abstract For readers new to as well as those familiar with the literature on classroom research, correctly sorting out how different terms are defined and used is crucial to developing expertise. The truth is that a lot of the key terms used in second language classroom research appear analogous. Adding to the potential confusion is the fact that some writers use terms rather loosely under the assumption that they are in fact parallel in meaning. In this chapter, I take up the challenge of defining key terms and attempting to show their relative positioning in TESOL research through a systemic analysis. The advantage of applying a systems approach to clarify classroom research categories is that this kind of analysis lays out a holistic view (i.e., systemic). The point of my chapter is to try to develop a common frame of reference among teachers and researchers interested in TESOL classroom research by sorting out the various boundaries of classroom research types in TESOL. This is important because making the practice of classroom research accessible to classroom teachers first requires clearly defining research categories.

Keywords Terminology · Classroom research · Practitioner research · Teacher research · Reflective practice · Classroom-based research · Classroom-oriented research · Soft systems approach

In this chapter, I examine the contemporary landscape of second language classroom research with an emphasis on terminology. I begin by laying out the various ways that classroom research is defined in the literature, concentrating on closely related terms. Drawing on my own experience teaching a graduate course on classroom research methods, I know that the number of overlapping terms used to define the area often leads to confusion. Clarity of terminology is essential to ensure understanding so that people with an interest in this area can "speak the same language" and communicate accurately to help develop it further. In the chapter I offer one way to sort out this hodgepodge, that is, through a "systems" perspective that

---

T. Stewart (✉)
Graduate School of Human and Environmental Studies, Kyoto University, Kyoto, Japan
e-mail: stewart.timothywilliam.3m@kyoto-u.ac.jp

A. Tajino (ed.), *A Systems Approach to Language Pedagogy*, Translational Systems Sciences 17, https://doi.org/10.1007/978-981-13-6272-9_5

lays out a holistic picture of second language classroom research. My hope is to further the creation of a common frame of reference for discourse among interested colleagues.

Terminology and Academic Writing Style in Flux

Every profession has specialized terminology, and a major aim of advanced courses in universities is, of course, to teach key terms. Graduate students of language education, linguistics, and Teaching English to Speakers of Other Languages (TESOL) need to learn the terminology that will gain them entry into professional discourse communities. But while academics need to learn the vocabulary of their specialization, it seems that how they express their disciplinary knowledge can lead less to enlightenment and more to confusion. The style of writing in academia has long been ridiculed (see Pinker 2014). Helen Sword, after doing research into academic writing style, described peer-reviewed journals as being filled with: "Impersonal, stodgy, jargon-laden, abstract prose" (2012, p. 3). Furthermore, she insisted:

> There is a massive gap between what most readers consider to be good writing and what academics typically produce and publish. I'm not talking about the kinds of formal strictures necessarily imposed by journal editors – article length, citation style, and the like – but about a deeper, duller kind of disciplinary monotony, a compulsive proclivity for discursive obscurantism and circumambulatory diction (translation: an addiction to big words and soggy syntax).

Manuscripts published in second language education and applied linguistics illustrate Sword's point quite well, unfortunately. The trend of writing in abstract, jargon-laden prose, crammed with citations, obscures rather than illuminates. Sometimes ideas are purposely written to be nearly inaccessible in order to try and impress readers with one's cleverness and level of sophistication. Sadly, the prose produced by university-based researchers often is inaccessible to the broad audience of classroom teachers (see Kerr 2005; Marsden and Kasprowicz 2017).

Of course, related to the obscurity of some academic prose is the sheer amount of specialized terminology and how terms are defined. Richards, Ross, and Seedhouse lament:

> One problem in research into language learning is that there is a proliferation of terminology, and terms are often associated with particular approaches or methodologies. Hence, the same phenomenon may have a different name when examined using a different methodology. (2012, p. 49)

Indeed, when surveying the contemporary landscape of classroom research in TESOL, the thing that quickly becomes clear is the lack of clarity in terminology. In the 50th anniversary issue of the *TESOL Quarterly*, Anne Burns (2016) laid out the journal's research guidelines for practitioner research. Burns described educational practitioner research as "situated at the interface of practice and theory, where participants are moving between the two in a designed process of intervention in response to participant-identified issues and challenges" (2016, p. 56). Her further explanation of the term identified significant overlap with other defined areas of research such as ethnography and case study. In addition to this, she emphasized the eclectic nature of data collection, as well as the variable formats and styles of reporting used which are "in flux" and "inevitably determined by the target audience" (Burns 2016, p. 57).

In this chapter, I wish to focus on research done by teacher-researchers in school contexts. For this type of research, authors have applied a number of labels in the literature: practitioner research, action research, self-study, collaborative inquiry, reflective practice, classroom research, and teacher research (see Roulston et al. 2005). Definitions of teacher research commonly state that it is inquiry conducted in a systematic way by teachers in schools and classrooms. Practitioner research, of course, is a broader term that refers to inquiry of practice generally by practitioners in any field. Naturally, classroom research is related to teacher research, but not all classroom research is teacher research as we know from classroom studies done by outside researchers.

Having established the point about the clutter of terms that have accumulated in relation to classroom research in second language teaching, the remainder of this chapter will be my attempt to organize the terminology in a systemic way.

Systems Thinking and Systemic Analysis for Holistic Understanding

Soft systems thinking was developed by systems theorists who were dissatisfied with *hard systems* and *organismic systems* approaches. Researchers encountered difficulties with the latter two approaches when dealing with data gathered in social situations. In social systems the problems that emerge often cannot be neatly categorized and appear ill-structured. Once convinced of the unsuitable nature of earlier approaches to resolving complex social issues, Checkland (1981) developed a soft systems approach.

Drawing on Checkland's model for research, Tajino, James, and Kijima (2005, p. 30) extended its use to second language education. In their article, they explained that a soft systems analysis of problematic situations provides researchers with "a structure or framework through which … accommodation among potentially conflicting perspectives" can be achieved. Peter Checkland's flexible soft systems approach to problem-solving promotes learning within· models by outlining the structure of the system under investigation in a holistic manner. Importantly, it is described as *systemic* since it focuses on "the whole, rather than the parts" (Tajino et al., 2005 p. 31).

By presenting a system holistically, researchers might avoid taking a selective focus that leads to piecemeal methods of analysis. Capra (1982) has emphasized how isolating elements of a system in order to analyze it will destroy its systemic properties since "the nature of the whole is always different from the mere sum of its parts" (p. 267). Fundamentally, it is the dynamic interdependence and interaction between components that define systems. Learning the relationships among the concepts helps researchers establish a set of principles. How the principles are related forms the basis for the systems model according to Banathy (1992).

Banathy was influenced by the "rich pictures" of Checkland (1981) and wanted to create more richly defined models. For research into educational systems, Banathy (1992) created three lenses or systems models: Systems-Environment Model, Functions-Structure Model, and Process Model. Banathy claims that researchers should use these models in tandem to "look at an educational activity system and understand, describe, and analyze it as an open, dynamic, and complex social system" (1992, p. 21).

Walton (2004) drew attention to the fact that Banathy's three lenses were never very specific about contents, examples, or notation. This flexibility of use is indicative of the organic approach that is the hallmark of soft systems. In this chapter, I will include aspects of all three lenses in my analysis of second language classroom research. I begin with Banathy's Systems-Environment Model and emphasize the larger social environment of classroom research. Next, I look more closely at the structure and functions of classroom research and end with a brief explanation of the process of classroom research practice. In my attempt to sort out the clutter of terminology associated with second language classroom research, a wide-view lens seems most appropriate. In other words, I hope to provide a comprehensive, but more importantly comprehensible, snapshot of the classroom research terrain.

Sorting Out Key Terminology

To achieve my goal of creating a snapshot of second language classroom research, I will build layers of understanding by addressing several questions. I focus on four key terms that are used interchangeably: practitioner research, teacher research, reflective practice, and classroom research.

What Is Research in Second Language Education?

The tensions between *psychometric* (experimental) and *naturalistic* (qualitative) research in studies of second language learning have been well-documented (e.g., Nunan and Bailey 2009). Both of these research traditions involve collecting and analyzing data; however, they use different methods and procedures to achieve results. Many published studies in the TESOL field combine elements from both traditions in fact. Nunan and Bailey (2009) emphasize this trend in their comprehensive guide to second language classroom research.

No matter which methods are used, all research is necessarily interpretive and, therefore, subjective. The worldview of the researcher always influences the questions asked and guides the selection of methods and interpretation of results. This reality challenges the imposed requirement of social science scholars who strive to highlight the "scientific" nature of their research, that is, the need for context-neutral research. This stance is impossible for classroom research.

As we know, research in the TESOL field draws heavily from psychology and general education models. It was in the 1980s that Schön (1983) revived and extended Dewey's (1933) conception of reflective practice based on his notion of education as social activity. Schön's research focused on how practitioners think when practicing, and he created an epistemology of practice that has served as a cornerstone of much classroom-based research. Schön's work, of course, reflects the evolution of practitioner research in education.

Practitioner research in general is simply research conducted by practitioners in some field (e.g., health-care workers, engineers, architects, lawyers, teachers). In their influential work, Cochran-Smith and Lytle (2009) use the terms "practitioner research" and "practitioner inquiry" interchangeably as umbrella terms for contemporary educational research. In education, practitioners can be teachers, students, teacher educators, administrators, and other stakeholders.

Stevick (1986) promoted humanism in language teaching and in his writing provided a holistic lens on learners and teachers. He called for a change of attitude that would allow classroom teachers to see others as whole, complex people, and as fellow practitioners. When the research community adopted ideas from Stenhouse (1975) and Lortie (1975) into second language research, teachers began to be positioned as researchers. This move encouraged some teachers to take control of their own professional development as the local knowledge of practitioners became valued more highly. Thus, teacher-researchers could contribute to the knowledge base of their field at long last.

Therefore, since at least the 1970s teachers of all subjects have wondered about the requirements of research. At the most basic level, research seeks answers to questions that we ask. To be considered "research" a study needs to be undertaken through a systematic process. Nunan and Bailey (2009, p. 16) describe four elements in the research process: (1) a research question, problem, puzzle, or hypothesis, (2) data, (3) analysis and interpretation, and (4) publication (written and/or oral) so as to add to the knowledge base of the field.

What Is Teacher Research?

As we know, second language research was preoccupied from the 1940s into the 1970s with the search for best methods of instruction. Researchers tended to compare different student groups studying languages through different methods and focused only on the outcomes (products) of the methods investigated. However, the large-scale studies conducted in search of methods that could be applied universally, produced inconclusive results. According to Allwright and Bailey (1991), these results stimulated researchers to focus on local, classroom-based research. What followed were a number of studies that focused on classroom processes of teaching and learning. These process-focused studies attempted to understand what happens in classrooms and did not make causal claims about best methods or materials.

Much of this early research on teaching and learning in TESOL, however, was done by outside researchers and could not be labeled teacher research. But the emergence of research focused on the process of teaching and learning led to "the next logical step in the evolution of language teaching research – that classroom studies would start to be conducted by teachers themselves" (Borg 2013, p. 11). This path was first promoted in general education by Stenhouse (1975) through his concept of "the teacher as researcher," as well as Lortie (1975). Stenhouse did not believe that private inquiry could be called research and defined research as "systematic inquiry made public" (p. 142) with a self-critical eye.

The ideas promoted by these educators paved the way for the contemporary rationale for the classroom as a research site and teachers as research practitioners (e.g., Zeichner and Noffke 2001). In the TESOL field, the idea of teachers doing research has steadily gained credence since Allwright and Bailey (1991) published their seminal volume. The underlying rationale for teacher research is that by exploring the activity in their own classrooms, teachers better understand their own practice. In this way, teacher research is often linked to the process of professional development.

The defining feature of teacher research is the researcher. The agent who conducts the research is the classroom teacher. This dominant variable is constant and is independent of research location and research methods. In sum, definitions of teacher research commonly describe self-initiated "inquiry conducted by teachers in their own professional contexts" systematically (Borg 2013, p. 8).

What Is Reflective Practice?

In its most basic form, reflective practice is simple curiosity about what you do as a professional. Asking *what* can be the beginning of research, but left at that it isn't research. Second language teachers would need to take a backward step, look inward further, and ask questions such as *how*, *why*, and *what might be changed* that would lead to improvement? In this way, reflection is seen as a process of both discovering and resolving problems.

According to Richards and Lockhart (1994), reflective practice in second language contexts is an "approach to teaching" wherein "teachers collect data about teaching, examine their attitudes, beliefs, assumptions, and teaching practices, and use the information obtained as a basis for critical reflection about teaching" (p. 1). The aim is to deepen awareness of teaching and learning.

Murphey (2014) paraphrases Dewey (1933) to say that reflective teaching requires practitioners to be aware, receptive, and take responsibility for the consequences of their actions in a wholehearted way. This means that teachers must adopt an attitude about their practice that will encourage them to reflect upon it.

The scholar whose work extended Dewey's concept of reflective thinking most is Schön (1983). Schön did research into how professionals think when engaged in practice and described three ways of reflective thinking: reflection-*in*-action, reflection-*on*-action, and reflection-*for*-action. Schön interpreted reflection-*in*-action as real-time decisions that interact with and modify current practices so that learning occurs, often tacitly. On the other hand, reflection-*on*-action is a deliberate and systematic process of retrospection about professional actions, while reflection-*for*-action goes beyond thinking about past or present classroom events to making plans about changing practice.

Schön's concept of reflective practice has been widely accepted by educational research communities, including TESOL. A lot of the research into reflective practice has focused on identifying conditions that enable its use. In addition, there are a number of books that tell teachers they should do it and explain how to do it. This is likely due to the fact that Schön's work was motivated by a perceived need to value the experiential knowledge of practitioners over the imposed technical knowledge of outside experts. This stance has motivated many classroom teachers to adopt reflective teaching as a method of taking control over their own professional development by learning more about their own practice and how it relates to their local context.

In fact, the practice of reflective language teaching (e.g., Farrell 2007) is quite exclusively focused on one actor in second language classrooms, the teacher, that is, teacher professional development and teacher understanding that might lead to modifications in teaching practice. While reflecting on your own practice is not necessarily teacher research, teacher research definitely has a reflective nature.

The concept has fuzzy edges which, as many researchers have noted, gives rise to divergent meanings (see Collins et al. 2013). Lack of theoretical consensus is partly a result of the fundamental schism along the line "between Schön's notion of practitioner-based intuition, on the one hand, and Dewey's notion of rational and scientific thinking on the other hand" (Fendler 2003, p. 19).

What Is Language Classroom Research?

Early proponents of classroom research in second language contexts pointed out that the term classroom research is often a cover term for "a whole range of research studies on classroom language learning and teaching" (Allwright and Bailey 1991, p. 2). My discussion above of several related terms indicates that this cross-referencing still occurs. Besides classroom research, other cover terms found in the literature are classroom-centered research, classroom-based research, and classroom-oriented research.

Defining what is meant by a classroom is necessary at this point. Leo van Lier (1988) provided a succinct definition of a classroom.

> The L2 classroom can be defined as the gathering, for a given period of time, of two or more persons (one of whom generally assumes the role of instructor) for the purposes of language learning. (p. 47)

While this definition covers traditional school settings adequately, van Lier did not anticipate today's hybrid and virtual classrooms. In other words, gathering together for the purposes of teaching and learning no longer indicates a physical space. In the domain of classroom research, "This redefinition of the classroom is also having an effect on language classroom researchers who now have to go beyond the four walls of the traditional classroom to conduct research" (Nunan and Bailey 2009, p. 21).

Classroom-based research is also referred to as classroom-centered research in the TESOL literature. When researchers use these interchangeable terms, they are thinking of the systematic research procedure of questioning, gathering data, and analyzing the data, using the classroom as the research site. According to Allwright (1983), classroom-centered research "simply tries to investigate what happens inside the classroom when learners and teachers come together" (p. 191). Allwright explained further that the main concern of classroom-centered/classroom-based research is the process and sequence of lessons, interaction between participants, and activity related to teaching and learning.

> At its most narrow, classroom-centred research is in fact research that treats the language classroom not just as the *setting for* investigation but, more importantly, as the *object of* investigation. (Allwright 1983, p. 191)

Classroom research then can be conducted by anyone and as a result can be related closely to the broad category practitioner research, where practitioners are defined as people who engage in research practices (see Fig. 2). This openness must be recognized because in the quest for making sense of what occurs in classrooms, classroom research is accommodating when it comes to questions of theory and methodology.

Finally, classroom-oriented research is studies done outside of classrooms that make some claims about the relevance of their findings for teaching and learning (see Fig. 2). Indeed, the cover term classroom research is the category that encompasses both classroom-oriented and classroom-based research in TESOL (see Nunan and Bailey 2009). Of course, most of the research conducted by classroom teachers is classified as classroom-based (Fig. 1, quadrant 4), but straddling quadrants 3 and 4 in Fig. 1 is research relevant to pedagogy that is conducted outside of classrooms.

Building the Model: How Do the Various Strands Connect?

Figure 1 depicts the types of practitioner research recognizable in the TESOL field. It is a view from the Systems-Environment perspective intended to simply map the space in which the system operates. This model is also referred to as the "bird's-eye-view" lens. The outer boundary of the environment is that of general practitioner

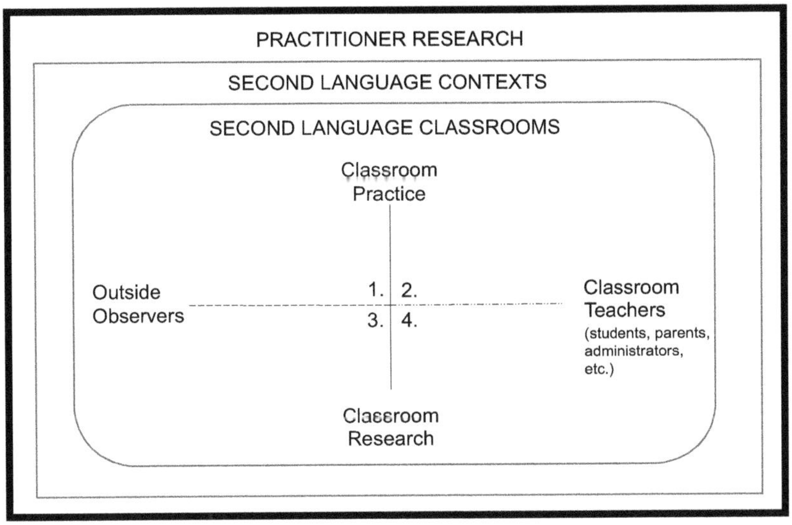

Fig. 1 Practitioner research landscape in TESOL

research. Nested within this larger social sphere is the space of second language teaching and learning in the broad sense. Finally, the activity of practitioner research in second language contexts mainly takes place in second language classrooms. Figure 1 reveals the basic outline of the landscape. This simple bird's-eye view shows at a basic level the relationship between practice and research as well as the actors most concerned. This view of the environment has a top half related to classroom practices and a bottom half related to classroom research.

Outside researchers do research related to classroom practice and can engage in classroom research. Classroom teachers, of course, directly engage in classroom practice and may at times choose to research their classrooms. From a systemic point of view, it is important to note that the divisions between practice and research quadrants in Fig. 1 are perforated to indicate the possibility for research to sustain practice and vice versa.

The next figure presents a more holistic picture of the practice-research environment in second language education contexts. It is an attempt at creating a snapshot of the system's probable structure at the moment (Banathy's Functions-Structure Model). Figure 2 is multilayered and shows both the wider view together with the more detailed view of the second language research landscape. This holistic view situates second language research within the broad category of practitioner research. Both outside researchers, as practitioners of research, and classroom teachers, as practitioners of teacher research and teaching (classroom practice), can engage in practitioner research.

Within the more detailed view, the type of research practice that typically occurs in quadrant 1 is labeled as *observation for evaluation*. This would involve outside observers coming into classrooms to analyze teaching practice. These kinds of

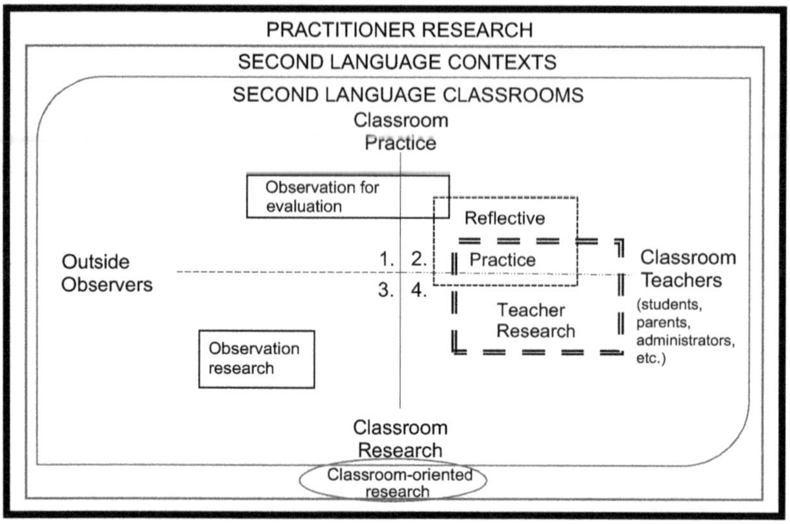

Fig. 2 Practitioner research and second language contexts

evaluations can be summative, formative, or both. They can also include self-evaluations on practice. This possibility for reflective input in evaluation of practice is indicated by the extension into quadrant 2 and the overlap there with reflective practice. Hirings, extensions, promotions, and teaching practicum are events that could require some evaluation of practice.

Quadrant 2 is the reflective analysis of teaching practice by the classroom teacher and can include students. Reflective practice could extend into evaluation as explained above, as well as into teacher research (quadrant 4). Zeichner and Liston (1996) created a five-level framework of teacher reflection. Quadrant 2 represents their levels 1–3: rapid reflection, repair, and review. Movement into quadrant 4 would indicate that the reflective practice is more systematic and conducted according to the tenets of "research." Often action research would be used in such cases. The size of the perforations in the dotted line dividing quadrants 2 and 4 illustrates how teacher research can feed back into and nurture classroom practice. Quadrant 4 is classroom research conducted by classroom teachers and is labeled as teacher research. Again, the defining factor for teacher research is the agent conducting the study. Feedback into classroom practice is also important since teacher research "needs to be conducted in teachers' own professional context and with the purpose of enhancing their understanding of some aspect of their work" (Borg 2013, p. 8). Finally, quadrant 3 represents classroom research conducted by outside practitioners of research (e.g., university faculty members).

There is possible overlap between quadrants 3 and 4 when outside observers collaborate with classroom teachers in their classroom research projects (see Cochran-Smith and Lytle 2009; Stewart 2006). Research *with* rather than research *on* classroom practitioners is favored in TESOL today. Finally, there is research done

Table 1 Types of research in second language contexts: actors, actions and perspectives

ETIC		EMIC
Who? Outside researchers	**Practitioner research**	*Who?* Classroom teachers (students, administrators, etc.)
What? Things outsiders see		*What?* Things insiders know
How? e.g., observation, recording		*How?* e.g., self-evaluation, reflective teaching, teacher research, classroom research
Who? Outside researchers	**Reflective practice**	*Who?* Classroom teachers (students, administrators, etc.)
What? Things outsiders see		*What?* Things insiders know
How? e.g., stimulated recall		*How?* e.g., journals, lesson reports, action research
Who? Outside researchers; teachers in collaboration	**Classroom research**	*Who?* Classroom teachers, researchers in collaboration (students, administrators, etc.)
What? Things outsiders see; combined with insider knowledge		*What?* Things insiders know; combined with researchers' knowledge
How? e.g., case study research, survey research, ethnography, narrative, interviews, discourse analysis		*How?* e.g., action research, think-aloud protocols, survey research, interviews, discourse analysis, exploratory practice
	Teacher research	*Who?* Classroom teachers (students, administrators, etc.)
		What? Things insiders know
		How? e.g., action research, autoethnography, narrative, survey research, exploratory practice

outside of second language classrooms, normally by those *not* engaged in second language teaching practice, that can have some influence on classrooms (classroom-oriented research).

Table 1 displays the four major terms featured in this chapter in a different light. The table is an attempt to create a process-behavior lens (Banathy 1992) that outlines systemically how contemporary research in second language contexts works. It describes activity related to the four key terms visible at two polar extremes, that of either *etic* or *emic* perspectives. The obvious point about Table 1 is that teacher research does not exist from the *etic* perspective. When teacher educators examine their own practice, they adopt the *emic* perspective. Another interesting point is that classroom research can include either the outsider or the insider view or both if organized as collaborative research or in professional learning communities. This means that a continuum of research perspectives exists in language classroom research.

The place of action research in TESOL classroom research is important as is evident in Table 1. Action research is a procedure, or method, for conducting classroom research. Not all classroom research follows the procedures that define action research, so they are not the same thing. However, action research is always a form of teacher research, and classroom research, when conducted by teachers in their professional contexts.

The popularity of action research in TESOL is largely due to it being seen by classroom teachers as an accessible research method. Part of the motivation underlying classroom teachers' research into their own practice is a result of outside researchers who maintain the mystification of research practices, which in turn marginalizes classroom teachers. Take for example the university researchers who were present in Schecter's (1997) classroom nearly every day.

> On the whole, I found them pleasant, even somewhat differential, as they stood or sat, their bodies tightening at my approach so as not to impede my access to their subjects. I remember remarking to a friend that not one of the university people returned to tell me what they had found, as though I were not a critical consumer of these concepts. However, I didn't find it odd at the time that none of the visitors bothered to ask me what I thought. (pp. 102–103)

Out of these kinds of unfortunate experiences, classroom teachers today, rather than waiting for outside researchers to ask them what they think, increasingly feel the need to explain classroom teaching and learning in their own words by conducting their own research projects and publishing (see, Stewart 2013 and the *TESOL Voices* series published by TESOL Press).

Ellis (2012, p. 26) contends that "the value of practitioner research lies more in the process of conducting it than in the product of the research." This crucial point cuts to the heart of the matter. It partially explains confusion of terminology because the objectives of "research" in second language classrooms, as conducted by researchers from the outside and teachers on the inside, are usually different. If different outcomes are valued by different types of practitioners of research, then understandings about what research is can easily be clouded. In short, if the fundamental questions about values related to classroom research differ between the various research agents, then research methods and related terminology are likely to be affected. For this reason, I turn back to the beginning and ask a basic question.

Why is classroom research important in the TESOL field? At the infancy of classroom research, Long (1984) answered this question by observing that early studies revealed "what actually goes on in ESL classrooms, as opposed to what is believed to go on, and as distinct from what writers on TESL methods tell us what ought to go on" (p. 422). This strongly suggests that the ultimate types of practitioner research in second language contexts are those in quadrants 3 and 4 of Fig. 2 that are classroom-based, with priority going to teacher research (quadrant 4), and collaborative classroom research (quadrants 3 and 4 combined).

Discussion

A central concept in soft systems analysis is Checkland's (1981) notion of the human activity system (HAS). This is fundamentally a system of relationships between people and exists in space and time within society in general. According to Banathy (1992), "The environment is the context within which a HAS exists" (p. 28). Of course, the activity changes over time. Banathy explained that it is not easy to draw the boundary between the general and the systemic environments. He suggested that analysts ask the question: "Which part, of the general environment, is that with which the HAS in question routinely interacts?" (p. 28). Second language classrooms are the place where the activity of practitioner research in TESOL routinely takes place, as shown in Figs. 1 and 2.

However, the boundary of classroom walls, whether physical or virtual, does not isolate the system from its environment. Banathy explained that there are a variety of boundaries: cultural, economic, social, psychological, ethical, technological, etc. This complexity means that: "Making boundary judgment is a significant task of people in the system" (Banathy 1992, p. 29). That quote sums up the point of this entire chapter as it involved sorting out the various boundaries of classroom research in TESOL.

Banathy (1991, pp. 35–37) claimed that there are several types of human activity systems that range from "rigidly controlled" to "purpose-seeking." The various systems are distinguished according to their position along four continua: closed-open, restricted-complex, mechanistic-systemic, and unitary-pluralistic. Examining second language classroom research as a human activity system reveals that it ranges between Banathy's definition of a purposive system and a heuristic system. Goal setting in second language classroom research ranges from unitary (quadrant 1) to somewhat pluralistic (quadrants 2 and 4). Change is certainly influenced by both the school and classroom environment but is often gradual which indicates that the system is moderately open. Control within the system is complex and systemic with a hierarchical structure that traditionally situates the outside observers (published authors) in the powerful position of knowledge creators of theory, while practitioners of teaching and learning are viewed as consumers of this knowledge. The fact that teacher-researchers challenge this positioning within the system indicates complex and systemic functional arrangements.

A useful way to characterize systems is by specifying their purpose, input, and output. When we examine Fig. 2, cross purposes are immediately apparent. Outside observers (quadrants 1 and 3) will often have purposes such as evaluating teachers or gathering data for later publication. Classroom teachers, on the other hand, engage in reflective practice and teacher research as a feedback into classroom practice with the purpose of professional development or deeper understanding about their practice. Naturally, these differing purposes influence the topics of research, the questions asked, the type of input sought, how it is gathered, and how it is analyzed and interpreted (Table 1). These differing research processes will often result in very different kinds of output and/or displays of knowledge. In fact, the type of knowledge that is often most valued in higher education research communities can be seen as something alien to practitioners and, therefore, of low value.

Human activity systems have to be sensitive to their environment and change accordingly. Feedback is the process whereby "the actual state of the output is continuously compared with its expected state" … [thereby enabling] "us to correct for differences between what is actually produced by the system and what was expected to be produced" (Banathy 1992, p. 32). We can attribute the evolution in second language classroom research in TESOL since the 1970s to this kind of feedback loop.

Conclusion: What Is the Picture for the Future?

The purpose of this chapter is to create a holistic picture of classroom research in second language teaching-learning contexts. Pica (1997) provided a holistic interpretation of how the relationship between second language teaching and research has evolved over time and addressed fundamental gaps in understanding between teachers and researchers. For many university-based researchers, beyond pure intellectual curiosity, a primary motivation for their research can be categorized as self-interest, that is, to further their career and/or financial interests through publication (Stewart 2006, 2014). This is because: "Career progression as an academic remains heavily influenced by one's performance as a researcher" (Borg 2013, p. 151). Whereas classroom practice is performed in the moment employing experiential knowledge to achieve very practical and immediate goals. This contrast in values has resulted in skepticism among classroom teachers about the applications of second language acquisition research to second language teaching. Indeed, "journal articles are very often linguistically, conceptually, and/or physically inaccessible to practitioners" (Marsden and Kasprowicz 2017, p. 614).

This divide became more apparent with the development and spread of specialist courses of study for TESOL educators. From the 1980s, a number of classroom teachers began enrolling in in-service and graduate programs where they read studies as part of their coursework, but many reported "a difficulty in connecting them with what goes on in their classrooms on a daily basis" (Pica, 1997, p. 53). This gap, as well as research requirements of graduate programs, led more teachers to engage in classroom research.

Although this development is typically viewed in a positive light, TESOL teachers today might feel excessive pressure to engage in research since reflective practice and teacher research are assumed to be so beneficial. For classroom teachers the potential conflict is that while "research is rarely obligatory […] the luxury of refusal is expensive if career development depends on evidence of research activity" (Richards, 2003, p. xx).

Allwright (2005) has long advocated for classroom teachers to engage in research. Worried about "the high risk of burnout associated with current proposals for classroom-based research" (2005, p. 27), he reconsidered the methods he had recommended for teachers in the 1980s and turned to a more soft systems type of approach to teacher research based on a set of guiding principles. The core of Allwright's exploratory practice is the notion of "classroom life," meaning how the quality of learning and the educational environment affect the general life of students and teachers.

Allwright's primary concerns with classroom research are that it has to be feasible, as well as sustainable. In fact, most classroom research is still not done by classroom teachers (Borg 2013), and this could partially be due to the impression that it is too demanding. The goal of exploratory practice is to deepen understanding of teaching-learning practice in a sustained way by integrating research on teaching and learning into daily practice. For students and teachers, understanding deepens through exploration into puzzling aspects of practice that arise in a given classroom. In this process, according to Allwright, university researchers should act as consultants on research practices, rather than as directors who control classroom research. This would situate exploratory practice across quadrants 3 and 4 in Fig. 2 with collegiality being a key principle (Allwright 2016).

Exploratory practice is one indication of where classroom research in TESOL might be heading. Overall, the picture for the future looks to be digital, multimodal, and collaborative. First of all, the Royal Statistical Society of the United Kingdom confirmed that the number of active phone connections has exceeded world population ("Kim Kardashian's tweet" 2017), signaling the ubiquity of digital cameras. Since recording devices are now less expensive, easier to use, extremely portable, and capable of storing a significant amount of high-quality audio-visual data, classroom teachers are likely to use them more often. In addition, digital recording is much easier to review than videotape. This advance is furthered by the availability of software that can help teacher-researchers analyze classroom data.

Second, the classroom lesson is no longer defined by simultaneously shared physical space and time. Learning in hybrid and virtual environments online will continue to expand in all fields. This will provide new opportunities for classroom research (Kessler 2018). For instance, course management systems store a large amount of data on student learning that can be retrieved at any time by teachers for analysis, including typed messages and conversations.

Related to the two points above, multimodality is likely to influence both classroom practice and classroom research. As digital technologies become embedded in classrooms, traditional books and writing will give way to screens and images. This means that literacy will become a much broader concept to include not only language but technological and social factors (Kress 2003). For classroom researchers, displays of learning about practice can provide an incredibly robust picture of teaching and learning in classrooms. Some academic journals are now supplementing article texts with interactive graphics and video. In fact, the *Journal of Visualized*

Experiments (JoVE) is the first peer-reviewed video journal; that is, video is the main medium of communication supplemented by text.

Finally, collaboration in classroom research between teachers, students, university researchers, and other stakeholders is likely to expand in the coming decade. Ubiquitous digital communication makes such collaboration much easier now than it was 10 years ago. Furthermore, credentialism means that there is growing pressure on second language teachers to upgrade their initial training and gain advanced qualifications. Again, digital connectivity means that the classroom has expanded beyond the traditional four physical walls so that teachers can now do advanced courses online or in hybrid mode while employed.

This situation seems ideal for advancing the vision Lortie (1975) had back in the 1970s wherein classroom teachers could form liaisons with "outside researchers in research institutes and universities. They could channel ideas for research and disseminate useful findings" (p. 243). Thinking about the place of classroom teachers in educational research has moved on since Lortie's groundbreaking work. Theorizing in general education (e.g., Cochran-Smith and Lytle 2009; Zeichner and Liston 1996) has led to valuing of teachers' experiential knowledge and their positioning as ideal to conduct classroom research in second language classrooms (e.g., Freeman 1998; Johnson and Golombek 2002). This stance obviously aligns with Allwright's educational philosophy, although it remains a contested position.

Despite the significant changes that the thinking of Dewey (1963) initiated in the twentieth century, it is apparent that there is still much more that needs to be done. Most schools do not offer much support for teachers wanting to do classroom research. The reason for this is the fact that in schools teaching effectiveness is valued and is often measured in terms of gains on standardized tests. The quantification of education has exploded since Dewey penned his idealistic vision. Dewey, of course, famously questioned the way science was taught in US schools and suggested that science needed to be an instrument for social progress. Today, there is renewed confidence in the ability of science to solve problems in education. The goal is to find universal answers to complex social problems using big data analytics under the name of "evidence-based education." This view of education reflects a *hard systems* approach to problem-solving by devaluing or ignoring qualitative inputs from classroom participants. Coupling this with the spread of computers in second language education could reinforce the construction of teachers as mere delivery systems of centrally planned curricula.

While evidence is essential and data is useful to educators, teaching is necessarily a very practical activity. This means that many teachers and administrators do not value theoretical knowledge as much as "personal and skill-related qualities acquired through experience and practical training" (Borg 2013, p. 151). Freeman has long argued that "teachers are constantly having what they know defined for them by others" (1996, p. 106) and advocates that teachers not blindly follow other research conventions but rather create their own ways of thinking, framing questions, and displaying results. However, the evidence-based education movement limits possibilities for classroom research by assuming the end of debate on:

> [T]he purpose of research, the questions that should be asked, the relationship between the researcher and the "objects" of research, the methods employed, standards for reporting research results, and relationships between research and practice. ... There is no question that the current regime of scientifically based research and evidence-based education positions practitioners as the recipients of other people's knowledge. (Cochran-Smith and Lytle 2009, pp. 10–11)

This informed perspective echoes the concerns voiced by scholars and teachers since the middle of the twentieth century. Questions about what research is, how it should be done, and who can do it have been central in discussions about classroom research and TESOL research in general (Holliday 2004; Shohamy 2004). To make the practice of classroom research accessible to teachers, we must first define research categories. This chapter was my meagre attempt to provide colleagues with more of a holistic picture of second language classroom research. There is still a great deal of work to be done to support classroom teachers doing research. But with commitment by schools to this goal and the creation of mutually productive partnerships between university researchers, under the condition that they include classroom teachers as full members of their research team, imagined barriers to classroom research can be removed to allow new knowledge to emerge.

References

Allwright, D. (1983). Classroom-centered research on language teaching and learning: A brief historical overview. *TESOL Quarterly, 17*(2), 191–204.

Allwright, D. (2005). From teaching points to learning opportunities and beyond. *TESOL Quarterly, 39*(1), 9–31.

Allwright, D. (2016). Foreword: Team teaching, team learning and the development of collegiality. In A. Tajino, T. Stewart, & D. Dalsky (Eds.), *Team teaching and team learning in the language classroom: Collaboration for innovation in ELT* (pp. xiv–xxx). New York: Routledge.

Allwright, D., & Bailey, K. M. (1991). *Focus on the language classroom: An introduction to classroom research for language teachers*. Cambridge, UK: Cambridge University Press.

Banathy, B. H. (1991). *Systems design of education*. Englewood Cliffs, NJ: Educational Technology Publications.

Banathy, B. H. (1992). *A systems view of education: Concepts and principles for effective practice*. Englewood Cliffs, NJ: Educational Technology Publication.

Borg, S. (2013). *Teacher research in language teaching*. Cambridge, UK: Cambridge University Press.

Burns, A. (2016). *TESOL Quarterly* research guidelines: Practitioner research. *TESOL Quarterly, 50*(1), 56–59. https://doi.org/10.1002/tesq.288.

Capra, F. (1982). *The turning point: Science, society, and the rising culture*. New York: Simon and Schuster.

Checkland, P. (1981). *Systems thinking, systems practice*. Chichester: John Wiley & Sons.

Cochran-Smith, M., & Lytle, S. L. (2009). *Inquiry as stance: Practitioner research for the next generation*. New York: Teachers College Press.

Collins, S., Karsenti, T., & Komis, V. (2013). Reflective practice in initial teacher training: Critiques and perspectives. *Reflective Practice, 14*(1), 104–117. https://doi.org/10.1080/14623943.2012.732935.

Dewey, J. (1933). *How we think: A restatement of the relation of reflective thinking to the educative process*. Boston, MA: Heath.

Dewey, J. (1963). *Experience and education*. New York: Collier Books.

Ellis, R. R. (2012). *Language teaching research and language pedagogy*. Oxford, UK: Wiley-Blackwell.

Farrell, T. S. C, (2007). *Reflective language teaching: From research to practice*. London: Continuum.

Fendler, L. (2003). Teacher reflection in a hall of mirrors: Historical influences and political reverberations. *Educational Researcher, 32*(3), 16–25.

Freeman, D. (1996). Redefining the relationship between research and what teachers know. In K. M. Bailey & D. Nunan (Eds.), *Voices from the language classroom* (pp. 88–115). New York: Cambridge University Press.

Freeman, D. (1998). *Doing teacher-research: From inquiry to understanding*. Pacific Grove: Heinle & Heinle.

Holliday, A. (2004). Issues of validity in progressive paradigms of qualitative research. *TESOL Quarterly, 38*(4), 731–734. https://doi.org/10.2307/3588292.

Johnson, K. E., & Golombek, P. R. (2002). *Teachers' narrative inquiry as professional development*. Cambridge: Cambridge University Press.

Kerr, P. (2005). The use of jargon in teacher education. *ELT Journal, 59*(2), 151–153. https://doi.org/10.1093/eltj/cci029.

Kessler, G. (Ed.). (2018). *TESOL voices: Insider accounts of classroom life – Online and hybrid classrooms*. Alexandria, VA: TESOL Press.

Kim Kardashian's tweet on lawnmower deaths is awarded stat of the year. (2017). *BBC Newsbeat*. Retrieved from http://www.bbc.co.uk/newsbeat/

Kress, G. (2003). *Literacy in the new media age*. London: Routledge.

Long, M. H. (1984). Process and product in ESL program evaluation. *TESOL Quarterly, 18*(3), 409–425. https://doi.org/10.2307/3586712.

Lortie, D. C. (1975). *Schoolteacher: A sociological study*. Chicago: University of Chicago Press.

Marsden, E., & Kasprowicz, R. (2017). Foreign language educators' exposure to research: Reported experiences, exposure via citations, and a proposal for action. *The Modern Language Journal, 101*(4), 613–642. https://doi.org/10.1111/modl.12426.

Murphey, J. M. (2014). Reflective teaching: Principles and practices. In M. Celce-Murcia, D. M. Brinton, & M. A. Snow (Eds.), *Teaching English as a second or foreign language* (4th ed., pp. 613–629). Boston: Heinle, Cengage Learning.

Nunan, D., & Bailey, K. M. (2009). *Exploring second language classroom research: A comprehensive guide*. Boston: Heinle, Cengage Learning.

Pica, T. (1997). Second language teaching and research relationships: A North American view. *Language Teaching Research, 1*(1), 48–72.

Pinker, S. (2014). *The sense of style: The thinking person's guide to writing in the 21st century*. New York: Viking Penguin.

Richards, K. (2003). *Qualitative inquiry in TESOL*. New York: Palgrave Macmillan.

Richards, J. C., & Lockhart, C. (1994). *Reflective teaching in second language classrooms*. Cambridge: Cambridge University Press.

Richards, K., Ross, S., & Seedhouse, P. (2012). *Research methods for applied language studies*. New York: Routledge.

Roulston, K., Legette, R., DeLoach, M., & Pittman, C. B. (2005). What is 'research' for teacher-researchers? *Educational Action Research, 13*(2), 169–190.

Schecter, S. R. (1997). My professional transformation. In C. P. Casanave & S. R. Schecter (Eds.), *On becoming a language educator: Personal essays on professional development* (pp. 101–108). Mahwah: Lawrence Erlbaum Associates.

Schön, D. (1983). *The reflective practitioner: How professionals think in action*. New York: Basic Books.

Shohamy, E. (2004). Reflections on research guidelines, categories, and responsibility. *TESOL Quarterly, 38*(4), 728–731. https://doi.org/10.2307/3588291.
Stenhouse, L. (1975). *An introduction to curriculum research and development*. London, UK: Heinemann.
Stevick, E. (1986). *Images and options in the language classroom*. New York: Cambridge University Press.
Stewart, T. (2006). Teacher-researcher collaboration or teachers' research? *TESOL Quarterly, 40*(2), 421–430. https://doi.org/10.2307/40264529.
Stewart, T. (2013). *Classroom research for language teachers*. Alexandria: TESOL Press.
Stewart, T. (2014). Playing the numbers game in academia. *The Language Teacher, 38*(1), 40–41.
Sword, H. (2012). *Stylish academic writing*. Cambridge, MA: Harvard University Press.
Tajino, A., James, R., & Kijima, K. (2005). Beyond needs analysis: Soft systems methodology for meaningful collaboration in EAP course design. *Journal of English for Academic Purposes, 4*, 27–42. https://doi.org/10.1016/j.jeap.2004.01.001.
van Lier, L. (1988). *The classroom and the language learner: Ethnography and second language classroom research*. London: Longman.
Walton, D. C. (2004). Modeling organizational systems: Banathy's three lenses revisited. *Systemic Practice and Action Research, 17*(4), 265–284.
Zeichner, K. M., & Liston, D. P. (1996). *Reflective teaching: An introduction*. Mahwah: Lawrence Erlbaum Associates.
Zeichner, K. M., & Noffke, S. E. (2001). Practitioner research. In V. Richardson (Ed.), *Handbook of research on teaching* (4th ed., pp. 298–330). New York: American Educational Research Association.

A Soft Systems Approach to Lifelong Learning

Ryan W. Smithers

Abstract Scholastic success has largely been associated with the ability to develop and utilize skills in students that reflect the kinds of traits that are typically found in successful lifelong learners. This has, however, been a complex task that has left education in a state of flux as teachers and administrators struggle to work out the best way to equip students with subject knowledge and metacognitive skills. In addition to the complexities found in formal educational systems, non-formal educational systems seem to have been marginalized, leaving these educators in a conundrum as to how best to address the needs of lifelong learners who have left formal schooling behind to peruse further education in non-formal contexts. This phenomenon is especially evident in non-formal classrooms where foreign languages like English are typically taught to Second and Third Age learners. Therefore, this chapter proposes Soft Systems Methodology (SSM) as an approach to take when trying to deal with problematical educational systems in general and also to offer guidance to practitioners from non-formal learning systems. To this end, a case study is presented to demonstrate how SSM can be used to deal with some of the messiness that exists in educational contexts. This case study, based on a sampling of Third Age learners studying English as a foreign language (EFL), reveals how SSM is a sustainable way to help all of the stakeholders of a system work together to take action that aims at improving their system, which, in the case study presented here, meant discovering how to take action to improve learning by trying a new way of learning English grammar.

Keywords English as a foreign language (EFL) · Lifelong learning · Older learners · Soft Systems Methodology (SSM) · Third Age learning

---

R. W. Smithers (✉)
Department of Intercultural Studies, Otani University, Kyoto, Japan

A. Tajino (ed.), *A Systems Approach to Language Pedagogy*, Translational Systems Sciences 17, https://doi.org/10.1007/978-981-13-6272-9_6

Introduction: The Messiness of Education

Within the field of education, the literature is not complacent about stressing to educators the need to empower learners to become autonomous and self-regulated so that their students will discover how accruing knowledge and skills are tantamount to finding greater reward and fulfillment in life—in addition to becoming more beneficial contributors to society. Therefore, practitioners working in formal schooling contexts (primary, secondary, and tertiary or university) should work toward creating lifelong learners in addition to teaching subject content. This need for the creation of capable lifelong learners is especially apparent in the field foreign language learning because of the vast amount of learning that needs to take place outside of the classroom so that a foreign language learner can acquire enough competency to communicate in a language other than his/her mother tongue.

Consequently, the rate at which students gain mastery over a skill or content, like fluency in a foreign language, is not only inextricably linked to qualities that are associated with being a lifelong learner, but it is also contingent upon receiving sufficient training to become a lifelong learner. Subsequently, this begs the question as to when and how one becomes a lifelong learner because of how this is essential to the acquisition of knowledge and skills. But, is it something that is guaranteed to happen during one's formal schooling years, and if it does happen at this time, during one's First Age (Laslett 1987), is there an age or grade in school when this is more likely to happen? Also, is it possible for someone to go through life without ever becoming a lifelong learner?

Although it is beyond the scope of this paper to engage in a debate over the intricacies of how, when, and why people become lifelong learners, at this juncture, however, it seems prudent to turn to the literature for some clarification on what it means to be a lifelong learner. Before doing that though, it should be said that humans are inherently curious beings and, as such, can be found directing their own learning at various times throughout their lives, for example, when they are faced with a problem that needs to be overcome or when they want to discover more about something that they find intriguing. Some of the greatest examples of this curiosity and drive can be seen very early on in life, like when a baby is trying to see how different objects taste or when a child begins speaking by asking for his or her favorite food or drink. London (2011) defines it this way:

> Lifelong learning is a dynamic process that varies depending on individual skills and motivation for self-regulated, generative learning and life events that impose challenges that sometimes demand incremental/adaptive change and at other times require frame breaking change and transformational learning. (p. 3)

Prior to London's (2011) definition above, it is worth noting that the Commission of the European Communities (2001, p. 9) declared that "all learning activity undertaken throughout life, with the aim of improving knowledge, skills, and competences within a personal, civic, social, and/or employment related perspective" is to be revered as lifelong learning. Therefore, it is fair to conclude that humans become lifelong learners at some point during their formal schooling years. However, for some, the skill will be seen exerting a positive influence over learning from adolescence (Alsop 2013), while others may not show any real signs of self-regulated, generative learning until adulthood. The reason for this is because learners need to "see themselves as learners, seek and engage life experiences with a learning attitude, and believe in their ability to learn" (Passarelli and Klob 2011, p. 80), which stresses the need to improve the tools to detect deficiencies in learning identities in students and the skills to develop learning identities in teachers.

Unfortunately, inconsistencies in pedagogies and theory, in addition to isolationism between academic disciplines, have resulted in a reactionary and often patchwork approach to pedagogies across all fields and disciplines. This is especially evident in the field of foreign language education (see, for example, Smithers and Gray 2018; Tajino, chapter "Toward Managing Language Pedagogy and Language Teaching Research", this volume). As a result, the learning that takes place inside and out of formal and non-formal institutions varies greatly, with only a small percentage of students getting the support they need to become lifelong learners. This disparity between those who are equipped to regulate their own learning and those who are not is especially apparent in higher education. In fact, Tajino (personal communication, June 15, 2017) aptly punctuated this point when discussing the difference between the qualities of freshmen students who enter different Japanese tertiary institutions. He declared that the freshmen at the most prestigious institutions know how to study on their own and will likely acquire the knowledge required to successfully complete a course irrespective of the kind of instruction they receive. That is, their ability to learn on their own has enabled them to accrue more knowledge than their peers, which is likely giving them a head start in life.

But because no one wants to see a student left behind or unequipped for life after graduation, educational stakeholders are constantly looking for new ways of empowering learners. Active learning (Bonwell and Eison 1991) is one such current trend that combines the subject matter to be learned with activities that seek to have students construct knowledge and understanding so that they engage in thinking about learning, which should lead to the creation of lifelong learners. The result being that when students leave formal schooling behind, they will be equipped to keep up with the learning and re-learning that this modern world demands of its citizens. Relatedly, this turn toward active learning is rapidly being promoted in tertiary institutions in Japan in the hopes that teacher-centered classes will be replaced with student-centered ones that utilize active learning strategies.

However, as mentioned above, current graduates are lacking lifelong learning skills and because the latest trend in education is still in its infancy, especially in Japan, there is no way of knowing when or if capable lifelong learners will be leaving formal institutions any time soon. Consequently, the task of creating lifelong learners falls heavily on the shoulders of practitioners who are educating adults in non-formal learning contexts. Not only is this where people go to acquire new or enhanced skills for occupations and life, but this is also where people commonly gather to learn skills for leisure-time enjoyment or hobbies like painting, singing, dancing, etc. Actually, non-formal learning contexts are great places for people to go to learning a foreign language, and Japan is no exception. In fact, the foreign language school market is the third largest non-formal education industry market in Japan, with market valuation at over 300 billion yen (US $2.6 billion) annually since 2013 (Yano Research Institute 2017).

In light of the fact that the literature on foreign language learning in non-formal contexts is necessitous, practitioners involved in non-formal education who want to learn more about related contexts and the applicability of pedagogical trends from formal education contexts to their own soon find that they have been marginalized. That is, the theory, research, and applications found in the literature have mostly been directed toward hierarchically structured formal contexts with seemingly little in common with settings where learners are typically adults who have either graduated or dropped out of formal institutions and have volunteered to engage in learning. Further complicating this is the fact that non-formal educational pedagogies can be burdened by the complexity of adult learning theory and psychology, such as transformative learning theory (Meziro 1991, 1995, 1996), andragogy (Knowles 1980, 1984), and the learning experience (Kolb 2015), to name a few. In addition, pedagogies for lifelong learners in this context quite likely necessitate different considerations, with age being one of the greatest. Specifically, students from the Second and Third Ages (Laslett 1987) will likely have different physiological and/or neurological strengths and weaknesses. Subsequently, the only way forward for non-formal practitioners to date has been to educate in ignorance or put on the cap of a researcher and investigate practice. For those that do put on the cap of a researcher, they will soon find the prospect of doing research in an understudied field overwhelming for many reasons; paramount of which is the task of managing and learning all of the variables that exert influence over their non-formal learning contexts. Further exacerbating the problem is the silo effect, how theory and the applicability of it seem to proceed in isolation of other fields and contexts (for more on this phenomenon, see Tajino, chapter "Toward Managing Language Pedagogy and Language Teaching Research", this volume). For practitioners looking for answers, however, this is likely going to be a source of frustration that may cause many to throw in the towel prematurely, further exacerbating the dearth of research on this context.

All of the problematical issues discussed up to here point to a lot of messiness in educational contexts, both formal and non-formal. As a result, this stresses the need for practitioners and related stakeholders to come up with a way to tackle the complexity of formal and non-formal educational systems. To do this, a systems approach needs to be used to provide a workable framework for dealing with this messiness. Soft Systems Methodology (SSM) could be such a system, and, to explore the feasibility of using SSM to deal with the educational problems discussed above, this paper will utilize the principles of SSM to investigate a problem that practitioners involved in the teaching of lifelong learners in non-formal contexts are likely to face. But because lifelong learning non-formally can span over more than 50 years of learning—the time from when a learner graduates from high school or university till the twilight years—this paper will specifically examine the Third Age (Laslett 1987). This is the time from when learners retire from full-time employment until they enter the Fourth Age (Laslett 1987), the time when they are unable to learn because of a neurological and/or physical impairment that makes it impossible to engage in learning.

Soft Systems Methodology: How to Address Messiness

Soft Systems Methodology (SSM), an approach that was created to solve problems related to business and, more recently, foreign language education, provides practitioners with a one-of-a-kind framework for improving practice. Based on the principles of action research, SSM allows practitioners to investigate and understand emergent properties so that solutions to problems can be found. That is, practitioners who utilize the SSM approach are able to see how microscopic activities (subsystems) are influencing the problematic, macroscopic phenomena (main system) that need to be understood so that practice can be improved or enhanced. According to Gasson (1994), SSM has many benefits for practitioners looking to discover how they can realize the *most effective way* to enhance a system such as a non-formal ESL classroom because SSM allows practitioners to learn what they need to do so that they can attain the most effective system. Accordingly,

> [t]he purpose of performing a Soft Systems Methodology **is** to define what a system is and what it **does**, before trying to design that system. Soft Systems Methodology (SSM) provides a set of tools to define a **human activity system**, not an information system. By using SSM, we can include multiple perspectives on what the system is and does, in order to make decisions as to which we want to include and those which we want to exclude. (Gasson 1994, p. 9)

In terms of practicality, within the field of EFL education, Tajino (2002) used SSM to discover how hidden expectations (a microscopic activity) were problematic in that they prevented native English speaker teachers from effectively collaborating with their Japanese non-native English speaker teacher counterparts (the macroscopic phenomenon). To do this, he conducted his case study based on the seven-stage model of SSM by Checkland and Scholes (1999; see Fig. 1).

In this model, Stages 1 and 2 are the discovery stages. In Stage 1, a practitioner puts on an investigator's cap and works to define the parameters of a problematic situation by determining all of the factors that are related to the problem, which is often done by having the investigator draw a schematic with as many details as possible so that it is easier to conduct an analysis of the problem in Stage 2. In Stage 2, the investigator will want to share his/her concerns about a problematic situation with relevant stakeholders to determine which systems are the most relevant to the problem at hand. Furthermore, it is advisable to encourage input from stakeholders and collaborate on the creation of more in-depth diagrams than in Stage 1. Specifically, these diagrams should show causation between related subsystems of human activity. Now that all related subsystems have been analyzed, Stage 3 involves taking this information and coming up with a "root definition" of the system being analyzed so that all of the stakeholders are able to understand exactly what the system does and how it works (Checkland and Poulter 2010). One key task

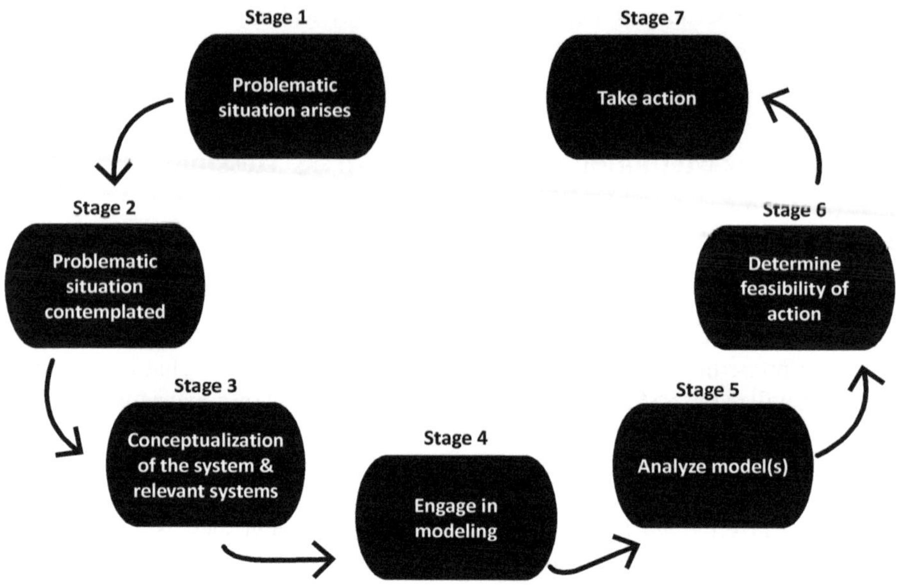

Fig. 1 Seven-stage model of SSM. (Adapted from Checkland and Scholes 1999)

to complete at this stage is the task of determining which subsystems are essential to the system that is problematic so that the less essential subsystems can be omitted. Also, to facilitate this "naming" of the system, the CATWOE acronym is to be used to enable stakeholders to better grasp the intricacies of the systems and prevent overlooking any of the functions of the subsystems. Following the CATWOE framework to define a system involves answering some questions related to this acronym as follows:

Customer(s)	→	Declare who the system is based on or for
Actor(s)	→	Determine who operates within the system
Transformation	→	Define what process is being transformed or modified to try and improve the system
Worldview(s)	→	Direct the transformation based on merit and vales of the Customers and Actors
Owner(s)	→	Decide who gives consent or has authority over the proposed transformation
Environment	→	Develop an understanding of the boundaries or parameters that the transformation must adhere to

After the system has been precisely defined, Stage 4 entails detailing what needs to take place so that the proposed transformation can be carried out and includes the steps that need to be taken to ensure that the treatment is effectively monitored and evaluated. Following this stage, Stage 5 necessitates that the model that has been constructed thus far go through a culling. That is, the stakeholders need to identify which subsystems are most likely to have the greatest influence over the problematical system and, conversely, those which have the least. Once the most important subsystems have been identified, it is time for Stage 6. In Stage 6, stakeholders will need to discuss the practicability of the proposed changes to the subsystems and determine if the changes can affect the proposed transformation in a manner that is agreeable to all. In doing this, it is important to look how the subsystems influence and are influenced by each other so that any possible conflicts can be resolved before moving on to the last stage. In the last stage, Stage 7, change is implemented with a couple of caveats: (1) make sure everyone is onboard and purposely working to help transform the system, and (2) be sure to progress at a pace that everyone is comfortable with when implementing one or more changes—slow and steady wins the race when it comes to SSM.

A Case Study: Tackling Some Messiness

As alluded to in the introduction, education is a messy business that can be problematic for formal and non-formal educators alike. To try and tackle some of this messiness and determine the fit of Soft Systems Methodology for practitioners involved in teaching in non-formal contexts, this section proposes to demonstrate how SSM can be used to address the problematical issue of how to teach English grammar to foreign language learners from the Third Age. It is further hoped that this will also provide a template for practitioners teaching First Age and Second Age learners to tackle problematic situations in their respective contexts.

The Context

This case study involves a native English speaker teacher (the author of this paper) and 11 Japanese lifelong learners who are Third Agers (mean age = 65.8). The learners are involved in learning *eikaiwa* (English conversation) in a non-formal setting, a community center. Their proficiencies range from false beginner to low intermediate, A1–A2 on the common European framework of reference (CEFR) scale (see Bonnah and Smithers 2017, for a sample transcript of classroom interaction for these learners).

The Problematic System

The problem that this paper seeks to address is likely one that is common to many in the field of English as a foreign language (EFL) education, how to teach English grammar. In short, the literature often reveals how practitioners can be found puzzling over how to teach grammar, while students are seen struggling to gain grammatical competency (for an in-depth discussion of the problem of grammar instruction, see Smithers and Gray 2018). Accordingly, this case study outlines how the SSM framework was used to plan a course of action for the abovementioned context. Detailed below will be the steps that were taken during the seven stages.

Working Through the Stages

Stage 1: Problematic Situation Arises

As mentioned above in section "Soft Systems Methodology: How to Address Messiness," this is the stage where the practitioner becomes an investigator to work out in as much detail as possible all of the factors that might be affecting the problematic situation. In the case of how to teach grammar to Third Age EFL learners, the author's brainstorming produced the first of two "rich pictures" (Fig. 2). By doing this, it visually captured the social and political context, which was helpful for identifying how everyone was related to each other and what the goals and motivations were for this community of learners. Of note, the comments expressed in quotations marks were ones that left an outstanding impression in the mind of the teacher over the course of 7 years of teaching this group.

Stage 2: Problematic Situation Contemplated

During Stage 2, the practitioner entered into dialogic discussions with all of the stakeholders (his students). In this case, the EFL learners were brought in to hear what their teacher had been contemplating, i.e., how he wants to improve their English grammar ability. Next, copies of the rich picture (Fig. 2) were given to all of the students so that they could give their input on the diagram. Specifically, comments were sought about how the practitioner/investigator viewed causation between the microscopic activities and the macroscopic phenomena (the need to help these learners improve at grammar). Imperative here is that students become empowered to join in the investigation for confirmation and/or correction(s) to the system. As a result of discussions during this stage, the rich picture was revised to incorporate the relationships and a more comprehensive network of subsystems (see Fig. 3).

Stage 3: Conceptualization of the System and Relevant Systems

When the SSM cycle reaches this stage, it is paramount that the stakeholders come up with a root definition so that the rich picture can be revised to as accurately as possible reflect the most relevant subsystems to the root definition. Because of the

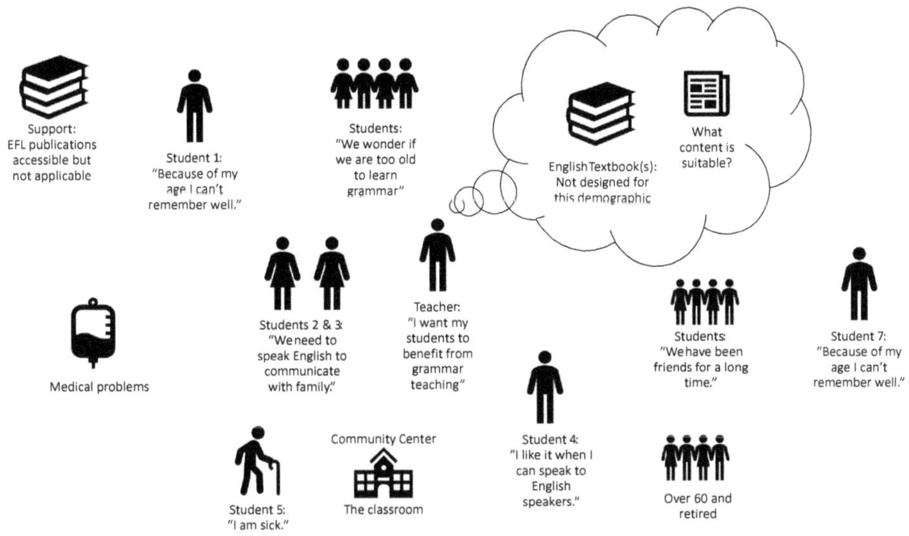

Fig. 2 An initial picture of the problem with teaching grammar to Third Age learners

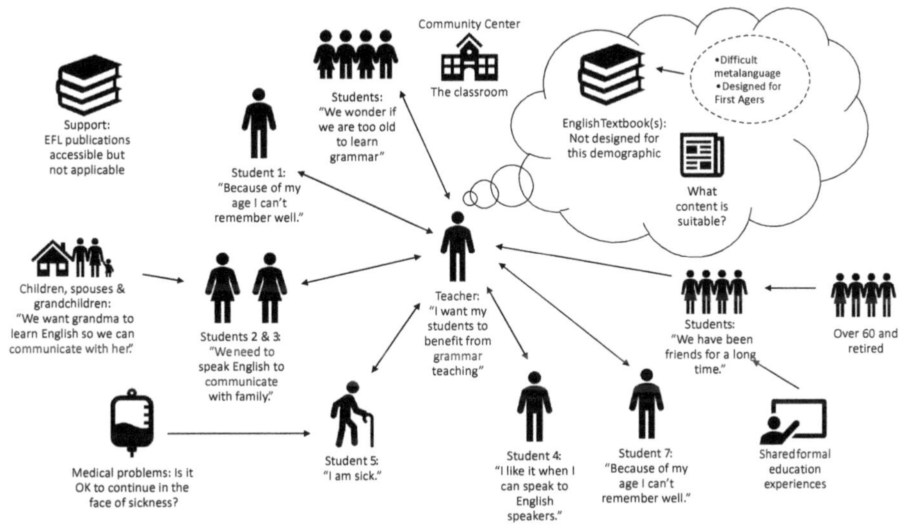

Fig. 3 A more-detailed rich picture of the problem with teaching grammar to Third Age learners (design adopted from Fig. 8, Team Teaching and Team Learning: SSM applied to the team-taught classroom, this volume)

need to make the root definition as rich as possible, this process required several revisions, with the final agreed upon definition as follows:

> A teacher-led grammar system[1] for older learners with age-related ailments who want to have fun studying English once a week, yet be able to improve at communication so that communication with classmates, the teacher, and family members could be facilitated.

Following the defining of systems, rich pictures sometimes require modification in a way that allows for all of the less essential subsystems to be omitted. For the stakeholders here, it was felt that the picture should remain as it is. The next thing that was done during this stage was establishing a model, based on CATWOE, of the purposeful activity that occurs within this system, which is listed below.

Customers	→	Customers equal the EFL students who are affected, for good or bad, by whatever changes are made to this system
Actor	→	This is the teacher who conducts the transformation
Transformation	→	The transformation is what transpires as a result for the action taken
Worldviews	→	These are the views (and suppositions) of the students and teacher that are influencing the transformation process (from beginning to end) and evaluate its success
Owner(s)	→	In this system, power resides with the teacher and the students, and anyone of these owners has the authority to stop the proposed transformation
Environment	→	The environment here is bound by the community center classroom, the physiological constraints of the students, and the available time that the teacher and students have for the transformation

Having completed the CATWOE acronym, the teacher and his students decided to revise the root definition to better reflect the proposed action. Accordingly, the revision became:

> A grammar system for learning English that is prepared by the teacher for older EFL learners with age-related ailments who do not want to spend lots of out-of-class time studying, but still hope to make some progress, want to have fun interacting in the English classroom once a week, and, should the occasion arise, be better able to communicate in English outside of the classroom with foreigners or family members should the opportunity arise.

Thus, with this updated definition, the stakeholders here have come up with better parameters by which they can effectively judge the success of the action.

---

[1] Note: A grammar system is not a soft system, rather it is a hard system because its boundaries are fixed and not subject to conflict or change like the soft, human activity system that SSM investigates.

Stage 4: Engaging in Modeling

In Stage 4, the Actor needs to determine the what and how for a proposed transformation. This could mean turning to peers and/or mentors for advice. It could also involve research on the part of the Actor to find solutions that might be able to provide options for which activities could be carried out so that the system can be transformed. In this case, the Actor relied on the education he was receiving in graduate school to come up with some ideas for how the transformation might take place. In fact, it was in graduate school where he was introduced to *the order of meanings* (see chapter "Teaching English Grammar for Communicative Purposes: A Systems Approach", this volume) by Professor Tajino as a possible alternative to traditional approaches to English grammar teaching. Furthermore, he also became aware of the principles of Exploratory Practice (Allwright 2003, 2005) as a sustainable way to value the lives of the Customers (EFL learners) while taking action. Accordingly, the following activities were proposed: (1) to use the principles of Exploratory Practice to guide a 6-week plan of action and (2) to learn about the order of meanings so that a proposed course of study could be conducted in the community classroom with these Customers (for a detailed outline of the specifics of this conceptual model, see Smithers and Gray 2018).

Stage 5: Analyzing the Model

During this stage, it is appropriate to compare the proposed model that was developed in Stage 4 with the "real world." To do this, the stakeholders were required to review what was proposed in Stage 4 to help determine what would most likely to have the greatest and least influence over implementing a course of study based on the order of meanings (also known as MAP Grammar) and Exploratory Practice. Points of discussion centered on how much time and effort would be required outside of the classroom. For the Actor (teacher), this meant managing other teaching, study, and family obligations to see that weekly one and a half hour lessons were properly prepared for. Included in this consideration was the need to provide resources to aid in a course of study. For the Customers (students), this meant finding time to review the homework and make diary entries so that the teacher could gauge moods and progress from week to week and address problems that were occurring as a result of the transformation. All in all, resources were committed, and the activities to be engaged in were agreed to (see Smithers and Gray 2018).

Stage 6: Determining the Feasibility of the Action

Stage 6, which necessitated that all of the stakeholders not only approve of the proposed action but also come to agreement on the feasibility of the action, was actually combined with the analyses that occurred in Stage 5. This was done out of expediency and because it was felt that analyzing the fitness of a model dictates feasibility considerations. In the end, however, everyone agreed to commit time and energy to the transformation for only as much as they felt motivated to do, so as to make allowances for whims and outside influences and demands.

Stage 7: Taking Action

After having progressed through the above listed six stages, action was taken. The result of which can be seen in a paper published by Smithers and Gray (2018). Highlighted in the study was the fact that the SSM transformation led to increased confidence in the ability to communicate in English and greater motivation to study English. In retrospect, it seems reasonable to conclude the success that occurred was the result of the principles of SSM because both the Actor and Customers were onboard and purposely working to help transform the system and because at every stage everyone was made comfortable with the proposed transformation.

Conclusion

This chapter has attempted to bring attention to the messiness of education, not just in formal contexts but also in non-formal ones. In formal educational context with high stakes, pedagogical pressures can be daunting. Likewise, the financial stresses of industry in the non-formal education sector can be equally as onerous to practitioners. Added to these contextual woes are the intricacies that learners and educational theory further burden teachers with. Indeed, educational systems are rife with systemic problems related to human activity systems, and those problems are not likely to disappear anytime soon.

To try and find a way through this messiness, this chapter proposed using Soft Systems Methodology as a means to begin. No, SSM did not—nor was it supposed to—show this practitioner the best way to teach English grammar, but what it did do was provide a way forward so that in the end, action for change could be taken. The problem of how to better teach English grammar to a class of Third Age lifelong learners who were learning English as a foreign language was solved because of the blueprint that SSM provided. SSM provided this practitioner with an understanding of how to study the system that he and his students found themselves in so that they could accurately define their system and then take purposeful steps toward the action that ultimately brought them closure, the discovery of how MAP Grammar would become the elixir that solved their problematical system.

References

Allwright, D. (2003). Exploratory practice: Rethinking practitioner research in language teaching. *Language Teaching Research, 7*(2), 113–141.

Allwright, D. (2005). Developing principles for practitioner research: The case of exploratory practice. *The Modern Language Journal, 89*(3), 353–366.

Alsop, A. (2013). *Continuing professional development in health and social care: Strategies for lifelong learning* (2nd ed.). Chichester: Wiley-Blackwell.

Bonnah, T., & Smithers, R. W. (2017). Reflecting on interaction: Using conversation analysis to improve ESL teacher reflection. *Kwansei Gakuin University Humanities Review, 21*, 123–126.

Bonwell, C. C., & Eison, J. A. (1991). *Active learning: Creating excitement in the classroom.* Washington, DC: The George Washington University, School of Education and Human Development.

Checkland, P., & Poulter, J. (2010). Soft systems methodology. In M. Reynolds & S. Holwell (Eds.), *Systems approach to managing change: A practical guide* (pp. 191–242). London: Springer.

Checkland, P., & Scholes, J. (1999). *Soft systems methodology in action*. Chichester: Wiley.

Commission of the European Communities. (2001). *Making a European area of lifelong learning a reality*. Brussels: EC. Retrieved from http://aei.pitt.edu/42878/1/com2001_0678.pdf

Gasson, S. (1994). *The use of soft systems methodology (SSM) as a tool for investigation.* Warrick Business School. Retrieved from https://cci.drexel.edu/faculty/sgasson/Vita/UseOfSSM.pdf

Knowles, M. S. (1980). *The modern practice of adult education: From pedagogy to andragogy.* Chicago: Follett.

Knowles, M. S. (1984). *Andragogy in action*. San Francisco: Jossey-Bass.

Kolb, D. A. (2015). *Experiential learning: Experience as the source of learning and development* (2nd ed.). Upper Saddle River: Pearson Education, Inc.

Laslett, P. (1987). The emergence of the third age. *Ageing and Society, 7*(2), 133–160. https://doi.org/10.1017/S0144686X00012538.

London, M. (2011). Lifelong learning: Introduction. In M. London (Ed.), *The Oxford handbook of lifelong learning* (pp. 3–11). New York: Oxford University Press, Inc.

Mezirow, J. (1991). *Transformative dimensions of adult learning*. San Francisco: Jossey-Bass.

Mezirow, J. (1995). Transformative theory of adult learning. In M. Welton (Ed.), *In defense of the lifeworld*. Albany: State University of New York Press.

Mezirow, J. (1996). Contemporary paradigms of learning. *Adult Education Quarterly, 46*(3), 158–172.

Passarelli, A. M., & Kolb, D. A. (2011). The learning way: Learning from experience as the path to lifelong learning and development. In M. London (Ed.), *The Oxford handbook of lifelong learning* (pp. 70–90). New York: Oxford University Press, Inc.

Smithers, R. W., & Gray, J. (2018). Enhancing the quality of life in lifelong learners: The influence of a meaning-order approach to pedagogical grammar on motivation and self-efficacy. *Applied Linguistics Review, 0*(0), 1–21. https://doi.org/10.1515/applirev-2017-0095.

Tajino, A. (2002). Transformation process models: A systemic approach to problematic team-teaching situations. *Prospect, 17*(3), 29–44.

Yano Research. (2017). *Educational industry market in Japan: Key research findings 2017.* Tokyo: Yanno Research Institute Ltd. Retrieved from http://www.yanoresearch.com/press/pdf/1744.pdf

A "Softer" Instructional Systems Design for Language Pedagogy

Kyoko Hosogoshi and Sachi Takahashi

Abstract This chapter examines the application of instructional systems design (ISD) in language pedagogy. ISD, a systematic approach to analyzing, designing, developing, implementing, and evaluating instruction, has been suggested to provide clear step-by-step models to instruction, thereby assisting instructors in the effective and efficient conveying of information and promotion of learning. Attempts at introducing ISD into language pedagogy have generally been praised in the literature of applied linguistics. On the other hand, some criticisms of ISD have surfaced in the field of general education, including the idea that ISD is *too* systematic and rigid and cannot account for the human element in the classroom. In this chapter, we revisit ISD in the language classroom, through review of a case study application of one iteration of ISD (the ADDIE model). Through examination of the theory and the case study present, we suggest that in language course design, it is beneficial to first take a rigid, systematic approach to course design, and rather it is in the implementation of the course that individual units necessarily have a degree of flexibility. We propose that a "softer" approach to ISD might be applied to the implementation of ISD in a language course, allowing for both a guided approach to instruction and the flexibility required in human interaction systems.

Keywords Gagné's nine instructional events · Instructional systems design (ISD) · Skill-integrated tasks · Task-based language teaching (TBLT) · ADDIE model

K. Hosogoshi (✉)
Faculty of Letters, Kyoto Prefectural University, Kyoto, Japan
e-mail: hosogoshi@kpu.ac.jp

S. Takahashi
Institute for Liberal Arts and Sciences, Kyoto University, Kyoto, Japan
e-mail: takahashi.sachi.4n@kyoto-u.ac.jp

A. Tajino (ed.), *A Systems Approach to Language Pedagogy*, Translational Systems Sciences 17, https://doi.org/10.1007/978-981-13-6272-9_7

What Is Instructional Systems Design?

Instructional systems design (ISD) is, simply put, a *systematic* approach to instruction that aims to encourage effective, efficient, and engaging learning. ISD is not a singular set-in-stone approach that can be applied as is across any educational context, but rather a set of principles that allow for systematic instruction.[1] It typically begins, therefore, with a needs analysis component, which assesses the needs of learners (not only scholastically but also psychologically), while also taking into account the unique factors of a particular educational context. Based on such needs analyses, ISD then sets out to devise a plan for choosing appropriate learning resources, implementing effective and stimulating instruction, and conducting reliable evaluation. It is also somewhat cyclical process, with knowledge gained from initial implementations of ISD informing subsequent cycles and thereby improving the quality of instruction and learning.

The merits of such a systematic approach to instruction have been well documented in the literature. Applied in numerous fields, including nursing (Robinson and Dearmon 2013), and business (Morrison et al. 2012), for example, ISD is touted as being of use in traditional classroom environments as well as distance or online learning, to provide a coherent framework for the support of teaching and learning. ISD typically is a clear process involving several steps or stages to ensure the successful achievement of learning objectives. Smith and Ragan (2005) define ISD as "[a] systematic and reflective process of translating principles of learning and instruction into plans for instructional materials, activities, information resources, and evaluation" (p. 4).

ISD in education has not, however, been free from criticisms. Bichelmeyer et al. (2006), for instance, citing the ADDIE model introduced in this chapter, point out the ISD is too rigid, too *systematic*, to be readily applied to instructional situations. Although the starting point of ISD is a needs analysis and is thus ostensibly learner-focused, the implementation of ISD beyond the needs analysis is too inflexible to readily adapt to unexpected occurrences in learning, even within a single task – and being a complex human endeavor, any type of educational enterprise is likely to encounter unexpected situations as often as on a daily basis. Another criticism that has been levelled at ISD has appeared within criticisms of a neoliberal view of education (the idea that education is and should be exposed to the same competitive forces as a free market, see Canaan and Shumar 2008). Such criticisms suggest that the "program management"-like features of ISD are too rigidly product-oriented and therefore may be more suited to business rather than primary, secondary, and tertiary education which (at least in ostensibly) should have broader aims than the purely pragmatic. Finally, some detractors have labelled ISD as being overly behavioristic, and that both instructors and learners are unlikely to fall into the neat "successful" behavioral patterns that it seems to suggest are possible.

---

[1] Indeed, there are many types of ISD including the ARCS model, CLER Model, and Goal-Based Instruction, among others.

The above criticisms of ISD are indeed valid if ISD principles are interpreted as dogma to be strictly adhered to. It is our position, however, that ISD is rather a set of guidelines that are useful for planning and implementing a course with clear goals and that taking a "softer" approach to the application of ISD may lead to some of the proposed benefits of ISD while also allowing for flexibility, individuality, and multiplicity in the classroom. Indeed, Bichelmeyer et al. (2006) suggest that this approach to the ADDIE model in particular is beneficial and that it should be viewed less as a model and more as a "conceptual framework" (p. 36).

In this chapter, we will begin with the aforementioned ADDIE model as an example of ISD, examining the individual phases of the model and the benefits they provide for planning/course design. Then, borrowing the idea of approaching the model as a more malleable *conceptual framework*, we will explore what aspects of the model can be made more flexible by borrowing from language education theory such as task-based language teaching (TBLT), before describing an instance of ISD-based instruction implemented by the authors.

Applying the ADDIE Model to an EAP Course Design

The ADDIE model is widely used in ISD and consists of five discrete *phases*, including *Analyze*, *Design*, *Develop*, *Implement*, and *Evaluate*. Although space precludes an in-depth description of each of the phases, they will be briefly outlined below (readers are directed to Dick and Carey 1996 or Takahashi et al. 2018 for more detailed explanations). This section describes our attempt to apply the ADDIE model to the design of a language course. Figure 1 is our model of a "softer" instructional systems design (ISD) for language pedagogy. This model is a combination of the ADDIE model and Gagné's nine instructional events.[2] The following case study will clarify how a "softer" ISD approach might be applied to the planning, conducting, and assessment of an English language course.

The semester-long (15 weeks) course introduced in this section was targeted to develop English for Academic Purposes (EAP) skills, as its participants were first-year students of a research-oriented university in Japan (see Hosogoshi and Takahashi (2015) for further details of the course). The type of EAP task implemented in the course was a skill-integrated task that consisted of (1) listening to a lecture, (2) reading an accompanying text, and (3) delivering a written or spoken summary of the two input sources. Such skill-integrated tasks have been receiving much attention in English language pedagogy worldwide. Oxford (2001), for example, introduces a *tapestry* approach in which the four macro skills (i.e., listening,

[2] Gagné's nine instructional events are nine events that occur in the process of classroom instruction and include *gaining the learners' attention*, *informing learners of the objective*, *stimulating recall of prior learning*, *presenting the stimulus*, *providing guidance for the learners*, *eliciting learner performance*, *providing feedback*, *assessing learners' performance*, and *enhancing retention and transfer*. For more, see (Gagné 1985; Takahashi et al. 2018).

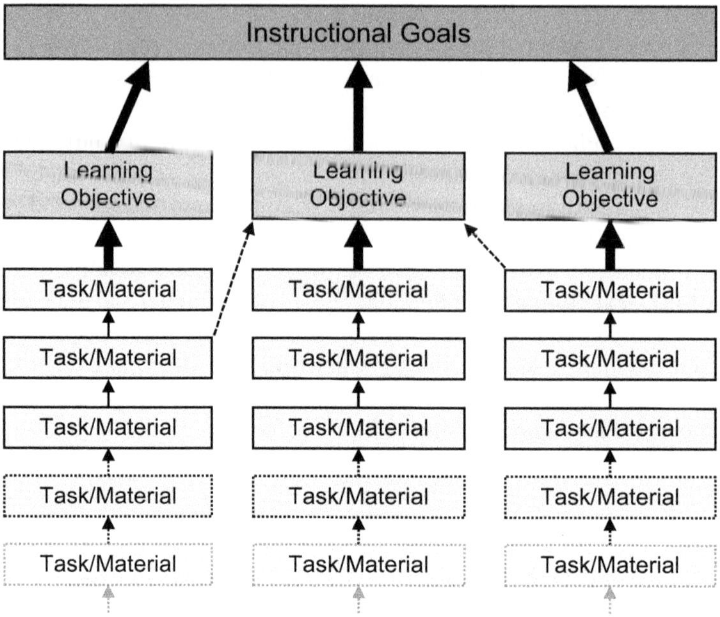

Fig. 1 A "softer" ISD to English language pedagogy

reading, writing, and speaking) can be taught synthetically. She points out that the traditional segregated-skill approach, which focuses on each of the four skills independently, would exclude language learning from its genuine context. According to her, holistic learning of the four skills is essential for students in becoming ready for authentic and skill-interactive communication outside classroom. Due to the complexity of teaching integrated skills, however, in order to maximize its pedagogical benefits, a thorough course design is necessary. The following sections report how the ADDIE model can fit with a skill-integrated course design in an English as a foreign language classroom.

Analyze Phase

The Analyze phase consists of a learner needs analysis, which includes both contextual factors as well as academic needs. From the analysis, overarching instructional goals for the course are decided upon, before tangible *learning objectives* which support the achievement of the instructional goals are plotted. The learning objectives should be categorized (and subcategorized) thoroughly and related back to the needs analysis outcomes, so that none are neglected.

In order to analyze the needs of the students participating the course, we conducted a questionnaire asking them to detail their previous experience of 18 sub-skills of academic listening, as designated by Richards (1983). The needs analysis questionnaire consisted of 18 can-do statements regarding academic listening skills, and students rated their familiarity with each sub-skill on a scale of 5, from 1 = *disagree* to 5 = *agree*. The results of the needs analysis suggested that the target students did not have adequate experience in academic listening in general, showing floor effects in eight of the total items:

Item 3 "I was able to identify relationships among units within discourse."
Item 4 "I was able to identify role of discourse markers in signaling structure of a lecture."
Item 9 "I was able to recognize function of intonation to signal information structure."
Item 11 "I was able to follow different modes of lecturing: spoken, audio, audio-visual."
Item 12 "I was able to follow lecture despite differences in accent and speed."
Item 13 "I was familiar with different styles of lecturing: formal, conversational, read, unplanned."
Item 14 "I was familiar with different registers: written versus colloquial."
Item 15 "I was able to recognize irrelevant matter: jokes, digressions, meanderings."

Of the above items, Items 3, 4, 9, and 15 concerned *top-down* processing during listening in which the listeners should understand the relationships among informational units in discourse and to grasp the gist of content by discriminating essential information from irrelevant matters (Rost 2011). Thus, we determined that our students were in greater need of tasks related to top-down processing than *bottom-up* processing, the latter referring to processing that requires phonological, lexical, and syntactic analyses, respectively, for comprehension (Vandergrift and Goh 2012). In addition, Items 11, 12, 13, and 14 highlighted some distinctive features of spoken lectures in contrast to written genre such as textbook and research papers. Based on a corpus research using the Spoken and Written Academic Language (T2K-SWAL) corpus, Biber (2006) argues that spoken registers tend to be heavily populated with verbs, while nouns dominantly occupy the written registers. The questionnaire results suggested that the students had rather limited experience of listening to academic discourse. Therefore, we decided to develop a number of supplemental activities before the lecture listening activity in order to allow the students to familiarize themselves with the listening mode.

Additionally, instructional analysis was conducted to isolate the cognitive goals of the course. A literature review on EAP education revealed that academic inquiry often requires students to employ the four linguistic macro skills in combination (see, for example, Flowerdew and Peacock 2001). For instance, university students are often assigned to read some text as homework and then listen to lectures during the class time, speak up their opinions about a topic in discussion sessions, and write essays on the topic as learning outcome. Thus, high-order cognitive skills (Bloom et al. 1956) such as summarizing the gist of sources, and synthesizing by combining ideas to form a new whole, were isolated to be the cognitive goals of the EAP task. Since such cognitive skills are often activated in task-based language teaching (TBLT), we adopted a TBLT approach to be conducted through ISD over the course.

TBLT, as the name implies, is an approach to English language pedagogy in which *tasks* tack a central role. According to Bygate et al. (2001), "[a] task is a contextualised, standardised activity which requires learners to use language, with emphasis on meaning, and with a connection to the real world, to attain an objective, and which will elicit data which can be used for purposes of measurement" (p. 12). Based on this definition, an EAP task should conform to five requisite criteria: *being contextualized*, *providing opportunity for use*, *focusing on meaning*, *being goal-oriented*, and *meeting assessment purposes*. For example, an EAP task should be contextualized to the real world (Long 2015). As Oxford (2001) claims, language skills should be treated as a whole, such as in communicative activities outside the classroom. Also, the format of an EAP task should encourage learners to use the language for both comprehension and production. In other words, learners should apply learned knowledge into practice and finally internalize it into their L2 repertoire for future use. In addition, an EAP task should be primarily concerned with meaning, not language forms. Long and Norris (2009) argue that traditional instruction focusing on forms, which would typically isolate and teach target linguistic items in decontextualized utterances, provides students with only "stilted language" (p. 135). Furthermore, an EAP task aims at attaining an objective; namely, it is goal-oriented. Thus, the outcome of such a task should be evaluated based on the content, or the achievement of the (non-linguistic) goal, rather than the language itself (Ellis 2003). Finally, an EAP task serves for assessment purposes as it helps teachers gain data of learners' performance in the form of its outcome. Such a task can help teachers and researchers grasp learners' degree of comprehension or production in L2.

As reviewed above, an EAP task was decided on as appropriate for our pedagogical purposes as it encourages learners to develop their English proficiency and cognitive skills through use of the target language in a similar manner to genuine communicative contexts. When the needs and goals of the tasks were set, a discrepancy was identified between the students' lack of EAP listening experience and the high-order cognitive demand of the EAP task. Thus, we decided to offer some meta-task modules which provided the students with detailed instructions on how to conduct the target EAP task before implementing it during the course. Also, we scheduled two 90-min lessons to complete one EAP task, which allowed for plenty of practice time.

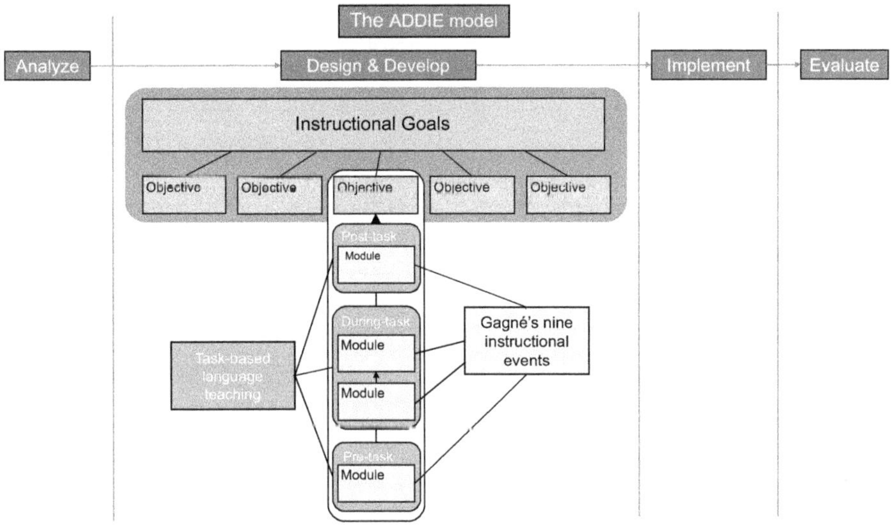

Fig. 2 Design and development of tasks and materials

Design Phase

The Design phase is where the learning objectives identified previously are plotted into concrete sets of tasks. Each individual learning objective is allotted a time frame in which to be achieved (although in many cases discrete objectives may overlap, or more holistic skills may be worked toward over the entirety of the course), and basic ideas for materials and tasks are conceived. This laying of tasks is shown in Fig. 2 and elaborated upon further below.

Based on the instructional analysis, we designed the EAP course first by setting goals of the target task in terms of the four linguistic skills as follows:

1. Students will be able to listen to an English lecture.
2. Students will be able to read an academic English text.
3. Students will be able to deliver a written or spoken summary of the two sources.

These goals illustrate EAP skills required for authentic academic communication (Flowerdew and Peacock 2001; section entitled 'Analyze Phase' above).

To achieve the above instructional goals, each lesson was designed by choosing the topics and time allotted for each task. Since the course was offered as a component of general liberal arts education for first-year students, the topics of each lesson ranged from social studies (e.g., *decision-making*, *global problems*) to science (e.g., *food environment*, *fetus learning*).

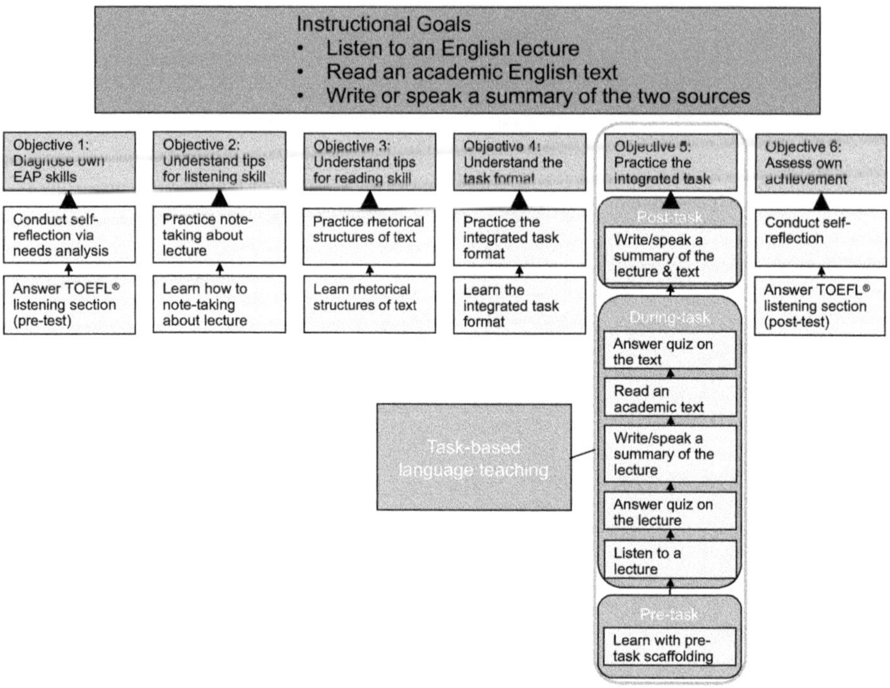

Fig. 3 English language course design

Figure 3 is a visualization of our EAP course design. The major instructional goals of the course were located on top. The three goals were further divided into six instructional objectives, which consisted of diagnosing one's own English skills, learning the target EAP skills, practicing the target skills, and reviewing the achievement. Specifically, Objective 1 intended to provide the students with an opportunity to check their EAP skills before taking the course by both attempting a TOEFL® listening section, as well as completing the needs analysis questionnaire. The next two objectives concerned understanding some key components of basic EAP receptive skills: note-taking for listening skills and understanding typical rhetorical structures and discourse markers for reading skills. These tips were instructed with, and practiced through, sample questions from TOEFL® integrated tasks with the aim of learning how to retain input information for subsequent output production during skill-integrated tasks. The following Objectives 4 and 5 encouraged the students to understand and practice the format of the target EAP task. For introducing the task format in Objective 4, sample questions from TOEFL® integrated tasks were employed (Phillips 2007). For instance, the students first read a short passage explaining general feature of the *Dead Sea*, listened to some unexpected facts about the sea, and wrote a summary of the two input sources. For Objective 5, students practiced with the target task format: listened to a short lecture, read a related text, and made a summary of the two sources in written or spoken forms, using materials from *OpenCourseWare*. For example, the first target EAP task, *food environment*, was based on a course material by Yale University professor Brownell (2008). The students first listened to a lecture proposing the importance of a worldwide view on food issues, then read a passage explaining the influence of American food culture onto the world's diet as a case study, and then wrote a summary of the two information sources. As we thought that a possible gap between students' English proficiency and the high demand of the target task may hinder their task completion, pre-task scaffolding (e.g., learning difficult vocabulary or outline of the lecture) and comprehension quiz of the two input sources were prepared as meta-task modules for Objective 5. Finally, Objective 6 was set to formatively assess the students' progress at the end of the course using another test set of TOEFL® listening section.

We allotted every single lesson for most of the six objectives except Objective 5 regarding the target EAP task practice. Each of the target tasks took two lessons to complete, so a total of eight lessons were spent for conducting two skill-integrated writing tasks and another two skill-integrated speaking tasks. As shown in Fig. 3, the seven modules for Objective 5 were first developed using the three-phase framework of TBLT and further elaborated on using Gagné's nine instructional events. The three-phase framework of TBLT consists of pre-task, during-task, and post-task. According to Ellis (2003), the pre-task phase "frames" the activity by establishing its goal, providing a model, or planning for it. Then, participants work on the activity as the during-task phase, sometimes under some time pressure so in authentic communication. The post-task phase follows it to reflect on one's performance, focus on linguistic form, and/or repeat similar task.

As for evaluation standards to assess participants' learning with the EAP tasks, we created an evaluation rubric with 14 criteria (see Hosogoshi and Takahashi 2015), based on the 6 components of skill-integrated tasks summarized by Knoch and Sitajalabhorn (2013). The rubric was a checklist to assess the degree of basic organizations of summaries (Criteria 1–4), qualities of input comprehension (Criteria 5 and 10–12), qualities of output production (Criteria 6–9), and accuracy of language use (Criteria 13 and 14). We used these criteria to give feedback on the students' summaries produced as outcome of Objective 5.

Develop Phase

The Develop phase is where the contents of the task sets described above are created. While each task should be specifically oriented toward a particular learning objective, human learning and interaction does not conform to such rigid, isolated learning, and thus some tasks will undoubtedly contain elements that lead to the achievement of more than one learning objective (as represented by the dotted arrows in Fig. 1 in the previous section). Nevertheless, keeping one main objective in mind often helps to make task development a more directed endeavor and therefore more likely to be successful. Task and materials development are ongoing processes, as represented by the faded boxes and arrows in Fig. 1.

In the Development phase, we first created a prototype of the target EAP task, which was targeted in Objective 5, referring to the format of TOEFL® integrated tasks. The prototype task consisted of seven modules, as shown in Fig. 3. Module 1 provided some pre-task scaffolding in advance of the main listening task. Reviewing literature on advance organizers[3] (e.g., Ausubel 1960; Chung and Huang 1998; Jafari and Hashim 2012; Mayer 2003), two varieties of scaffoldings were created: a selection of difficult vocabulary and an outline of the lecture to be introduced. The difficult vocabulary was decided to be 5 to 10 words from the lecture of 3000 words frequency level or more (Zeeland and Schmitt 2013). These difficult words were presented alongside the Japanese meaning, the students' first language (L1), with the hope that this coverage would allow the students to achieve 95% vocabulary coverage of the listening material (Bonk 2000). The outline of the lecture involved five L1 sentences introducing the topics of the lecture but did not include the thoughts or opinions conveyed by the lecturer in the listening (Herron 1994). These sentences were displayed in the order of appearance in the lecture to provide its outline. Module 2 was lecture listening, so a consistent segment of lecture which lasted for 60–90 s was chosen from *OpenCourseWare*. Module 3 offered a comprehension quiz of the listening input. Presented in English, the students' target language (L2), each quiz had five comprehension questions with four multiple choice options each. Module 4 required students to summarize the single input in written or spoken forms. Module 5 was text reading; a subsequent segment of the lecture passage was transcribed to function as the reading text (at a length of 400–600 words). Module 6 again offered another comprehension quiz of the reading with several questions of four multiple choices each. Lastly, students were assigned a composition as final product of the task, either a written or spoken summary of the two input sources in Module 7.

Adopting the above prototype, four sets of EAP tasks were prepared for the course: two for skill-integrated writing and another two for skill-integrated speaking. The materials developed for each module were devised on *BeeDance*, a learning management system (LMS) for iPads in order for the students to be able to work on the task on an individual basis. Although we did not pilot all of the developed course materials before implementation, we mutually checked their appropriateness as well as procedure of the task modules.

[3] Advance organizers may take many forms but are typically defined as information presented prior to learning, in such a way that a learner may orient themselves to properly interpret and understand new information.

Implement Phase

The Implement phase is where all of the previous steps come to fruition; it is where instruction is carried out, usually, but not always, in a classroom environment. This is where we believe that a "softer" approach to ISD becomes relevant. Even the most meticulous planning cannot account for the wide variety of experiences, opinions, and attitudes that learners will bring into the classroom (which are labelled "worldviews" in Soft Systems Methodology; see chapter Toward Managing Language Pedagogy and Language Teaching Research, this volume). Instructors will inevitably have to adapt to situations on the fly, perhaps rejected pre-planned materials, or changing the planned courses of individual lessons, and this is where the "art" of teaching comes into play, with instructors making the best use of their knowledge and experience. This should not discourage instructors from conducting the analysis through design phases, however, as the preparation required in those stages will more than likely equip an instructor to be able to deal with deviations from the plotted course.

Once the course had started, we implemented the task materials developed for the course. The target EAP task was implemented following the three-phase framework of TBLT, with further elaboration using Gagné's nine instructional events in order to address the discrepancy found in the students' English proficiency and the requirement of the EAP tasks after the initial instructional analysis.

Figure 4 highlights some correspondence of our task design between TBLT and Gagné's nine instructional events. The main flow of the target EAP task was indeed

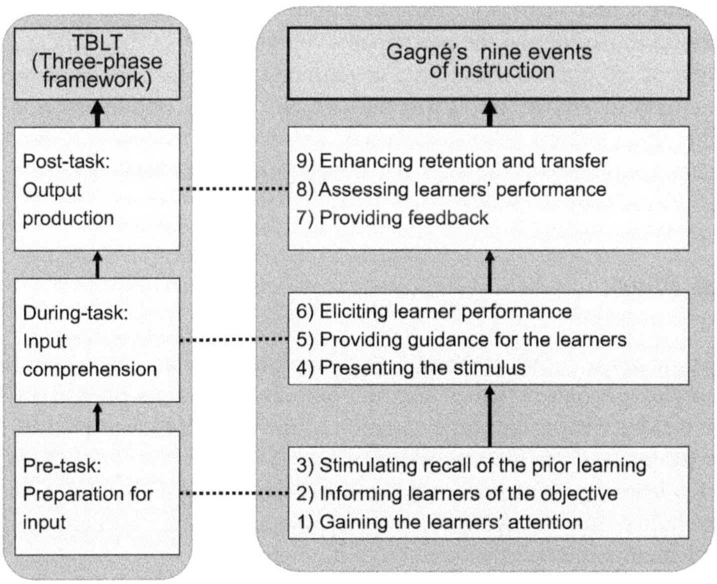

Fig. 4 Correspondence of TBLT and Gagné's nine instructional events

(1) a preparation of the input source, (2) main receptive activity, and (3) post-productive activity. As illustrated, while TBLT framework may be efficient in grasping overall form of the task, Gagné's nine instructional events, one of ISD frameworks, would even be more suitable for describing the task procedure in further detail. Gagné's model helped the course elaborate supplemental modules, such as answering quiz on the lecture and writing or speaking summary of the lecture. Also, the course utilized various scaffoldings as form of pre-task instruction and other preliminary learning activities (e.g., understanding tips for listening) before conducting the EAP task practice. These modules were added in hope of scaffolding students with relatively low English proficiency by providing opportunities to reflect on their progress even during the main task. For example, we provided pre-task scaffolding (e.g., learning keywords of the lecture) for gaining the learner's attention (Gagné's 1) in the pre-task phase of TBLT. Then, we let learners watch lecture video for presenting the stimulus (Gagné's 4) in the during-task phase. Finally, we conducted rubric-based assessment on learners' summary for assessing learners' performance (Gagné's 8) and for enhancing retention and transfer (Gagné's 9) in the post-task phase. Thus, ISD models can be said to elaborate each of the three task phases of TBLT with its flexibility and rich sub-components.

During this Implement phase, the participants sometimes showed confusion over the content provided in the course, and it is here that we had to take a "softer" approach. For instance, even though we offered rubric-based feedback with a model summary after completion of the first set of skill-integrated tasks, some participants did not seem to grasp the aspects they needed to revise. Therefore, from the second trial, we further conducted a "softer" instructional design. We edited the model summaries to be more visually instructive ones, by underlining discourse markers or highlighting report verbs, for example. These flexible modifications were generally successful in facilitating the participants' understating of the content as well as the structure of anticipated summary. Nevertheless, they had not been included in our original task inventory, and it was through observation and interaction with the learners that these matters were discovered. This will be discussed in the following section, after a summary of the learners' development over the course.

Evaluate Phase

The evaluation phase comes at the end of an individual course. The aim of this phase is to determine not only whether learning outcomes in terms of instruction goals have been met but also entails an evaluation of the preceding four phases. Here, an instructor (or team of instructors) will evaluate the appropriateness of the instructional goals, learning objectives, tasks and materials, and their implementation of these. The evaluation of the ADDIE model as practiced conducted in this will inform future implementations in a cyclical, ongoing manner.

As student evaluation, we assessed the outcome of the four EAP tasks. In other words, students' summary produced at the end of each EAP task was evaluated using

Table 1 Results of the pre- and post-tests

	Pre-test		Post-test		
	M	*SD*	*M*	*SD*	*t*
Part A	0.545	0.157	0.580	0.102	2.420*
Part B	0.520	0.187	0.408	0.199	3.290**
Part C	0.493	0.175	0.571	0.207	2.932**
Total	0.529	0.129	0.554	0.117	2.272*

Note. $N = 56$. $+p < .10$, $*p < .05$, $**p < .01$

an evaluation rubric (see Hosogoshi and Takahashi (2015)). Also, we presented a model summary for each task in the hope of raising participants' attention toward linguistic features applicable to the six components of integrated tasks (Knoch and Sitajalabhorn 2013). We could have gathered the students' self-reports on their learning experience during the course possibly by interview or questionnaire.

As course evaluation, we collected data of students' progress during the course by assigning TOEFL® listening questions (Educational Testing Service 1997) in the first and last lessons. Specifically, data of 56 students who participated both of the lessons were compared to assess the efficacy of the course on their language skills development. Each test had 50 questions in total; these were subdivided into three parts: 30 questions on short conversations between two speakers (Part A), 7–8 questions on longer conversations between two speakers (Part B), and 12–13 questions on short talks of a single speaker (Part C). The individual students' total scores for the three parts were converted into percentile scores since the number of questions in each part was different in the two tests. The percentile scores of each part as well total were statistically compared using a paired *t*-test to examine the efficacy of the designed course in EAP skills development (Table 1).

The overall students' average score was found to be significantly increased (t $(55) = 2.272$, $p < .05$, with a small effect size of $d = .21$). As for Part A about short conversations, the average score also improved significantly after the EAP course (t $(55) = 2.420$, $p < .05$, with a small effect size of $d = .26$). On the contrary, regarding Part B on longer conversations, the percentile score significantly decreased (t $(55) = 3.290$, $p < .01$, with a medium effect size of $d = .58$). The score for Part C on short lectures significantly improved (t $(55) = 2.932$, $p < .01$, with a small effect size of $d = .42$).

These results suggest that the designed EAP course was helpful for the majority of the students to acquire not only the academic listening skill applicable to lecture listening but also to deal with short dialogs on campus-related topics. However, the ability to listen to longer dialogs on academic-related topics declined after the course, possibly because the focus of the present EAP course was on listening to monologs, not dialogs.

Finally, we recycled some of the task materials for other EAP courses offered in the following semester. Also, we presented on the development and evaluation of the target EAP task at several conference and journal article (Hosogoshi and Takahashi 2015) in the hope to preserve the course for future use.

As for our evaluation of the implantation of the ADDIE model itself, both instructors felt that it had been largely successful. While there were some instances in the actual teaching that were not accounted for in the design and develop phases (see section "Implement phase" above), we would argue that these were not a failing of the ADDIE model. On the contrary, the thorough planning of the ADDIE model perhaps allowed the instructors to pay more attention to the learners in action and therefore to be more readily able to respond to their needs. It is in this sense that some of the criticisms of ISD seem to fall short. While it is true (and evident from our own implementation) that instructors cannot possibly account for all of the human factors that occur in the classroom, having planned a course using ADDIE as a conceptual framework rather than a set-in-stone outline for the course allowed the instructors to address those human factors when they arose.

A Softer ISD

This chapter has introduced a case study of an implementation of ISD. In the first section we addressed some of the prior criticisms of ISD, such as its inflexibility and inability to address the human element in learning situations. Through our execution and analysis of the ADDIE model in particular, however, we proposed a softer approach to ISD and argued that it can indeed achieve its proposed benefits as a framework to support learning and teaching. We contend that criticisms of ISD are certainly compelling if ISD in application is taken as a set of rigid rules for instruction. Understanding that, of course, plans tend not to be flawless, we approached our implantation with the idea that things might change.

Our particular case study focused on a TBLT implementation, but it may (and is) of course applied in a much wider variety of contexts. Furthermore, while the only slight hiccup in our implementation involved an adjustment to materials already planned, the development of task inventories and the updates to the plans that can occur as a result of human factors in the classroom can of course allow for entire lessons, or, even if necessary, learning objectives, to be altered. This possibility, we argue, is not a failing of ISDs, such as the ADDIE model, themselves. Rather, these are the times in which the human experience of the individual teacher is most important. As touched upon in chapter Toward Managing Language Pedagogy and Language Teaching Research of this volume, as well as several other chapters, learning (perhaps especially language learning) is an inherently *human endeavor*, and over-systematizing learning deprives it of the emergent properties that can result from genuine human interaction. Nevertheless, a degree of "hard-system" thinking, such as that provided by the ADDIE model, allows for an instructor to control for as many of the controllable factors that they may while taking a softer and therefore more human approach to their implementation.

References

Ausubel, D. P. (1960). The use of advance organizers in the learning and retention of meaningful verbal material. *Journal of Educational Psychology, 51*(5), 267–272.

Biber, D. (2006). *University language: A corpus-based study of spoken and written registers*. Amsterdam: John Benjamins Publishing.

Bichelmeyer, B., Boling, E., & Gibbons, A. S. (2006). Instructional design and technology models: Their impact on research and teaching in instructional design and technology. *Educational media and technology yearbook, 31*, 33–73.

Bloom, B. S., Engelhart, M. D., Furst, E. J., Hill, W. H., & Krathwohl, D. R. (1956). *Taxonomy of educational objectives, handbook I: The cognitive domain*. New York: David McKay Co.

Bonk, W. J. (2000). Second language lexical knowledge and listening comprehension. *International Journal of Listening, 14*(1), 14–31.

Brownell, K. D. (2008). *Introduction: What we eat, why we eat, and the key role of food in modern life*. Retrieved from http://oyc.yale.edu/psychology/psyc-123/lecture-1

Bygate, M., Skehan, P., & Swain, M. (2001). Introduction. In M. Bygate, P. Skehan, & M. Swain (Eds.), *Researching pedagogic tasks: Second language learning. Teaching and testing* (pp. 1–22). Harlow: Pearson Education.

Canaan, J. E., & Shumar, W. (2008). Higher education in the era of globalization and neoliberalism. In J. E. Canaan & E. Shumar (Eds.), *Structure and agency in the neoliberal university*. London: Routledge.

Chung, J. M., & Huang, S. C. (1998). The effects of three aural advance organizers for video viewing in a foreign language classroom. *System, 26*, 553–565.

Dick, W., & Carey, L. (1996). *The systematic design of instruction* (4th ed.). New York: Harper Collins College Publishers.

Educational Testing Service. (1997). *TOEFL® practice tests vol. 2*. Princeton: Educational Testing Service.

Ellis, R. (2003). *Task-based language learning and teaching*. Oxford: Oxford University Press.

Flowerdew, J., & Peacock, M. (2001). Issues in EAP: A preliminary perspective. In J. Flowerdew & M. Peacock (Eds.), *Research perspectives on English for academic purposes* (pp. 8–24). Cambridge: Cambridge University Press.

Gagné, R. M. (1985). *The conditions of learning* (4th ed.). New York: Holt, Rinehart & Winston.

Herron, C. (1994). An investigation of the effectiveness of using an advance organizer to introduce video in the foreign language classroom. *The Modern Language Journal, 78*(2), 190–198.

Hosogoshi, K., & Takahashi, S. (2015). The use of integrated listening, reading, speaking and writing tasks on students' productive skills in a university EAP course. *Professional and Academic English, 45*, 22–30.

Jafari, K., & Hashim, F. (2012). The effects of using advance organizers on improving EFL learners' listening comprehension: A mixed method study. *System, 40*, 270–281.

Knoch, U., & Sitajalabhorn, W. (2013). A closer look at integrated tasks: Towards a more focused definition for assessment purposes. *Assessing Writing, 18*, 300–308.

Long, M. (2015). *Second language acquisition and task-based language teaching*. West Sussex: Wiley.

Long, M., & Norris, J. (2009). Task-based teaching and assessment. In K. Van den Branden, M. Bygate, & J. M. Norris (Eds.), *Task-based language teaching: A reader* (pp. 135–142). Amsterdam: John Benjamins.

Mayer, R. (2003). *Learning and instruction*. Upper Saddle River: Pearson Education.

Morrison, G. R., Ross, S. M., Kalman, H. K., & Kemp, J. E. (2012). *Designing effective instruction*. New York: Wiley.

Oxford, R. (2001). Integrated skills in the ESL/EFL classroom. *ESL Magazine, 6*(1). Reprinted in ERIC/CLL Digest, EDO-FL-01-05.

Phillips, D. (2007). *Longman preparation for the TOEFL® test : iBT*. White Plains: Pearson Education.

Richards, J. (1983). Listening comprehension: Approach, design, procedure. *TESOL Quarterly, 17*(2), 219–240.
Robinson, B. K., & Dearmon, V. (2013). Evidence-based nursing education: Effective use of instructional design and simulated learning environments to enhance knowledge transfer in undergraduate nursing students. *Journal of Professional Nursing, 29*(4), 203–209.
Rost, M. (2011). *Teaching and researching listening* (2nd ed.). Harlow: Pearson Education.
Smith, P. L., & Ragan, T. J. (2005). *Instructional design* (3rd ed.). Hoboken: Wiley.
Takahashi, S., Pearce, D. R., & Dalsky, D. (2018). MAP grammar and instructional design. In A. Tajino (Ed.), *A new approach to English pedagogical grammar : The order of meanings* (pp. 103–115). Oxford: Routledge.
Vandergrift, L., & Goh, C. C. M. (2012). *Teaching and learning second language listening: Metacognition in action*. New York: Routledge.
Zeeland, H. V., & Schmitt, N. (2013). Lexical coverage in L1 and L2 listening comprehension: The same or different from reading comprehension? *Applied Linguistics, 34*(4), 457–479.

Team Teaching and Team Learning: SSM Applied to the Team-Taught Classroom

Daniel Roy Pearce

Abstract The benefits of team teaching in language education have largely been recognized in the literature. Nevertheless, there remain many barriers to achieving adequate teacher collaboration in the classroom. Such barriers may be a result of real-world constraints, such as a lack of time for preparation, or may be caused by personal or cultural factors. This chapter takes a managerial systems approach to the team-taught language classroom and suggests a methodology to help teachers overcome these issues. First, the ideal form of team teaching, *Team Learning*, is introduced, and the concept of a *shared value* in the classroom is discussed. *Soft systems methodology* (SSM) is then proposed as a tool for team-teaching practitioners to overcome hurdles in collaborative teaching. It is suggested that the implementation of SSM may assist practitioners in achieving Team Learning by inspiring systemic change in the team-taught classroom. This change should lead to emergent properties beyond those that might be expected in a traditional one-teacher classroom.

Keywords Team teaching · Team learning · Value-centered classroom · SSM · Collaboration

Introduction

Team Teaching (sometimes referred to as co-teaching) is a broad term that has been given a great number of definitions in the literature of education. Perhaps the loosest definition of team teaching might include out-of-class collaboration before or after lessons, while instruction in the classroom is carried out by a solo teacher. On the opposite end of the spectrum, team teaching may refer to a sharing of roles in the classroom, with little collaboration outside of lessons (Copland et al. 2016). The author of this chapter believes that effective team teaching requires collaboration both within the classroom and outside of lessons. As such, for the purposes of this discussion, we will borrow a definition of team teaching (co-teaching) from Villa

D. R. Pearce (✉)
Graduate School of Human and Environmental Studies, Kyoto University, Kyoto, Japan
e-mail: pearce.roy.26e@st.kyoto-u.ac.jp

A. Tajino (ed.), *A Systems Approach to Language Pedagogy*, Translational Systems Sciences 17, https://doi.org/10.1007/978-981-13-6272-9_8

et al. (2004), in which team teaching is "two or more people sharing responsibility for teaching… it involves the distribution of responsibility among people for planning, instruction, and evaluation for a classroom of students" (p.3).

In English language education, team teaching exists in varying forms. It may take the form of team-taught classes conducted by a native-English-speaking teacher (or NEST, typically of differing nationality to the other classroom participants) and a local, nonnative-English-speaking teacher (or NNEST, who usually shares a cultural background with the students). This form of team teaching is particularly prevalent at secondary schools in East Asia, beginning with precursors to Japan's JET Program, established in 1987, and since spreading to Korea, mainland China, and Taiwan, among other countries and territories (see, e.g., Carless 2006; Jang 2006; Liu 2008). Similar types of team teaching may occur between two NNESTs, with the objective of increasing opportunities for interaction in EFL environments (see Carley III 2013). In Japan, NESTs often teach along homeroom teachers at elementary schools, who are usually not trained in language teaching (see, e.g., Aline and Hosoda 2006). Other forms of team teaching include CLIL, or content and language integrated learning, in which the target of lessons is typically a different field (such as history or biology) and instruction in such lessons is often shared between a content specialist and a language specialist. This form of team teaching is more often conducted at the tertiary level (see, e.g., Gladman 2015; Perry and Stewart 2005).

Collaboration in teaching is not easy to achieve, and each form of team teaching brings with it its own unique issues. Team teachers in CLIL contexts may experience clashes over the importance of language instruction versus content instruction, whereas NNESTs might experience frustration with NESTs who are often not accustomed to the local educational setting (Ogawa 2010). In either setting, conflict may occur due to a difference in culture between teachers (be it a result of differing nationalities or a divergence in culture due to different institutional backgrounds). The mere presence of another teacher in the classroom can also be a stressful factor, potentially threatening the authority of the individual teachers involved. This is particularly conspicuous when teachers are thrust into team teaching situations involuntarily, as is often the case at the primary or secondary level (see Miyazato 2009). Overcoming such clashes is a difficult, although necessary, factor in achieving effective collaboration in the language classroom.

Team teaching is thought to be most effective when it takes the form of *Team Learning*, in which all participants (both teachers and learners) embrace a "shared value" (see Tajino and Smith 2016, and the section entitled Value-centered Team Learning, below) in the classroom. Fostering such a shared value is perhaps easier said than done, however, as each participant in the classroom brings with them their own views on language and learning, views that have been shaped by their individual cultures and life histories and continue to be influenced by different factors. Indeed, far from sharing, teachers and learners may at times find their values at odds with each other. As each team-teaching situation is inherently context-bound (no assortment of factors is shared between two classrooms, even in the same institution), there is no panacea for issues that may disrupt collaboration in the classroom. Nevertheless, while complicated, and at times even messy, achieving a shared value

(or something close to it) in the classroom is by no means an impossible task. It is the aim of this chapter to equip the reader with a powerful tool through which they might nurture shared values that are relevant to their own educational contexts, be they teacher, student, or administrator. That tool is *soft systems methodology.*

As a means to achieve deeper understandings of situations, participants, and motivations, soft systems methodology (SSM) is a process of inquiry that is uniquely suited to addressing issues in complex social undertakings, such as team teaching. This chapter will first explore the "ideal" form of team teaching, *Team Learning*, before giving a general overview of SSM alongside a hypothetical team-teaching scenario to demonstrate how the methodology might be applied. It should be noted that while the idea of applying SSM to achieve Team Learning originally stemmed from a consideration of team teaching between a NEST and NNEST, this chapter should nonetheless have implications for practitioners involved in any form of team teaching.

From Team Teaching to Team Learning

The concept of Team Learning first entered the literature in 1997 in response to several issues in team teaching in Japan (Tajino 1997). In the Japanese EFL context, team teachers had fallen into certain specific roles that did not realize the full potential of team teaching (such as NESTs being used as simple "tape recorders" to provide "more accurate" pronunciation models, see Kumabe 1996). The fossilization of such roles may have come about due to a hierarchy of power relations in the classroom, identified in later research (Lee 2015; Pearce 2017), in which the NNEST, who often has a better understanding of the education system and the local students, usually occupies a dominant role as instructor, and the NEST tends to operate within a provided framework (see Fig. 1).

Whatever the cause behind this trend, Team Learning was a call to reconsider these roles and recommended a form of team teaching that focused on teachers' strengths, recognizing the potential emergent properties in teacher collaboration that could achieve much richer lessons than just a sum of the teachers' efforts. Later, Tajino and Tajino (2000) described these emergent properties through a metaphor of a duet between a pianist and a singer on stage – much more powerful than the pianist and singer performing on the same stage at different times.

In the same article, a set of concrete models for how teachers might interact in classroom activities is proposed – some of which are shown in Fig. 2. These activity patterns were suggested to be most effective when each party (NNEST, NEST, or student) might act as "cultural informants" to the others, by perhaps sharing the local culture to the NEST as a "guest" or having the NNEST and students fulfill "learner" roles as the NEST introduced their culture to the classroom – all using the English language as a vehicle (see Tajino and Tajino 2000). In such a way, these

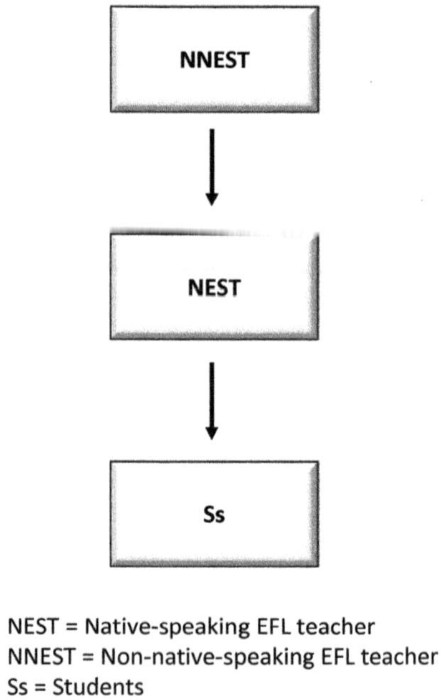

Fig. 1 Hierarchy in the team-taught classroom

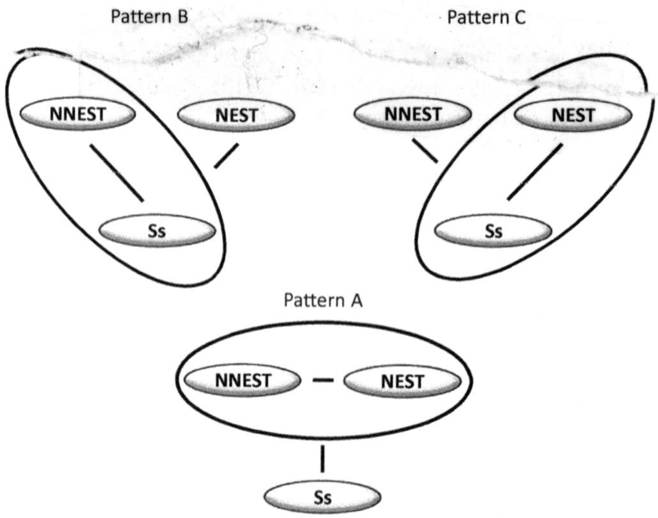

Fig. 2 Some team patterns (Adapted from Tajino and Tajino 2000. Copyright 2000 by Oxford University Press)

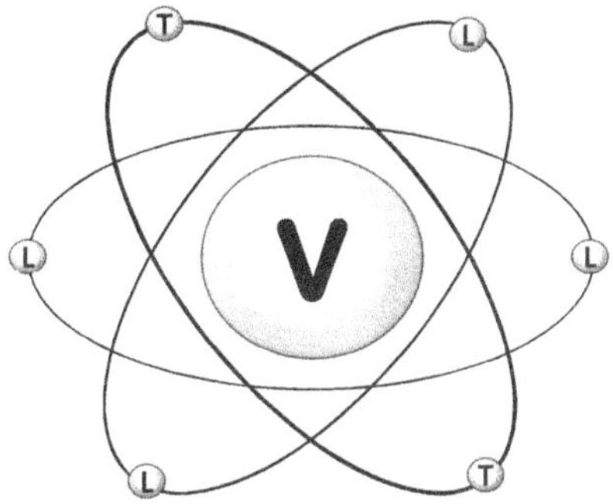

Fig. 3 Value: The "nucleus" of the classroom with teachers and students in changing roles

patterns were intended to play to the strengths of the individuals, by relying on the unique knowledge and experience that both teachers brought to the classroom.[1]

In the two decades since team learning was first proposed, language teaching (and education in general) has undergone somewhat of a paradigm shift toward a learner-centered classroom (see Anton 1999; McCombs and Whisler 1997). Team Learning, too, has evolved beyond its original conception, influenced also by ongoing research into teaching methodologies such as *Exploratory Practice* (see Allwright 2003; Hanks 2017). Earlier conceptions of Team Learning were ostensibly teacher-focused, with models centered on what unique attributes individual *teachers* brought into the classroom with them. More recent Team Learning theory recognizes all members of the classroom as practitioners of learning and further posits that in order for Team Learning to succeed, both teachers and learners must approach the classroom with "shared values" (see Tajino and Smith 2016).

Value-Centered Team Learning

Team Learning recognizes that, as stated above, in a heterogeneous classroom, just as in any other collaborative endeavor, participants should share a common *value*. Such a value may be as simple as a shared goal for a particular task or may be as complex as "developing mutual understanding" or "build[ing] and maintain[ing] comfortable relationships between classmates and teachers" (Tajino and Smith 2016, p. 21). Striving toward realization of such shared values may allow for the focus of the classroom to become less teacher- or learner-centered but rather *value-centered* (visualized in Fig. 3). In the language classroom, this approach should allow for both teachers and learners to break out of power hierarchies that impede equality in communication and thus provide more opportunities for both teachers and learners to engage in a more meaningful interaction, learning from, and with,

[1] It should be noted that while these patterns were proposed for team teaching between native- and nonnative-speaking English teachers, they may be equally applicable to the CLIL classroom, with content and language specialists taking the places of NESTs and NNESTs.

each other, as a team. As the classroom is often necessarily a rigidly hierarchical institution (see McHoul 1978, 1990; Pearce 2017), and teachers must regularly assume more rights to interaction (e.g., for classroom management purposes), teachers must be able to perform the challenging task of moving in and out of certain roles (i.e., teacher, learner, or facilitator). On the other hand, learners also need to be prepared to face a similar challenge as they may be required to take on the role of "teacher."

Here, three conditions are posited as prerequisites for the achievement of the shared values which are required for effective Team Learning:

1. A mutual understanding and respect between the two teachers (who are both in positions of authority in the classroom) and their learners
2. The ability of teachers to move in and out of roles with relative fluidity (learner, teacher, mediator, etc.)
3. Teachers' ability to guide students in taking on the roles of teachers and mediators where necessary

It was primarily the first prerequisite that inspired the author of this chapter to consider SSM – not only because it provides a possible framework for developing mutual understanding (which should eventually lead to the achievement of prerequisites 2 and 3) but because it also considers real-world factors (such as preparation time, curriculum or institutional constraints, etc.) that might be barriers toward the realization of Team Learning.

The next section will give a brief overview of SSM, alongside a hypothetical team-teaching context to which the methodology may be applied. The hypothetical situation involves a NEST and NNEST in an EFL setting, but the reader should once again be reminded that SSM may be applied equally readily to other team-teaching contexts.

Soft Systems Methodology

Soft systems methodology (SSM) is somewhat unique in systems thinking, as it was originally conceived as an organized process for exploring particularly the type of messy, complex situations that are inherent to social interaction. Since its original conception in the early 1980s by Peter Checkland (Checkland and Poulter 2010), it has been refined over several decades of practice in various institutions, including the UK's National Health Service (Checkland and Poulter 2010). SSM recognizes that any situation in everyday life, and particularly social situations, can give rise to events that we feel need to be improved upon. SSM labels such events *problematic situations*, rather than problems, a term which suggests a definitive solution – whereas real life is generally more complex (Checkland and Poulter 2006). Problematic situations occur because people approach situations with different *worldviews*, and these worldviews inform any action they might take. One can easily imagine such situations occurring in a classroom in which two teachers have different teaching priorities (influenced by their worldviews), and we cannot forget that the students, of course, have their own worldviews which determine how they react to what is happening in the classroom. What a messy situation indeed!

In a nutshell, SSM is a methodology for arriving at *accommodations* of (or compromises between) worldviews. It is an active process of inquiry to bring about improvement in complex, real-life situations. Space unfortunately precludes a comprehensive introduction of SSM, and readers are directed to Checkland and Poulter (2006, 2010), from which much of this section has been summarized for more detailed discussions of the methodology. This section will, however, attempt to give an overview of the process of SSM before the following section describes how it may be implemented in a team-teaching context to achieve that elusive *shared value*.

The SSM Learning Cycle

SSM consists of a *learning cycle* comprised of four actions to address problematic situations. According to Checkland and Poulter, such situations not only contain different worldviews but also invariably involve people who are "trying to act purposefully, with intention" (2010, p.192). A typical example in the classroom might be a NEST who hopes to teach English for communicative purposes and a NNEST who wishes to prepare learners for university entrance examinations. SSM is a process that would help these teachers to accommodate these worldviews to the benefit of both themselves and their learners. The learning cycle is as follows:

1. Finding out about the problematical situation: This action involves not only identifying a problematical situation but also the characteristics of the situation, which may include personal, cultural, and political factors.
2. Modeling relevant purposeful activities: Here the aim is to develop a model for possible action to improve a situation, with relevance to the characteristics identified in action 1. Purposeful activities should be expressed using models which incorporate "declared worldviews." Such models will be simplified versions of the complex real-world situation but will serve to facilitate discussion, by making worldviews tangible.
3. Deriving questions from the models: The models created in action 2 provide structure for coherent discussion about the situation. Such discussion will inevitably touch on how the situation might be changed.
4. Finding changes: The purpose of this action is to find changes based on the previous steps that are both desirable to all participants involved and culturally feasible (in terms of both personal and institutional history and politics and culture). Here, changes should be actions that participants with conflicting worldviews can agree upon and live with (i.e., *accommodations*). Such changes should ultimately affect individual worldviews. (adapted from Checkland and Poulter 2010, pp.192–193)

As is evidenced by action 4, above, SSM is an ongoing process. It has necessarily been outlined in a linear manner here, but the actions are not rigid, standalone steps, and should be viewed rather as a back-and-forth process, in which each action influences the others. SSM practitioners will likely wish to revisit individual actions several times before proceeding to the next. In the case of team-teaching, in which an NEST and NNEST (or content specialist and language specialist) may have busy schedules that provide little opportunity for discussing questions and finding changes, for example, each teacher may carry out actions 1 and 2 individually, which will enable well-ordered, productive discussion on the occasions when they are able to meet and talk.

The remainder of this section will describe how SSM practitioners might carry out actions 1 through 4, providing guidelines for identifying characteristics of problematic situations, how to make models of the situations, and how to derive questions from the models. Based on these three steps, the final accommodations made in action 4 should help to lead to the development of *shared values* between the practitioners.

The SSM Learning Cycle: Four Actions

This section will outline in more detail how the actions above generate deeper understandings of complex situations and allow participants to take into account other perspectives in a structured, systematic manner. Continued application of these steps should lead to *systemic* change in the team-taught classroom which should bring about more genuine collaboration.

Action 1: Finding Out and Analyzing

The first action consists of four stages – referred to as "making Rich Pictures" and conducting *interventional*, *social*, and *political* analyses. The Rich Picture stage, from which the analyses are subsequently conducted, originally stemmed from the following two questions:

1. What resources are deployed in what operational processes under what planning procedures within what structures, in what environments and wider systems, by whom?
2. How is resource deployment monitored and controlled?(Checkland and Poulter 2010, p. 209)

A cursory glance at these two questions shows that they cover the necessary background information to understand a situation as outlined by Tajino, Smith, and Kanamaru in chapter Toward Managing Language Pedagogy and Language Teaching Research of this volume (i.e., the "who," "what," "where," "when," "by whom," and "how"). Also, just as Tajino presents a useful visualization of such systems, SSM suggests creating actual pictures to grasp a situation. According to Checkland and Poulter, the aim of making a Rich Picture is "to capture, informally, the main entities, structures and viewpoints in the situation, the processes going on, the current recognized issues and any potential ones" (Checkland and Poulter 2010, p. 210).

In a team-teaching context, a real-world problematic situation might be as follows:

> A NNEST Head of English (HoE) at an elementary school is in charge of the curriculum and liaising with a NEST assistant language teacher (hereafter, ALT) who visits the school once each week. The ALT is a newly-arrived teacher with no experience or qualifications in education but is highly motivated and offers to create lesson plans for his visits to the school. The HoE is aware that the elementary school teachers are legally responsible for their lesson content and must conform to the Ministry of Education guidelines regarding the curriculum. A considerable amount of content needs to be covered within a limited number of lessons, for which the head teacher creates a general lesson plan as a guideline for teachers from grades 1 to 6. On the other hand, several teachers in the English department are happy to accept the ALT's lesson plans in their entirety due to a lack of confidence in their own ability to teach English or overly hectic work schedules. The students are enthusiastic regarding lessons that involve the ALT and spend a few lessons preparing for his visits. The head teacher wishes to include input from the ALT but does not feel it is appropriate to relinquish control of entire lessons to the ALT.

This situation is better represented as a Rich Picture, as in Fig. 4.

Physically making such rich pictures has a twofold benefit, in that it succinctly summarizes the relationships between all invested parties while also being light on textual data. They may be particularly useful in some team-teaching situations (such as the above hypothetical), in which language ability can sometimes be a barrier to communication.

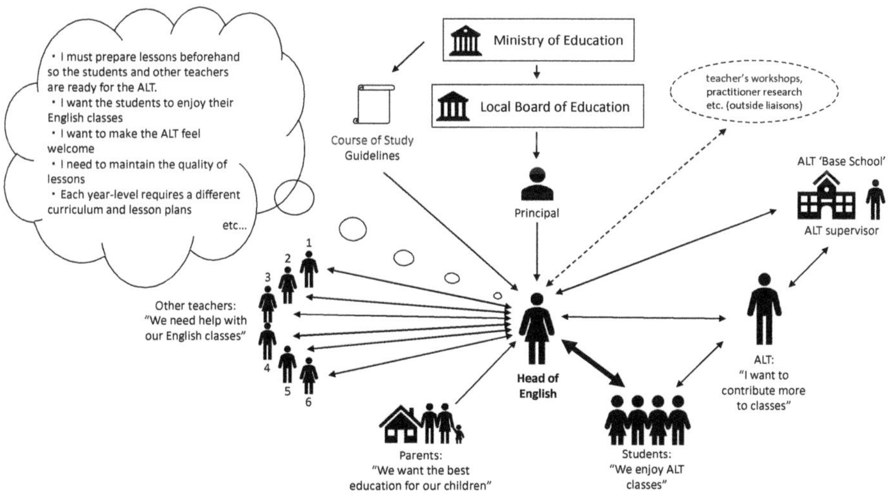

Fig. 4 Rich picture of a hypothetical team-teaching situation

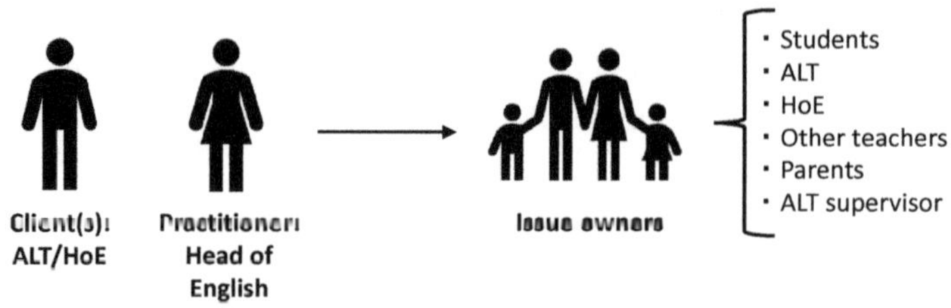

Fig. 5 Analysis 1: the intervention

Carrying out Analyses

The second part of the finding out action consists of three different ways of analyzing the problematic situation: interventional, social, and political. The goal of these analyses is to identify key "roles" in a problematic situation, to examine the social relationships therein, as well to ascertain relevant power relationships. The analyses will inform models for purposeful action, and cognizant discussion of those models. The following subsections will give a brief guide to these interventions while referring to the hypothetical problematic situation above as a point of reference.

Analysis 1: Identifying the Situation

The first analysis is based on the assumption that in a problematic situation, three key roles will always be present (see Checkland and Poulter 2006, 2010); the *client* (a person or persons that caused the intervention to happen), the *practitioner* (the person or persons who carry out the investigation), and *issue owners* (those affected by the situation and any efforts to improve it). An interventional analysis of our hypothetical situation is shown in Fig. 5.

Analysis 1 is the process of identifying such roles. It is recommended to use the label "role" rather than specific individuals as particular individuals may simultaneously inhabit multiple roles (the head teacher in our hypothetical may simultaneously be all three of these roles). Once the client, practitioner, and issue owner roles have been identified, the second analysis may be undertaken.

Analysis 2: Exploring the Social

This second analysis addresses one of the "messier" aspects of human situations. It is also where SSM takes a departure from traditional "hard" systems approaches, in that it recognizes, and compensates for, the fact that humans are often motivated by factors that are *not* logical – factors such as emotions and cultural norms.[2] For any

[2] Cultural norms may differ on a macroscale, i.e., between nationalities, or be much more local differences, such as between different institutions. Both kinds of cultural norms are equally relevant to human situations.

intervention or attempted improvement to be successful, the changes that occur will need to be *culturally feasible* (Checkland and Poulter 2006, 2010). In our hypothetical situation, for example, it would likely not be culturally feasible for the HoE to relinquish control of full lessons to the ALT, while neither would be the exclusion of the ALT's input entirely. According to SSM, three elements must be investigated before any culturally feasible change is attempted. These elements are intertwined in any human situation: *roles*, *norms*, and *values*.

Roles are the positions that distinguish members of a group or institution. In our hypothetical, this might include, for example, the Head of English, the Principal, and the ALT. There is a second type of role, however, which is equally important: informal roles. In a school setting, examples might be the "strict teacher" or the "motivated ALT."

Norms are the expected behaviors that accompany formal roles. These are particularly worth paying attention to in an intercultural team-teaching context, as it is a near certainty that individual issue owners will have different "commonsense" ideas regarding these norms.

Values are the criteria by which an individual's behavior is judged with respect to their role. Our ALT might be appraised as "punctual" at his base school for arriving exactly on time every day. He might on the other hand be criticized as "uncooperative" for not showing up 15 min early to his elementary school visits.

These three elements ceaselessly influence and change the others. Keeping a working record of such roles, norms, and values (Fig. 6) allows for richer, more informed action plans for enacting change. When carrying out this analysis, it is recommended to keep physical records of such observations, which will become a powerful tool for reflection.

As all three elements are constantly present in human situations, this analysis can be undertaken in a wide variety of contexts. For example, a chat over drinks after work may enlighten one about another individual's values in a different way to observing her or him in the staffroom or in the classroom.

Analysis 3: Investigating the Political

This third analysis is conducted in an almost identical way to the exploration of social roles, although with a different focus – on *politics*. Every human interaction involves individuals pursuing different agendas, and for any system of human interaction to function smoothly, these agendas must be accommodated. These agendas are also inevitably influenced by structures of power. The amount of political power an individual wields is influenced by numerous factors. The most obvious among these is an overt position in an institution – at a school, a principal is much more likely (but not necessarily always or in every situation!) to hold more political sway than a regular teacher, for example. Other factors that influence power relationships include the amount of information an individual has access to, their reputation (as

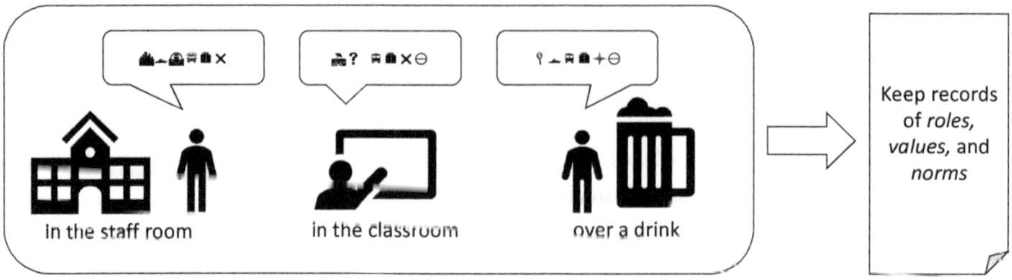

Fig. 6 Analysis 2: social aspects

competent or incompetent, for example), or personal connections within a certain institution.

In a primary or secondary school situation, power relationships may be relatively straightforward, as they tend to be somewhat insulated institutions, although, as our Rich Picture above (Fig. 4) makes clear, there are outside influences as well – including boards of education or parents, for example. In a tertiary institution, power relationships may be more complex, including, for instance, interdepartmental as well as administrative politics.

In our hypothetical, the ALT is unlikely to hold much political power, being a new arrival and a "guest" at the school once a week. As time progresses, however, he develops relationships with other teachers and learns more about his position. A total lack of political power may make the ALT feel unwelcome, and be a demotivating factor, so it is important for our practitioner to conduct this analysis thoroughly.

In order to successfully enact change, an SSM practitioner will want to be aware of power structures and continually observe how they might be changing. It is therefore recommended that, just as in analysis 2, the practitioner keeps physical records of her or his analysis – preferably dated, as a record to refer to over the course of an investigation (Checkland and Poulter 2006, 2010).

Action 2: Making Purposeful Action Models

With the above analyses completed, the practitioner should now be informed enough to begin building purposeful action models. These models will provide a framework for asking questions about the real-world situation. It must be noted that as each model is constructed on the foundation of a particular *worldview*, they are not definitive descriptions but rather guides to the *learning process* of SSM. As such, these models facilitate the learning process by providing a structure.

The first step in creating an action model is to come up with a statement that defines the action to be modeled. In SSM, these are known as *root definitions* (RDs), based on a particular worldview, and are a particular way of viewing an action to be modeled, which will later help to form organized discussions of problematic situations.

Let us first begin with an inadequate RD for the change to be enacted in our hypothetical situation: "A system to improve communication between English teachers." This definition lacks the key components of human situations that our practitioner has investigated in the finding out step. In order to flesh out this RD to model an action for improvement, the PQR Formula is used. In SSM, this is defined as "do P, by Q, in order to help achieve R" (Checkland and Poulter 2010, p.219).[3]

The PQR formula may provide the following RD: "A HoE-lead cooperative system to enhance communication between Japanese English teachers and the ALT, to ensure that each party is aware of the others' educational obligations, in order to allow more input from the ALT and improve collaboration, thus increasing participation, learning, and enjoyment in our English classes."

This definition can be further enriched by applying the mnemonic "CATWOE" to the RD. The letters in CATWOE represent:

C: Customers, those who stand to benefit (or become victims of) the transformation process (in our hypothetical, this would primarily be the students but may include other English teachers and the ALT).

A: Actors, those who conduct the actions that make up the transformation process (primarily the HoE but also the ALT).

T: Transformation process, the transformation that results from the purposeful action being undertaken.

W: Worldview, the defined worldview behind the transformation process (if this SSM is being conducted initially with just the HoE as a practitioner, the entailing worldview may be something like: "Team-taught classes at elementary school are most effective when managed primarily by the homeroom teachers, with constructive input from the ALT").

O: Owners, those who have the power to stop the transformation process (in our example this would include the HoE herself, the principal, and potentially the ALT, his supervisor, or other teachers).

E: Environmental constraints, which are taken as given in the transformation process (in our situation, this would include physical dimensions of time-and-space; the HoE is tied up in other classes for the entirety of the ALT's visits, while the ALT spends most of the workweek at different schools).

Having applied the mnemonic to the RD, the practitioner may update the RD, and once satisfactory, the RD will form the basis of a purposeful action model. An updated RD after applying PQR and CATWOE may be something like the following: "A HoE-lead cooperative system to enhance communication between Japanese English teachers and the ALT by encouraging input from each party within mutually agreed-upon guidelines, to ensure that each party is aware that the Japanese teachers are obligated to be the main teacher in lessons, but also to improve collaboration, thus increasing participation, learning, and enjoyment for our students in their English classes in a manner that is not overly burdensome for anyone involved."

[3] Here the letters PQR do not have any particular meaning (aside from being sequential in the alphabet). They simply refer to the "what, how, and why."

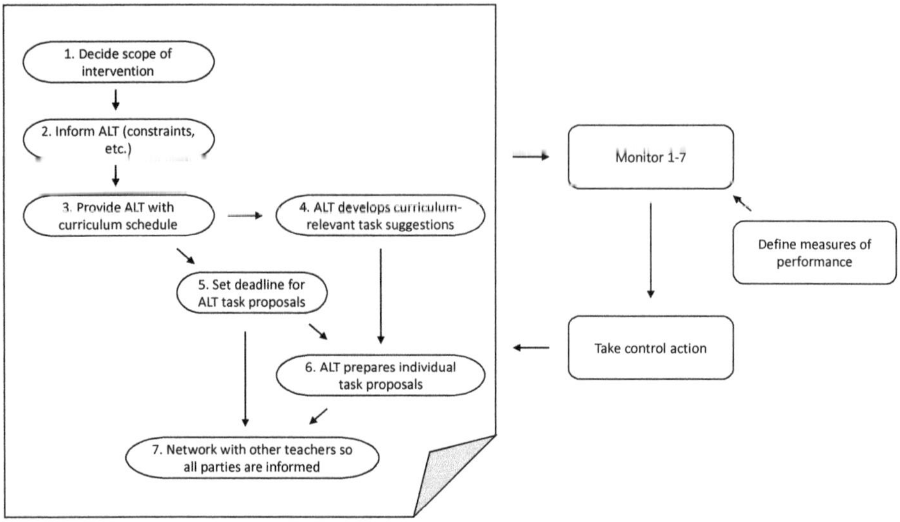

Fig. 7 Purposeful action model to improve collaboration in elementary school team teaching

A visualization of an action model for our hypothetical situation based on the reformulated RD is shown in Fig. 7. On the right-hand side of the figure are three steps external to the action model. These will inform the model, and if any of the steps are unsatisfactory, the model may be updated. The measures of performance will be influenced by both checking the model against the guidelines above (the PQR formula, CATWOE, and the RD) and by questioning the models (action three in SSM, discussed in the following section).

It must be noted that during the model-building phase, new questions may arise that require more "finding out." The practitioner should be aware that this is a natural part of the SSM process, and that there may often be much back-and-forth between the steps before reaching the next part of the SSM cycle: *Questioning the models* in structured discussion.

Action 3: Questioning the Models

Now that the practitioner has developed a relevant model, the invested parties are ready to have an informed discussion about the problematic situation, and how change might be enacted, which should lead to concrete action being taken. What the models do for our invested parties is to ensure that all parties are discussing the same issues, focalized on the same worldview. The model provides a framework from which relevant questions might develop. In our hypothetical, our ALT might raise a relevant question regarding Step 4 in the model: "What kind of tasks should I prepare? Cultural or linguistic?" or perhaps questions about Step 2: "Are these constraints truly binding? What degree of freedom do we have in the curriculum?"

An important way in which the models facilitate discussion is that they are based on an overt worldview. Making the worldview explicit allows participants to avoid the complications that arise when one or more parties are arguing from different worldviews. This is not to say that worldviews will not conflict, they might, and this in fact may even be a desirable outcome! Emotions tend to inspire enthusiastic discussion, and as worldviews are inherently influenced by emotion, such structured discussions are likely to at least stimulate interest in the problematic situation at hand. If an action model is not stimulating enthusiastic discussion, it should be reformulated.

Action 4: Defining Action for Change

The structured discussions above should lead to an agreement about what actions will be taken to change the problematic situation. It is important to note here that this process is not about consensus but rather finding *accommodations* between different worldviews. This does not mean, of course, that consensus *cannot* happen, although the literature suggests that true consensus typically only occurs around trivial issues (Checkland and Poulter 2010). As team teaching is inherently bound to the context of education, discussions about problematic situations are often likely to be decidedly nontrivial, and thus it would be exceedingly unwise to strive for consensus. Accommodations should lead to action for change that is cultural feasible and agreeable to each party. In Checkland and Poulters words, change should be aimed toward achieving "a version of the situation which [involved parties] can all live with" (2010, p. 229). Finding this accommodation is a necessary condition for deciding upon what action is to be taken.

It is worth noting here that enacting change in a complex situation will usually involve three different types of change: change to *structures* (in our hypothetical, perhaps how role distribution in the classroom, or in preparation, might be reorganized), *processes* (perhaps how, and by whom, the content of classes is decided by), and *attitudes* (the attitude of the HoE to ALT and vice versa and also potentially the attitude of students toward a class as a whole). Fig. 8 is a visualization of these three types of change.

With the action for change now decided upon, our invested parties are able to enact it.

A Brief Recap

This section has provided a brief introduction of the SSM process, and how it might be applied to a hypothetical team-teaching situation. Space has precluded a fuller explanation of SSM and thus some of the intricacies of the methodology. For a more detailed introduction, readers are directed to Checkland and Poulter (2006, 2010).[4]

[4] A fifth action, *reflection*, although of relevance to teachers, has been omitted from this overview of SSM. For more details, see Checkland and Poulter 2006, 2010.

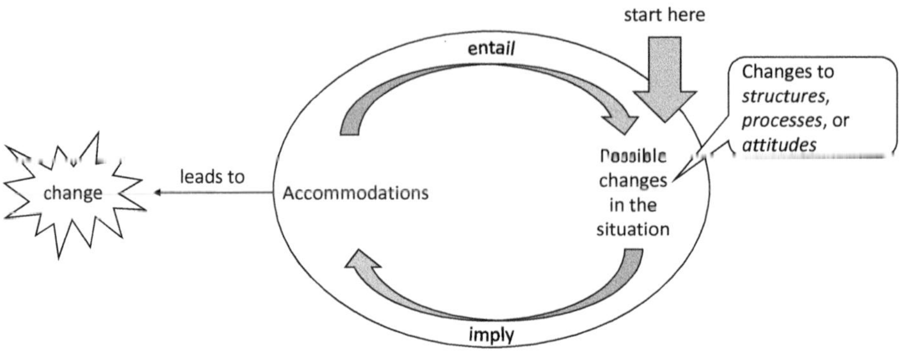

Fig. 8 Seeking accommodations leading to change

To recap this brief introduction, below is a simple description of the four actions outlined in this chapter:

1. Finding out and analyzing: Making *Rich Pictures* (visualizations) of a *problematic situation* to identify key relationships and conducting analyses on the social and political elements of the intervention.
2. Making purposeful action models: Establishing a *root definition* of the problematic situation, from a declared worldview, based on the rich pictures and analyses, to create a *purposeful action model.*
3. Questioning the models: Using the action model as a framework, orderly discussions are carried out and relevant questions raised.
4. Defining action for change: Having come to an *accommodation* between differing worldviews, a plan is conceived to enact change in a way that everybody involved can live with.

Once again, it is important to note that SSM is not a linear process. Each of the steps influence the other, analyses will affect worldviews, questioning models may encourage further finding out, or action for change may bring about a new problematic situation. During the SSM process, many of the actions may be carried out simultaneously by one or more practitioners. This is why the SSM process is referred to as a learning cycle – SSM should be conducted cyclically and once started will ideally be a continuous process.

The cyclical nature of SSM, the number of actions involved, and the above suggestion that it should be a perpetual process may seem daunting to novice SSM practitioners. This might be particularly true for team teachers, who have the added burden of collaboration to what is likely an already very busy schedule (keep in mind that our HoE above also must prepare and teach lessons in math, Japanese, science, social studies, ethics, music, and physical education!). The novice user should be aware, however, that not every action needs to be conducted to the full complexity described above. Indeed, Checkland and Poulter suggest that some of the most effective implementations of SSM arrive from informal, abbreviated learning cycles (2010). Furthermore, as the practitioner becomes more familiar with the cycle, each action will become easier to carry out. For team teachers, this is likely to be of genuine benefit – successful implementation of the SSM cycle – and the explication of the worldviews of involved parties should lead to more congenial, and therefore more efficient, working relationships, reducing the time needed for class preparation as both teachers end up on "the same page."

In section "From team teaching to team learning" above, the concept of team learning was introduced, as was the necessity of all participants in the classroom (teachers and learners) achieving a "shared value." The remainder of this chapter will discuss how the SSM learning cycle can function as a tool to help our teachers and learners get closer to sharing such values while remaining conscious of the real-world limitations that make accomplishing this task difficult.

SSM as a Tool to Achieve "Team Learning"

In team learning, the "value" at the center of the classroom is a somewhat intangible concept and an elusive one. Similar to the worldviews of SSM, it is likely also to be constantly changing. Tajino and Smith (2016) suggested that one example of a value might be "the acquisition of language skills in order to communicate with people from other cultures will promote the achievement of 'quality of life' through learning" (p. 19). Other possible values certainly exist, but as a general concept, this "value" might be defined as a shared outlook on learning that facilitates collaborative learning. It is, in any case, an emic phenomenon that cannot readily be generalized for every classroom but something that must be developed by individual practitioners (teachers and learners) themselves. Any given value may be an implicit, even undefined, yet shared, understanding. Despite the difficulty of giving a general definition of shared values, when achieved, they are said to be able to "enhance intercultural understanding and intercultural communication skill development" (Tajino and Smith 2016, p. 20).

Achieving such a state is much easier said than done, however, as often teachers themselves have difficulty with collaboration, which has been discussed at length in this chapter. In fact, perhaps the most regularly raised issue in the literature is confusion about shared roles and the conflict this confusion can engender (see, e.g., Glasgow 2013; Liu 2008; Mahoney 2004; Miyazato 2009; Pearce and Oyama Forthcoming; Sakui 2004; Wada and Cominos 1994). In a recent study compiled by the British Council, it was suggested that among team teachers, the definition of collaboration itself was open to interpretation and encouraged teachers to "discuss their own understandings of collaboration with each other to ensure that both parties at least understand each other's position" (Copland et al. 2016, p. 27). SSM thinking suggests that different interpretations of collaboration may be arising from different worldviews and provides a unique framework to organize of these discussions between teachers. Furthermore, SSM takes into account other environmental factors such as time constraints, cultural differences, and political agendas. Only by making these factors explicit in discussion can they be meaningfully addressed and work toward generating a shared value begins. *Accommodations* between worldviews may be where the elusive value lies. Sustained implementation of the SSM cycle should bring about *systemic change* to the classroom environment that allows participants to overcome such barriers to collaboration and achieve team learning and the emergent properties that result.

In Section 2.2 of this chapter, we conceived of three prerequisites for the successful realization of shared values in team teaching. Let us briefly revisit these with a new understanding of the SSM process, and see how it might help to fulfill them:

1. A mutual understanding and respect between the two teachers (hopefully developed through grounded discussions) and their learners (built upon the teachers' mutual respect).
2. The ability of teachers to move in and out of roles with relative fluidity (undeniably a very difficult task, although it is hoped that through the analyses conducted during the SSM learning cycle, and the understandings of roles, norms, and values that result, both teachers should become more comfortable with their own roles and thus more able to adapt to occasional changes to them).
3. Teachers' ability to guide students in taking on the roles of teachers and mediators where necessary (having explored and explicated the relationships and conditions of certain roles, teachers should be more readily equipped to guide others into assuming the same roles).

As participants deepen understandings through the SSM cycle, they may become more comfortable with role fluidity, while relationships of trust are being built. After years of reflection on the nature of team learning, here we take a modest stance toward the shared value and understand that, just as SSM recognizes that consensus is essentially impossible to achieve, it is highly unlikely that every participant in the classroom will be able to achieve a completely shared value. Nevertheless, as participants become more used to the processes involved, and deepen understandings of each other, it might be possible for them to become infinitely closer to developing such values. This process over time is visualized in Fig. 9, below.

It must be made clear here that certain structures of power in the classroom (and the resulting hierarchy mentioned in the section above) may well be intentional (Miyazato 2009) and sometimes even determined by law (such is the case in Japan). Achieving the shared values and collaboration in team learning is *not* intended to overturn these structures but rather allow for certain activities and explorations in the classroom in which these structures no longer present a barrier to collaborative learning efforts.

Finally, it would be remiss not to introduce a final emergent property that might result from an SSM approach to team teaching. Team learning is a concept that is not just limited to the classroom but has the potential to extend beyond it. The SSM questioning of models, and the discussions that result, should allow for reflection on individuals' teaching practices – indeed, this is a form of "covert" team teaching as first intimated by Tajino and Tajino (2000). These SSM actions should be considered as a part of team learning itself, as the actions entail teachers learning about each other, and each other's worldviews, both inside and outside of the classroom. Such learning may cause individual teachers to reflect on their own teaching practices. In the hypothetical that we have discussed in this chapter, the discussions might lead to new insights that our ALT could implement in classes at his "base school", or our HoE might gain novel understandings that could bring out positive change in her own solo classes. It is exactly this type of emergent property that team learning has been endeavoring to bring about for the last two decades!

Team Learning: Not Just for Teachers

Given the fact that in team teaching contexts, practitioners of SSM are likely to be the teachers involved, as a matter of necessity, this chapter has been considerably teacher-centered. As practitioners, however, we must not forget perhaps the most important "issue owners" in the team-taught classroom – the learners. With all the politics of the workplace, and the busy nature of schools, it can be easy for teachers to lose sight of their learners in discussions of teaching practice and teacher relationships, but we cannot forget that it is the learners for whom we are here! Without the learners, teaching cannot exist. Indeed, as stated in above sections, the most recent iterations of team learning theory suggest that team learning is most pedagogically potent when learners can become equal partners in the classroom, perhaps adopting the role of teacher, or facilitator, periodically.

Including learners as equal partners in team learning may take some time, but as SSM cycles are conducted, and teachers are able to develop more collaborative relationships, teachers will become more able to turn their attention to fostering an inclusive environment for their learners. Ideally, learners would also become active practitioners of SSM, but as this is often likely to be impractical, different approaches to the classroom, such as Exploratory Practice (see Allwright 2003; Hanks 2017) might be considered. Regardless of the practicalities involved, the process of SSM,

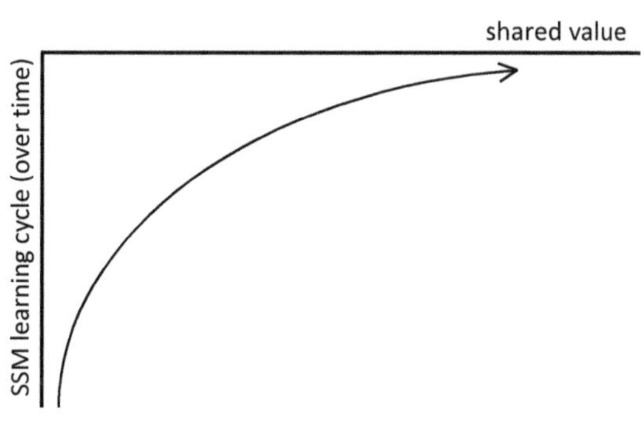

Fig. 9 Approaching shared values over time

and its focus on understanding roles, norms, and values, as well as the cultural, political, and emotional factors that influence them should allow teachers to view their learners through the same lenses and thus enhance their ability to create environments that allow their learners to engage in team learning.

Concluding Remarks

To reiterate what was stated in the introduction to this chapter, there is no easy remedy for all of the issues of team-teaching situations. Each situation is unique, and thus each individual teacher and learner must find a balance between conflicting opinions, beliefs, and values in order for team teaching to be successful.

This chapter has introduced soft systems methodology as an encouraging tool for team teachers to overcome many of the barriers that can prevent effective collaboration. Furthermore, the concept of Team Learning, as an ideal form of team teaching, has been expanded upon, and the nature of shared values in the classroom has been made a little more transparent. It is the author's hope that practicing teachers will attempt to adopt SSM practices in their institutions, and that this will bring about systemic change in the classroom, leading to more fruitful team learning endeavors.

Acknowledgments The author would like to extend his gratitude to Mrs. Maiko Ikegami for her insightful comments regarding our hypothetical team-teaching situation.

References

Aline, D., & Hosoda, Y. (2006). Team teaching participation patterns of homeroom teachers in English activities classes in Japanese public elementary schools. *JALT Journal, 28*(1), 5–22.

Allwright, D. (2003). Exploratory practice: Rethinking practitioner research in language teaching. *Language Teaching Research, 7*(2), 113–141. https://doi.org/10.1191/1362168803lr118oa.

Anton, M. (1999). The discourse of a learner-centered classroom: Sociocultural perspectives on teacher-learner interaction in the second-language classroom. *The Modern Language Journal, 83*(3), 303–318. https://doi.org/10.1111/0026-7902.00024.

Carless, D. R. (2006). Good practices in team teaching in Japan, South Korea and Hong Kong. *System, 34*(3), 341–351. https://doi.org/10.1016/j.system.2006.02.001.

Carley, H. F., III. (2013). Team teaching styles utilized in Japan: Do they really work? *Journal of International Education Research, 9*(3), 247–252.

Checkland, P., & Poulter, J. (2006). *Learning for action: A short definitive account of soft systems methodology and its use for practitioners, teachers and students*. West Sussex: Wiley.

Checkland, P., & Poulter, J. (2010). Soft systems methodology. In M. Reynolds & S. Holwell (Eds.), *Systems approaches to managing change: A practical guide* (pp. 191–242). London: Springer. https://doi.org/10.1007/978-1-84882-8094_1.

Copland, F., Davis, M., Garton, S., & Mann, S. (2016). *Investigating NEST schemes around the world: Supporting NEST/LET collaborative practices*. Resource document. British Council.

http://www.teachingenglish.org.uk/sites/teacheng/files/BC_Report_online_screen_res_final_te.pdf. Accessed 12 Nov 2017.

Gladman, A. (2015). Team teaching is not just for teachers! Student perspectives on the collaborative classroom. *TESOL Journal, 6*(1), 130–148. https://doi.org/10.1002/tesj.144.

Glasgow, G. P. (2013). The impact of the new national senior high school English curriculum on collaboration between Japanese teachers and native speakers. *JALT Journal, 35*(2), 191–204.

Hanks, J. (2017). *Exploratory practice in language teaching: Puzzling about principles and practices*. London: Palgrave Macmillan.

Jang, S. J. (2006). Research on the effects of team teaching upon two secondary school teachers. *Educational Research, 48*(2), 177–194. https://doi.org/10.1080/00131880600732272.

Kumabe, N. (1996). ALT donyu ga motarashitamono [What the introduction of ALTs has brought about]. *Modern English Teaching, 33*(6), 13.

Lee, J. (2015). *The interactional organization of bilingual co-teaching in South Korea* (Unpublished doctoral dissertation). Hawaii: University of Hawaii.

Liu, L. (2008). Co-teaching between native and non-native English teachers: An exploration of co-teaching models and strategies in the Chinese primary school context. *Reflections on English Language Teaching, 7*(2), 103–118.

Mahoney, S. (2004). Role controversy among team teachers in the JET Programme. *JALT Journal, 26*(2), 223–261.

McCombs, B. L., & Whisler, J. S. (1997). *The learner-centered classroom and school: Strategies for increasing student motivation and achievement*. San Francisco: Jossey-Bass Publishers.

McHoul, A. (1978). The organization of turns at formal talk in the classroom. *Language in Society, 7*, 183–213. https://doi.org/10.1017/S0047404500005522.

McHoul, A. (1990). The organization of repair in classroom talk. *Language in Society, 19*(3), 349–377. https://doi.org/10.1017/S004740450001455X.

Miyazato, K. (2009). Power-sharing between NS and NNS teachers: Linguistically powerful AETs vs. culturally powerful JTEs. *JALT Journal, 31*(1), 35–62.

Ogawa, C. (2010). Perceptions about team teaching: From assistant language teachers and Japanese teachers of English. In A. Stewart (Ed.), *JALT 2010: Creativity: Thinking outside the box* (pp. 473–486). Tokyo: JALT.

Pearce, D. R. (2017). *A conversation analysis of interaction in the team-taught EFL classroom*. Unpublished master's thesis. Kyoto University, Kyoto.

Pearce, D. R., & Oyama, M. (Forthcoming). Team teaching for EFL at the university level: Student and teacher perspectives. *Ritsumeikan Higher Educational Studies, 19*.

Perry, B., & Stewart, T. (2005). Insights into effective partnership in interdisciplinary team teaching. *System, 33*(4), 563–573. https://doi.org/10.1016/j.system.2005.01.006.

Sakui, K. (2004). Wearing two pairs of shoes: Language teaching in Japan. *ELT Journal, 58*(2), 155–163. https://doi.org/10.1093/elt/58.2.155.

Tajino, A. (1997). Team-teaching kara team-learning e – komyunikeshon katsudo kasseika ni mukete 'team' no saihen o [From team teaching to team learning – Reformulating the 'team' to encourage communicative activities]. *Modern English Teaching, 34*(9), 20–23.

Tajino, A., & Smith, C. (2016). Beyond team teaching: An introduction to team learning in language education. In A. Tajino, T. Stewart, & D. Dalsky (Eds.), *Team teaching and team learning in the language classroom: Collaboration for innovation in ELT* (pp. 11–28). Abingdon: Routledge.

Tajino, A., & Tajino, Y. (2000). Native and non-native: What can they offer? Lessons from team-teaching in Japan. *ELT Journal, 54*(1), 3–11.

Villa, R. A., Thousand, J. S., & Nevin, A. I. (2004). *A guide to co-teaching*. Thousand Oaks: Corwin Press.

Wada, M., & Cominos, A. (1994). *Studies in team teaching*. Tokyo: Kenkyusha.

Interaction in the Language Classroom: A Systems Approach

Yoshitaka Kato and David Dalsky

Abstract Interaction has long been considered to be one of the key factors in language learning and teaching. Previous studies have investigated how interaction influences second or foreign language (L2) development in the language classroom; however, the nature of "interaction" itself is still elusive. This lack of a holistic picture makes it difficult to apply research findings in the classroom. Here, we attempt to clarify the system of the interactive language classroom, especially by applying a *soft* systems approach. First, we propose that interaction can be defined as a system consisting of the two core elements: tasks and participants. Assuming that language pedagogy is a human activity system, we argue that interaction can be viewed as something created through the negotiation of *worldviews* among the class participants. We then demonstrate how participants' worldviews can affect decision-making processes in the classroom, specifically by exemplifying two core values of interaction: *cooperation* and *collaboration*. We believe that this attempt to understand interaction from a systems approach has the potential to help practitioners realize meaningful interaction in their own unique classrooms.

Keywords Interaction · A systems approach · Worldview · Value · Cooperation · Collaboration

---

Y. Kato (✉)
Faculty of General Education, Chubu University, Kasugai, Aichi, Japan
e-mail: kato44taka@isc.chubu.ac.jp

D. Dalsky
Institute for Liberal Arts and Sciences, Kyoto University, Kyoto, Japan
e-mail: dalsky.davidjerome.8u@kyoto.u.ac.jp

A. Tajino (ed.), *A Systems Approach to Language Pedagogy*, Translational Systems Sciences 17, https://doi.org/10.1007/978-981-13-6272-9_9

Introduction

Understanding interaction in the language classroom has long been considered a key to understanding life in the classroom (e.g., Allwright 1984). Supported by both cognitive and sociocultural theories in second language acquisition (SLA), interaction has been a focal point of several major teaching methods of English language teaching (ELT) such as communicative language teaching (CLT), task-based language teaching (TBLT), and content language integrated learning (CLIL). Recent ELT researchers and practitioners have thus given additional weight to the roles of interaction in the language classroom.

However, despite the focus on the interactive aspects of language teaching, what we have lacked is a holistic understanding of the "system" in interaction. Previous studies have so far investigated effects and nature of a variety of interaction (see Sato and Ballinger 2016, for a summary of these studies). Pedagogical implications elicited from these studies are certainly useful for language practitioners, although would be even more so if these results were interpreted in a meta-framework of the interactive classroom. In other words, without a holistic picture, it is difficult to understand how each part contributes to the whole.

This paper thus attempts to describe the system of the interactive classroom. Proposing that interaction can be viewed as a system consisting of tasks and participants, we first attempt to describe interaction from a "hard" systems approach. This approach assumes that improving individual elements of tasks (e.g., task type) and participants (e.g., group size) should help us realize the "best" interaction in the classroom. Through examination of several limitations of this approach, we point out that what may be considered "best" can be profoundly affected by *worldviews* of the class participants (e.g., Checkland & Poulter, 2006). From this "soft" systems approach, we discuss how interaction can be created in a systemic and purposeful manner among the class participants. We then demonstrate how classroom values could affect the decisions language teachers and learners make regarding task selection and the way class participants interact. Through a systems approach, this paper aims to contribute to our holistic understanding of interaction in the language classroom.

Toward a Holistic Understanding: Two Core Elements of Interaction

In order to depict a holistic picture of interaction in the language classroom, it would be pertinent to reconsider the necessary conditions for interaction to occur. Interaction in the language classroom does not occur spontaneously. It materializes when there are multiple class participants engaging in a shared task. It can be contrasted with individual learning, in which the participants do not share a task and thus they do not necessarily get involved with each other to complete the task

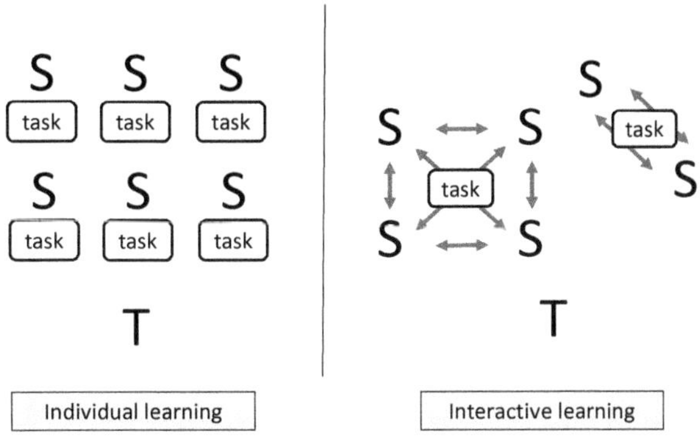

Fig. 1 Individual learning versus interactive learning

(Fig. 1). For interaction to occur in the language classroom, therefore, class participants must share the same task with their peers.

The following sections will briefly review what previous studies have clarified regarding the elements of tasks and participants.

Tasks

Research on tasks in language education has been conducted primarily within the framework of task-based language teaching (e.g., Ellis 2003; Long 2015; Skehan 1998; Willis and Willis 2007). The definition of task here broadly indicates a piece of work to be done with others, describing a picture, solving a puzzle, or discussing an issue in a group, for instance. One of the earliest task studies was conducted by Pica et al. (1993), which categorized tasks into five types: information gap, jigsaw, problem-solving, decision-making, and opinion exchange. Among them, they argued that the information gap and the jigsaw tasks encouraged more beneficial interactions than the other tasks, since such tasks require dividing learner roles to produce a single outcome. The significance of giving an equal role to each learner in peer activities and requiring learners to reach a single conclusion (i.e., closed tasks) has been supported by other studies in the field (e.g., Gass et al. 2005). As such, these studies have clarified the nature of tasks that are likely to elicit negotiation of form and meaning that is beneficial for the purpose of language learning.

Participants

Task implementation cannot be discussed, however, without considering the participants of the tasks. Along this line, Breen (1989) proposes a valuable framework to understand task-based interaction, which distinguishes the *task-as-workplan* from the *task-as-process*: the former refers to the teaching materials which intend to elicit a certain expected interaction among students, while the latter is the actual performance of the task. It is often the case that a certain task does not flow as teachers expect. Success of the interactive classroom largely depends on how the participants act in the task. SLA studies on learner-learner interaction, or peer interaction, thus far have investigated several influential factors regarding class participants such as proficiency differences among peers (e.g., Kim and McDonough 2008; Leeser 2004; Watanabe and Swain 2007), patterns of peer interaction (Storch 2002, 2013; Tan et al. 2010), and group size (e.g., Dobao 2012, 2014, Dobao and Blum 2013). The previous literature has emphasized the need to take these elements into consideration in order to utilize small group activities effectively in terms of L2 development.

For better understanding of interaction, however, we need to consider how both tasks and participants function interactionally in the classroom. Interaction is not a static state but rather something dynamically created among the class participants. Unless this dynamic process is taken into consideration, the findings of the above-mentioned independent research on interaction cannot be fully utilized in the actual classroom. In order to describe how interaction can be generated in a more dynamic sense, the next section applies a systems approach to the interactive language classroom.

A Systems Approach to Exploring Interaction

What we call here "a systems approach" actually encompasses two approaches: *hard* and *soft*. Whereas a *hard* systems approach has a goal-seeking element and decides "how" the goal might be achieved, a *soft* systems approach attempts to determine "what" the goal is, or how it is understood among the participants (see Checkland and Holwell 1998, for the hard and soft systems thinking). This section first describes a hard systems approach and its limitations in realizing meaningful interaction in the language classroom. It then discusses the possibilities of a soft systems approach and attempts to depict a holistic and dynamic process of the interactive classroom.

A "Hard" Systems Approach

The hard approach generally assumes that the class participants, including students and their teacher(s), share "precise objectives" of a certain action. It presupposes a common understanding of the goals of the class. If this were true in the language classroom, that is, all the participants knew what they should do to develop their L2, classroom management would be fairly easy as the role of the teacher(s) can be simply defined as selecting and arranging interactive tasks aligned with the needs, interests, and proficiency of their students.

Given that language pedagogy is a human activity system (see Tajino chapter "Toward Managing Language Pedagogy and Language Teaching Research" of this volume), however, realizing ideal interaction is in actuality far more difficult because the meaning of "ideal" or "best" can differ among the stakeholders of the classroom. This discussion is reminiscent of the Prabhu's (1990) statement: "There is no best method" in the language classroom. He argued that every classroom is based on their own context, and thus ultimately it would be the *sense of plausibility* of the class participants that decides what "best" means in a specific context. As interaction necessarily involves multiple persons who have different attitudes toward working together, it is not easy to decide upon or plan a specific form of interaction in line with what everybody wants. In this sense, interaction in the language classroom may be realized in a more meaningful way through not *hard* but *soft* systems approach.

A "Soft" Systems Approach

Class participants do not come to the classroom in the state of *tabula rasa*. Every participant has their own *worldviews (Weltanschauung)* (e.g., Checkland and Poulter 2006) regarding language learning and teaching, which shape the classroom values. In order to comprehend interaction in the language classroom, these invisible aspects need to be taken into consideration. Having an in-depth understanding of classroom dynamics is one of the most crucial factors for successful L2 learning in the classroom (Dörnyei and Murphey 2003).

A soft systems approach emphasizes the dynamic process of creating a common understanding among the participants. Given that the interactive classroom necessarily involves multiple and complicated worldviews of the class participants, we need some sort of methodology to accommodate those different views and shape the direction the participants will take together. Potential methodologies might include soft systems methodology (see Checkland and Poulter 2006) and exploratory practice (see Allwright and Hanks 2009; Hanks, 2017), which have in common a respect for the participants and seek to elicit their voices in the process of creating a shared understanding among them. As such, interaction can be viewed as something created through the negotiation of worldviews among the class participants (i.e., both learners and teachers).

When the individual components are viewed together, a holistic picture of the interactive language classroom can be described as in Fig. 2. For interaction to occur, there must be multiple participants and a shared task. Taking a soft systems approach, students and teachers are assumed to have different personal worldviews on language learning and teaching, which collectively shape the classroom values (represented by the dotted lines in Fig. 2). When these values are negotiated appropriately, the types of interaction that they desire, and are beneficial for them, can be determined for the first time.

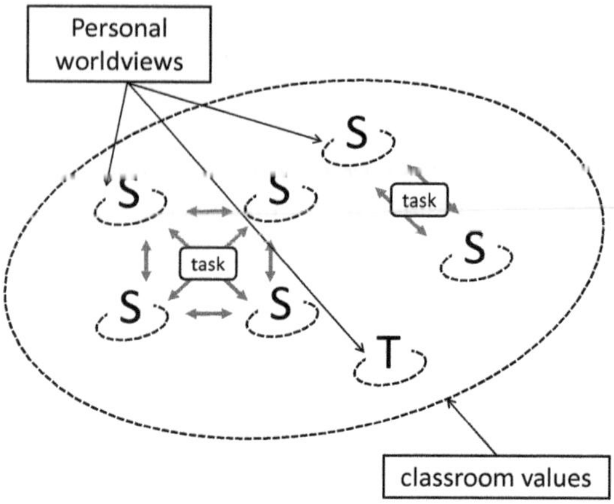

Fig. 2 A holistic picture of the interactive language classroom

This paper has so far argued the necessity of considering and adjusting worldviews on interaction among the class participants.[1] The next section then demonstrates how the worldviews can affect the decision-making process in the actual classroom, specifically by exemplifying the two core values of interaction (i.e., *cooperation* and *collaboration*).

Two Core Values of Interaction: Cooperation and Collaboration

This section elaborates on the notion of interaction by disentangling it into two centric ideas of cooperation and collaboration. First, the definitions of the terms will be described with reference to dictionaries and previous studies in learning sciences as well as language pedagogy. Second, the two concepts are compared in a holistic picture of the interactive classroom, which demonstrates how the values make an influence on other elements of interaction such as tasks and participants.

Defining Cooperation and Collaboration

According to the *Oxford Dictionary of English* (2003), cooperation is defined as "the action or process of working together to the same end," and collaboration is referred to as "the action of working with someone to produce something." At least in this dictionary, cooperation emphasizes the harmonious process of working

[1] For an in-depth explanation of how this might be achieved, through an example of teacher collaboration, see chapter "Team Teaching and Team Learning: SSM Applied to the Team-Taught Classroom" of this volume.

together toward the same end, whereas collaboration seems to focus on the products made through working together.

The definitions provided by educational researchers may have something in common with the definitions above, but the researchers are more likely to articulate the differences between the two concepts. For example, Roschelle and Teasley (1995) in the field of learning sciences differentiated collaboration from cooperation as follows:

> "cooperative work is accomplished by the division of labor among participants, as an activity where each person is responsible for a portion of the problem solving. We focus on collaboration as the mutual engagement of participants in a coordinated effort to solve the problem together." (p. 70)

Roschelle and Teasley defined collaboration more specifically as "a coordinated, synchronous activity that is the result of a continued attempt to construct and maintain a shared conception of a problem" (p. 70). While cooperation can be achieved through individual endeavor at different times, collaboration cannot be realized without synchronous mutual engagement among participants. Following this line of thought, Kozar (2010), in an article on foreign language teaching, describes the difference of the two terms in a similar manner:

> "cooperation can be achieved if all participants do their assigned parts separately and bring their results to the table; collaboration, in contrast, implies direct interaction among individuals to produce a product and involves negotiations, discussions, and accommodating others' perspectives." (p. 16–17)

Likewise, in SLA, Storch (2013) also makes a theoretical distinction between cooperation and collaboration. Quoting Dillenbourg, Baker, Blaye, and O'Malley (1996), she explains "whereas cooperation involves the division of labor between individuals in order to complete a task, collaboration involves individuals in a coordinated effort to complete a task together" (p. 3). Her main interest being research into writing, she states that in collaborative writing (i.e., not cooperative writing) "there is mutual engagement and a coordinated effort by all members of the group or pair throughout the composing process" (p. 3).

The above researchers' attempts seem to share the same foundation when distinguishing between cooperation and collaboration, that is, the division of labor. When interaction involves division of labor, which induces an asynchronous and limited level of engagement, the interaction is likely to be labelled cooperation. Products made as a result of cooperation are likely to be predictable to some extent before conducting work together. In contrast, when interaction does not include division of labor and facilitates synchronous and elaborate levels of engagement among participants, the interaction is likely to be called collaboration. In contrast to cooperation, it is difficult to predict the results of collaborative interaction beforehand. When collaboration goes well, its products can be better than expected; when it does not, however, its products can be somewhat disappointing. It should be noted, however, that the relationship between these terms should be understood not as a clear-cut dichotomy but as a continuum.

Bringing These Values into the Classroom

When the concepts of cooperation and collaboration are applied to the holistic picture of the interactive language classroom, they could be described as follows.

The Cooperative Classroom

The cooperative language classroom (Fig. 3) puts value on building a harmonious relationship among participants. Teachers in this type of classroom engage themselves in managing the classroom to maximize the benefits of students working together. Supported by the value of cooperation, teachers tend to adopt the types of tasks that can be dividable among group members as the division of labor can make the assigned role fair to everyone. Students are thus typically given a clearly defined role so that they are likely to interact with peers without unnecessary conflicts, gradually getting used to joint activities as structured by their teachers. The cooperative classroom may thus work well, especially when participants do not have much experience of working together before or when the relationship in the classroom has yet to be established typically at the beginning of the new semester. Furthermore, the structured tasks are unlikely to generate noncooperative students, so-called free-riders, in the classroom. It would be therefore a good choice for novice teachers unfamiliar with the interactive classroom to start with cooperation in mind as a value of the classroom.

Task examples in this cooperative classroom include (1) picture description and (2) jigsaw reading as shown in the right half of Fig. 3. When pairs perform a picture

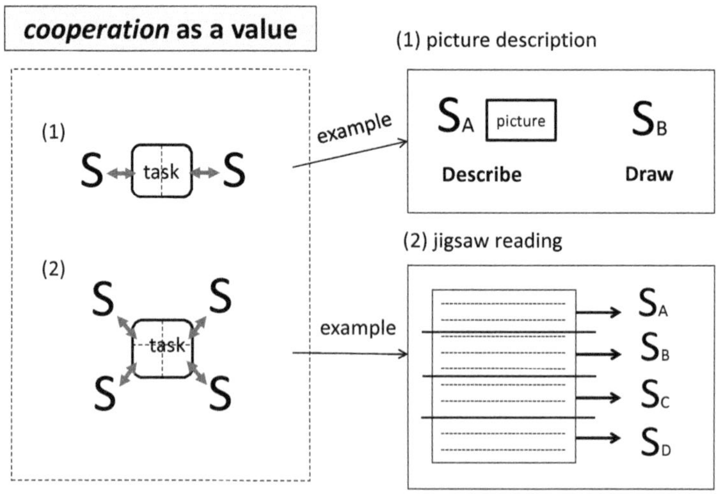

Fig. 3 Cooperation as a value in the interactive classroom. Every student has a specific role to play in a shared task

description task, for example, a student needs to describe a certain picture so that the other student can replicate it on his or her paper. As students are required to perform their assigned roles respectively in this type of task, the structure of the task enables them to work together in a concerted way. Likewise, in jigsaw reading, students are first required to understand their assigned parts of a text individually. This step is then usually followed by mutual consultation among members who have the same assigned part (called an *expert group*), and then upon returning to the original group (called a *home group*), they explain the meaning of their assigned text to their group members in turn (see Aronson et al. 1978). It is obvious that jigsaw reading is a fairly structured task with a clear division of labor. As referenced in an earlier part of this chapter, Pica et al. (1993) demonstrated that information gap (e.g., picture description) and jigsaw tasks are more likely to elicit meaningful interaction in comparison with three other (noncooperative) tasks. This result could be explained by the structured nature of the tasks, which requires every student to interact. Having said so, it is not that the other three tasks (i.e., problem-solving, decision-making, and opinion exchange) are meaningless, which leads to the following discussion.

The Collaborative Classroom

The collaborative language classroom (Fig. 4) puts a value on dynamic interaction among the participants as well as the products themselves, and thus it does not structure the process of working together as much as cooperative tasks do so. The collaborative classroom expects its members to produce something that exceeds simple addition of what each of them can do on their own (i.e., it expects more than a sum of the individual parts). It thus may risk conflict occurring in relationships among the group members due to the less structured nature of the tasks. The participants would need to negotiate their own roles in a group. Even so, the collaborative classroom encourages the participants to exert their full resources with synchronous and mutual engagement among them. This increased interaction is expressed in Fig. 4 as bidirectional arrows among students (and teachers).

Another difference between cooperation and collaboration as a value in the classroom is the role of teachers. As expressed in (5)'s relationship in Fig. 4, teachers could be sometimes regarded as one of the learners in the classroom. This line of thought comes from the idea of *team learning* (Tajino et al. 2016; Tajino and Tajino 2000), which is also discussed in the chapter,"Team Teaching and Team Learning: SSM Applied to the Team-Taught Classroom" of this book. While the cooperative classroom tends to regard teachers as classroom organizers who manage the classroom through the structured tasks with division of labor, the collaborative classroom may at times allow for the authority to shift between every class participant. In this latter style of classroom, the border between learners and teachers could disappear, which sometimes allows teachers to join in the students' discussion as "learners" (Kato et al. 2018). This could not happen in the cooperative classroom.

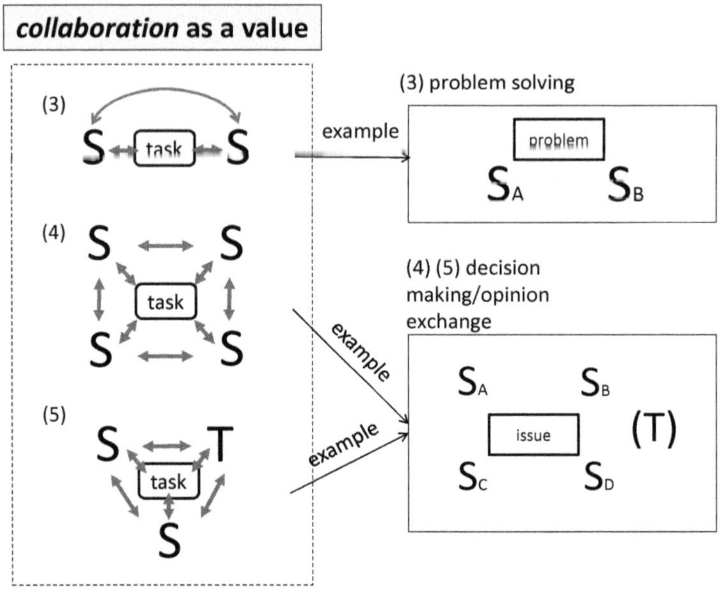

Fig. 4 Collaboration as a value in the interactive classroom. The teacher does not specify the roles of students beforehand

The task examples in the collaborative classroom include problem-solving, decision-making, and opinion exchange tasks. As you may notice from the right side of Fig. 4, the teacher does not give every student a specific role as in the cooperative classroom. In these collaborative tasks, they are only provided with a problem or a quiz (e.g., a math riddle) or an issue to be discussed (e.g., a travel plan). They are required to negotiate their responsibility in the task. Since the task completion is usually prioritized over building a harmonious relationship among group members, this collaborative work may put more pressure on each member, and thus they need to be more autonomous than they would be in conducting cooperative work. These activities are thus likely to succeed when the participants know each other well and have a positive mind-set toward working together with others. This could be part of the reason why these collaborative tasks sometimes do not work well in the classroom (Pica et al. 1993).

Whether cooperative or collaborative, the two types of the values inform us of the fact that classroom values can have a strong influence on the tasks and the way the participants work together. In other words, language teachers and researchers should be aware of the influence of their own, and their learners', values on interaction. In this post-method era, the final decision of what "works" in the actual classroom will be made based on the *sense of plausibility* (Prabhu 1990) of the class participants. Constant reflections of our own values could help us to understand our unique classrooms in a better sense. The framework of cooperation and collaboration may facilitate the process of understanding the values of the classroom.

Conclusion

This chapter discussed how we might better understand the nature of interaction in the language classroom by an application of a systems approach. The significance of considering the worldview of the participants was emphasized. Also, two major values in the interactive classroom, *cooperation* and *collaboration*, were highlighted. Exemplifying how the participants in each value type interact with each other, this paper demonstrated the influence of classroom values on the decisions the class participants make regarding the tasks and how they work together. Understanding the classroom from a macro perspective including values as well as tasks and participants could help us to interpret the interwoven elements that previous studies on interaction have offered. In this regard, viewing interaction from the framework of cooperation and collaboration could be a useful starting point toward realizing meaningful interaction in the language classroom.

References

Allwright, R. L. (1984). The importance of interaction in classroom language learning. *Applied Linguistics, 5*(2), 156–171. https://doi.org/10.1093/applin/5.2.156.

Allwright, D., & Hanks, J. (2009). *The developing language learner: An introduction to exploratory practice*. Basingstoke: Palgrave Macmillan.

Aronson, E., Blaney, N., Stephan, C., Sikes, J., & Snapp, M. (1978). *The jigsaw classroom*. Beverly Hills: Sage.

Breen, M. P. (1989). The evaluation cycle for language learning tasks. In R. K. Johnson (Ed.), *The second language curriculum* (pp. 187–206). Cambridge: Cambridge University Press.

Checkland, P., & Holwell, S. (1998). *Information, systems, and information systems: Making sense of the field*. Chichester: John Wiley & Sons.

Checkland, P., & Poulter, J. (2006). *Learning for action: A short definitive account of soft systems methodology and its use, for practitioners, teachers and students*. Chichester: John Wiley & Sons.

Dillenbourg, P., Baker, M., Blaye, A., & O'Malley, C. (1996). The evolution of research on collaborative writing. In E. Spada & P. Reiman (Eds.), *Learning in humans and machine: Towards an interdisciplinary learning science* (pp. 189–211). Oxford: Elsevier.

Dobao, A. F. (2012). Collaborative writing tasks in the L2 classroom: Comparing group, pair, and individual work. *Journal of Second Language Writing, 21*(1), 40–58. https://doi.org/10.1177/1362168813519730.

Dobao, A. F. (2014). Vocabulary learning in collaborative tasks: A comparison of pair and small group work. *Language Teaching Research, 18*(4), 497–520. https://doi.org/10.1177/1362168813519730.

Dobao, A. F., & Blum, A. (2013). Collaborative writing in pairs and small groups: Learners' attitudes and perceptions. *System, 41*(2), 365–378. https://doi.org/10.1016/j.system.2013.02.002.

Dörnyei, Z., & Murphey, T. (2003). *Group dynamics in the language classroom*. Cambridge: Cambridge University Press.

Ellis, R. (2003). *Task-based language learning and teaching*. Oxford: Oxford University Press.

Gass, S., Mackey, A., & Ross-Feldman, L. (2005). Task-based interactions in classroom and laboratory settings. *Language Learning, 55*(4), 575–611. https://doi.org/10.1111/j.0023-8333.2005.00318.x.

Hanks, J. (2017). *Exploratory practice in language teaching: Puzzling about principles and practices*. London: Palgrave Macmillan.

Kato, Y., Watari, H., & Bolstad, F. (2018). Voices from "practitioners": A collaborative exploration of MAP grammar in an EFL classroom. In A. Tajino (Ed.), *A new approach to English pedagogical grammar: The order of meanings* (pp. 160–171). Oxford: Routledge.

Kim, Y., & McDonough, K. (2008). The effect of interlocutor proficiency on the collaborative dialogue between Korean as a second language learners. *Language Teaching Research, 12*(2), 211–234. https://doi.org/10.1177/1362168807086288.

Kozar, O. (2010). Towards better group work: Seeing the difference between cooperation and collaboration. *English Teaching Forum, 48*(2), 16–23.

Leeser, M. J. (2004). Learner proficiency and focus on form during collaborative dialogue. *Language Teaching Research, 8*(1), 55–82. https://doi.org/10.1191/1362168804lr134oa.

Long, M. H. (2015). *Second language acquisition and task-based language teaching*. Oxford: Wiley-Blackwell.

Oxford Dictionary of English. (2003). *Oxford dictionary of English*. Oxford: Oxford University Press.

Pica, T., Kanagy, R., & Falodun, J. (1993). Choosing and using communication tasks for second language instruction. In G. Crookes & S. Gass (Eds.), *Tasks and language learning* (pp. 9–34). Clevedon: Multilingual Matters.

Prabhu, N. S. (1990). There is no best method—Why? *TESOL Quarterly, 24*(2), 161–176. https://doi.org/10.2307/3586897.

Roschelle, J., & Teasley, S. D. (1995). The construction of shared knowledge in collaborative problem solving. In C. O'Malley (Ed.), *Computer supported collaborative learning* (pp. 69–97). Berlin/Heidelberg: Springer.

Sato, M., & Ballinger, S. (Eds.). (2016). *Peer interaction and second language learning: Pedagogical potential and research agenda*. Amsterdam: John Benjamins.

Skehan, P. (1998). Task-based instruction. *Annual Review of Applied Linguistics, 18*, 268–286. https://doi.org/10.1017/S0267190500003585.

Storch, N. (2002). Patterns of interaction in ESL pair work. *Language Learning, 52*(1), 119–158. https://doi.org/10.1111/1467-9922.00179.

Storch, N. (2013). *Collaborative writing in L2 classrooms*. Bristol: Multilingual Matters.

Tajino, A., & Tajino, Y. (2000). Native and non-native: What can they offer? Lessons from team-teaching in Japan. *ELT Journal, 54*(1), 3–11. https://doi.org/10.1093/elt/54.

Tajino, A., Stewart, T., & Dalsky, D. (Eds.). (2016). *Team teaching and team learning in the language classroom: Collaboration for innovation in ELT*. Oxford: Routledge.

Tan, L. L., Wigglesworth, G., & Storch, N. (2010). Pair interactions and mode of communication: Comparing face-to-face and computer mediated communication. *Australian Review of Applied Linguistics, 33*(3), 1–27. https://doi.org/10.2104/aral1027.

Watanabe, Y., & Swain, M. (2007). Effects of proficiency differences and patterns of pair interaction on second language learning: Collaborative dialogue between adult ESL learners. *Language Teaching Research, 11*(2), 121–142. https://doi.org/10.1177/136216880607074599.

Willis, J., & Willis, D. (2007). *Doing task-based teaching: A practical guide to task-based teaching for ELT training courses and practicing teachers*. Oxford: Oxford University Press.

Systems Thinking: An ESP Genre Approach

Hajime Terauchi and Sayako Maswana

Abstract Although there has been increasing pedagogical attention to the English for Specific Purposes (ESP) in Japanese English education, ESP theory, and specifically its concept of genre, is not well understood by teachers and learners. Using some examples, we explain genre models and genre systems as hard systems and suggest that adding the perspective of systemic functional grammar to current ESP teaching and learning practices will be beneficial for English learners. In a genre system, the interconnectivity of genres in terms of discourse communities and language functions is key to understanding that composing elements of genres and language use do not have much meaning as parts but are crucial for the whole. An ESP genre approach not only clarifies English learning objectives but also equips learners with the skills to analyze genre text and to make sense of complex discourse realities. We argue that in ESP classrooms, a soft systems methodology helps reveal different perceptions held by stakeholders, and an ESP genre-based approach can be applied to improve a problematic situation in ESP classrooms based on a soft systems framework.

Keywords ESP · Genre · Discourse community · Systemic functional grammar · Genre system

Introduction

Students in Japan usually learn English by focusing on grammar and separate skills, such as listening, speaking, reading, and writing for general purposes, throughout their formal education. These English skills and knowledge are thought to be fundamental, generic, and usable in any situation. However, there have been urgent calls to improve these abilities and communicative ability in English of Japanese students

H. Terauchi (✉)
Faculty of Commerce, Takachiho University, Tokyo, Japan

S. Maswana
Faculty of Foreign Language Studies, Mejiro University, Tokyo, Japan

A. Tajino (ed.), *A Systems Approach to Language Pedagogy*, Translational Systems Sciences 17, https://doi.org/10.1007/978-981-13-6272-9_10

(Noguchi 2015). In recent years, the theory of English for Specific Purposes (ESP) has been introduced to Japanese English teaching practices to facilitate better communicative abilities and enable students to understand both the English needed for communication in a specific situation and the social aspects of the language. In other words, students learn why the language is used the way it is. Dudley-Evans and St. John (1998, pp. 4–5) define ESP as follows: "ESP is designed to meet specific needs of the learner; ESP makes use of the underlying methodology and activities of the disciplines it serves; ESP is centred on the language (grammar, lexis, register), skills, discourse and genres appropriate to these activities." As shown in the latter part of the definition, ESP is closely related to sociolinguistics as a discipline for its interest in holistically understanding how language is used in specific situations because communication is not simply composed of language skills and knowledge. ESP has also been influenced by systemic functional grammar (SFG) in terms of understanding a language and its descriptive approach (see Terauchi and Maswana 2018). A problem remains, however, in that ESP and its genre-based approach are not well understood by some teachers, learners, and educational institutions in Japan (Terauchi et al. 2010).

ESP and its genre-based approach to learning enable us to view conventional English education differently because we know the goal of learning and understand how to approach English teaching. More importantly, the understanding of the "how and why" in addition to the "what" of language use of a particular genre is necessary in ESP learning because it can lead students to lifelong learning endeavors by applying the approach to many emerging situations (Noguchi 2009). Because ESP offers a perspective from which to see language as a dynamic system, we suggest that the ESP approach encompasses an aspect of systems thinking. Systems thinking here refers to the understanding that any system consists of interacting and interdependent parts that function as a whole rather than as a collection of independent elements. According to Checkland and Scholes (1990), there are two complementary traditions in systems thinking. The first is "hard" systems thinking, which considers the world to be systemic. In contrast, "soft" systems thinking creates "a systemic process of enquiry" (Checkland and Scholes 1990, p. 25) to solve ill-defined problems. In Japanese English education, Tajino et al. (2005) applied soft systems methodology to an English for Academic Purposes (EAP) course design at a national university in Japan and demonstrated the usefulness of the methodology in English education.

In this chapter, we discuss hard systems in ESP genre theory and illustrate how the genre system could be used to promote actions to resolve problematic situations in ESP classrooms through a soft systems methodology. First, we provide an overview of ESP and explain genre models whose focus is on a single genre as well as the genre systems whose focus is on a set of genres. We argue that adding an SFG perspective to current ESP teaching and learning practices will be beneficial for English learners. Finally, we argue that a soft systems methodology helps reveal different perceptions involved in ESP writing classrooms, and ESP genre-based approaches, namely, OCHA and PAIL (observe, classify, hypothesize, and apply; purpose, audience, information, and language features) proposed by Noguchi (1997, 2003), can be applied to improve problematic situations in English education. It will be suggested that the ESP perspective has implications for both systems thinking traditions.

Background

In the past, English taught in school and universities could be mostly termed English for General Purposes (EGP) in Japan. In the 2000s, however, shifts in the purpose of English learning from EGP to ESP have been introduced to secondary and tertiary school English education, which has had a significant impact on English education programs and curricula (Noguchi 2015; Terauchi et al. 2010). For example, programs based on EAP, a subcategory of ESP, have been implemented after 2000 in Japan in response to a demand for the internationalization of universities. Curriculum directors of English education at several universities have clarified and defined the English skills needed for students' academic success and course objectives in accordance with their university's mission and the results of needs analyses (Iijima et al. 2016). In English education based on EGP, the purpose and goals tend to be not only unclear but also different across teachers and other parties involved in the English curriculum. The introduction of an EAP approach has influenced institutions and teachers when deciding the objectives, content, materials, and teaching styles of their English courses (Tajino and Suiko 2005). With clear course objectives often explicitly outlined in "can-do" statements in syllabi, the results students obtain from attending these English courses have been more concrete and relevant.

As the examples of EAP education show, ESP is considered more applicable to higher education because it is related to the professional use of language. Although it may now seem natural that at some point, most likely in tertiary education, we will have to employ the ESP perspective, many books on English language teaching and applied linguistics in the 1960s and the 1970s did not mention ESP (e.g., Corder 1973; Lado 1964). It could be argued that the need for ESP grew exponentially from the 1980s to the end of the twentieth century because world trade, international business, and human mobility have increased and academic institutions and research have been subjected to international influence and pressure. We could therefore say that ESP is a product of the second half of the twentieth century and continues to be of interest for English teaching.

The ESP approach in practice usually starts with a needs analysis of the learner (e.g., Hutchinson and Waters 1987). Based on the needs analysis, instructors or administrators determine the text type of English (i.e., genre) that the learners will need in their current and future professional communities. The ESP approach then proceeds to genre analysis, which describes and examines the language use of the important genres identified in the needs analysis, and centers on learning the characteristics of the target genre. Genre is defined in ESP as a recurring communicative event with specific communication goals identified by the discourse community that has distinct rhetorical and lexico/grammatical patterns (Noguchi 2017; Swales 1990). For an efficient transmission of information, discourse communities develop "genres." The crucial element of ESP genre-based teaching is its focus on the genre whose language is used by a group of people (i.e., a discourse community) whose members display a mutual interest in a specific area. The discourse community, another key term in ESP, is a group of people who are connected by discourse and share a means of communication (i.e., a genre). The discourse community is not bound by location, and it shares and constructs information and knowledge through appropriate genres in the relevant domain. The ESP approach and genre analyses are largely descriptive and explanatory, with no prescribed correct means of language use.

The pedagogically oriented ESP approach is a way to learn or teach the language needed to participate actively in discourse community environments through shared genres based on systemic literacy. Here, systemic literacy refers to "the understanding of the processes and consequences of complex social systems" (Brown, as cited in Noguchi 2009, p. 17); it is an ability that university graduates are expected to have and also an ability that ESP genre-based learning is expected to foster. Therefore, it is important to raise awareness of the genre, even at earlier stages of learning, so that learners can be prepared for the goals they would like to achieve at any time in their professional lives. In the following section, we explain multilayered genre models and theoretical genre systems to illustrate hard systems perspectives found in the ESP approach.

Genre Model

Knowledge of genre, an essential concept in ESP, comprises "textual knowledge, the awareness and understanding of the shared practices of professional and discourse communities" (Swales, as cited in Bhatia 2004, p. 20). The discourse community defines and characterizes a genre, and the interpretation of the text depends on the discourse community members (see Swales 2016, for a recent review of the concept of discourse community). For example, a group of people attending a conference on physics would display distinctly different features in the use of professional language at their conference presentations than journalists at a press conference due to differences in their professional practices. Additionally, genres are communicative events with patterns of rhetorical structure called "moves" (Swales 1990). These moves are signaled by "hint expressions" that inform the reader of a written text (or the listener of a spoken text) of the type of information being transmitted (Noguchi 2017). For example, scholars can expect the abstract section of a research paper to generally have the following move structure: (1) background of the research, (2) aim, (3) the methods used, (4) results, and (5) conclusions. Each section is signaled by hint expressions such as "the purpose of this study was to" for the aim of the research or "from these results, we conclude that" for the concluding statement.

Traditional ESP genre understanding centers on the discourse community and the linguistic features required to achieve specific communicative objectives. Bhatia

(2002) proposed a further genre-based understanding of discourse with the multi-perspective model, which consists of three views of discourse: discourse as text (textual knowledge), discourse as genre (genre knowledge), and discourse as social practice (social knowledge). Textual knowledge focuses on the language use of the discourse at the surface level, such as its lexico/grammatical and phonological aspects; students tend to learn only the linguistic features of a particular genre using this view. Next, genre knowledge is the common understanding of any genre theory. It includes both text and context in a broader sense. It means that to be able to function appropriately in professional domains, professional knowledge and experience are required in addition to genre textual knowledge. Social knowledge views context within a deeper social context. Analysis no longer focuses on textual analysis but rather on social contextual analysis, such as the identities and the professional relationships of the discourse members in the genres in which one may need socially pragmatic knowledge to be effectively functional. According to Bhatia (2002), "the three interacting views of discourse are not mutually exclusive, but essentially complementary to each other" (p. 18). Furthermore, the genre is not an isolated entity with a clear-cut boundary in relation to other genres. It consists of overlapping and interconnected elements, which imply that genres are constantly evolving and emerging, making them difficult to define based solely on their textual characteristics.

Referring to Bhatia's (2002) three-space model of genre analysis, we provide a new genre model specifically proposed for ESP learners (see Fig. 1) that focuses on a single genre in which multilayered genre-centered discourse overlaps against the backdrop of different but connected cultures. The focused genre is shown with black lines, and another genre is shown with gray lines. By simplifying terminology and the figure itself, this model aims to reach a wide range of English learners, from the novice to proficient learners, for use in English learning.

Here, the concept of culture is rather broad and diverse, including national or regional customs as well as professional, socioeconomic, and linguistic cultures and practices. A genre could belong to more than one culture, and culture goes beyond the boundary of a genre and its discourse community. Thus, understanding the

Fig. 1 Genre model for ESP learners

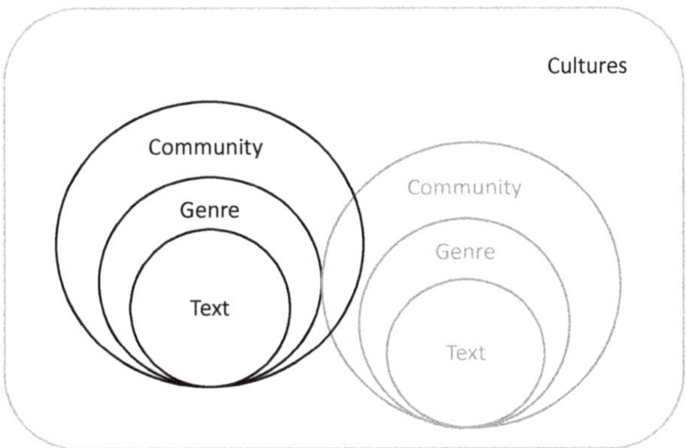

broader culture is important for moving actively across different genres, which should be taken into consideration in educational settings. Acquiring cultural and genre knowledge is difficult because it often contains subjective interpretation by each individual in addition to general cultural and genre conventions.

However, learners at any level can refer to the proposed model to set their learning objectives. An example is business meetings in English (Terauchi et al. 2015), which is considered one of the difficult business genres. At first, novice learners of business English can focus only on the text (the language use of the genre), the smallest core circle in the figure. They could focus on listening accurately to the words being pronounced or prepare a script to read in a meeting. After participating in meetings effectively and gaining confidence, they could then move on to understanding the genre and discourse community, represented by the three-layered circle in the figure. At this stage, in addition to their language skills, they need to be able to understand the context of the business meeting, the features of a good meeting, and how to achieve the meeting's objective; they also need to know how to control the meeting through facilitation skills, with consideration given to the participants' professional and linguistic backgrounds. To put the model fully into practice, one needs to be at the management level, where a person can work outside the meeting framework—the outer space in the figure labeled "cultures." It could include building trusting relationships through dinners or giving another opportunity to those who cannot linguistically participate in the meeting.

This addition of culture as an element of a genre model seems to complicate the fluid situation further; however, it more accurately represents the reality of the language used, particularly in this changing environment. The model shows that each element is crucial but cannot dictate the whole. This loose definition of each element in the genre model allows speakers and writers to be creative and provides space for them to change the genre's practices. In the next section, we broaden our discussion from a single genre and its surrounding elements to the system of genres, multiple genres, and their relationships.

Genre System

We have seen that an ESP approach and its genre-based hard systems perspective can organize discourse realities to provide a larger picture for understanding complicated English language use. The idea of genre explains various elements involved in the language used in specific situations. A genre does not exist in a vacuum, and it is more reasonable and pedagogically effective to think that genres are related, with varying degrees and varying factors, as in a set of genre groups, which is sometimes called the system of genres or genre set (Tardy 2003). We call it a genre system, a hard system that consists of multiple genres in a discourse community. See Fig. 2 for an example of a genre system in a legal discourse community. It should be noted that although the members of a legal discourse community practice the set of

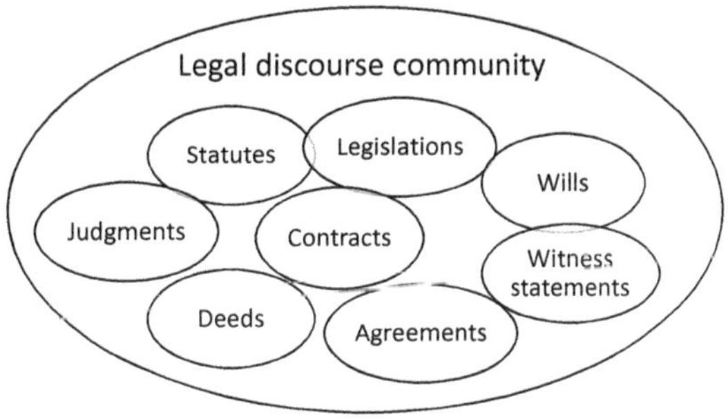

Fig. 2 System of genres in a legal discourse community

genres, they also communicate with people outside the discourse community through the genre system.

According to Bazerman (1994), a system of genres consists of "interrelated genres that interact with each other in specific settings" (p. 97). Orlikowski and Yates (1994) proposed a similar idea of genre repertoire, which is "the set of genres that are routinely enacted by the members of a community" (p. 542). These scholars placed a different degree of emphasis on interactions between genres and the involvement of discourse community members, but they agree that genres interact with each other within the discourse community.

For example, in the domain of law, the system of genres includes cases, judgments, contracts, agreements, wills, witness statements, and law reviews, whereas the system of genres in a business discourse community includes memos, reports, proposals, case studies, meetings, and letters. In academic settings, the system of genres includes research proposals, grant proposals, research papers, conference proposals, conference presentations, and conference proceedings. The obvious common denominator in each system is the domain or the specialization, that is, the expert knowledge. Therefore, the genres in a system are likely to have the same or largely overlapping discourse community members, even though each genre has a distinct communicative purpose and rhetorical structure. Legal case notes and law reviews can be very different in their rhetorical patterns and communicative purposes, even though they can be constructed and shared by the same discourse community and the terminologies can be quite similar.

The language used across genres in the same discourse community shows certain characteristics. For example, the English used across the genres in Fig. 2 generally has consistent grammatical, lexical, and phraseological characteristics, including the particular use of the conjunctions "and" and "or," as well as prepositions of time and boilerplate in opening sentences (see Terauchi 2001, for an overview of the legal English). These characteristics make it difficult for people outside the discourse community to understand the language of the law. We could treat these genres with similar discourse community members as one genre set, or a genre system.

At the same time, even in a single genre, some variations might occur in the terminology and rhetorical structure, depending on sub-domain. For example, a well-established academic genre of research papers could have different rhetorical patterns according to their academic disciplines and even within a single discipline (e.g., Hyland 2017; Ozturk 2007). Depending on the type of research, there is also variation among research articles, such as the differences between theoretical and applied disciplines. In addition, a single genre can be comprised of mixed genres such as the corporate annual report, which consists of a performance report and company promotion (Bhatia 2002). The pedagogical implications drawn from these findings should be considered in teaching. Understanding the organic relationship among genres would allow us to better learn and teach the variations within a system of genres. This understanding of genre is based on the ESP genre perspective, which focuses on the target discourse community.

Here, we discuss another way to see a genre system that focuses on language functions, rather than the discourse community or specialization. Because the language used in a specific genre is largely influenced by the purpose, audience, and information and the language feature is only a part of the whole, it is natural that the categorization of genres based primarily on language functions has rarely been explored in the ESP tradition. In reality, language features, one very important element comprising a genre, are sometimes interrelated even across distant ESP genres, as implied by systemic functional linguists (e.g., Bloor and Bloor 2013; Martin 1999, 2009). The genres with similar linguistic features can comprise different levels of English and be used by seemingly different discourse communities.

Let us examine three sample genres with language functions that convey "procedural information:" the recipe, the instruction manual, and the research article method section. These instructional genres share certain language features and a broad purpose (as opposed to a specific purpose in ESP): to give sufficiently detailed procedures for the replication. Although the target discourse communities are very different, we can categorize these genres as a system of procedural genres (see Fig. 3). These genres with similar language functions can be organized based on the linguistic difficulty of the text for English learners as indicated with the arrow in the figure.

The recipe genre is linguistically simple compared to the other two genres. Recipes describe the procedure for cooking a dish, often with help of pictures. The sentences used in recipes are usually short and easy to follow by anyone in the general public who would like to make the dish. The next genre in the figure is instruction manuals, such as evacuation manuals for school staff or DIY shelf assembly manuals that provide a procedure to follow. The language and terminology might appear a little difficult to people who are not familiar with the situation described.

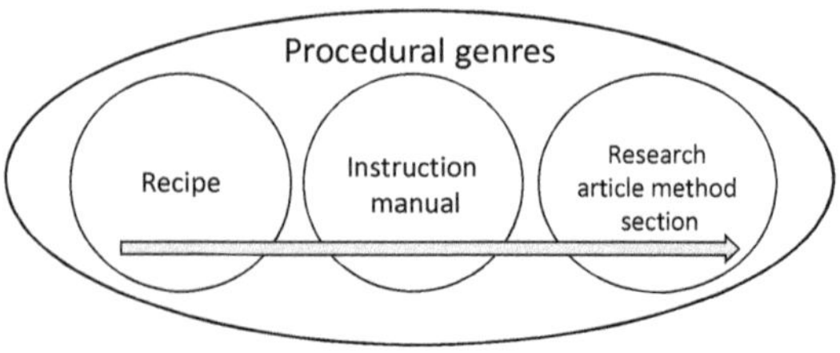

Fig. 3 System of procedural genres for English learners

The most linguistically difficult level in the figure is the method section of a research paper, which includes an explanation of the procedure. The terminology and the sentence structure are more complex than those of the previous two genres, and it would be difficult to understand the text without knowledge of the described topic. Below are text examples for each genre.

(1) Oyako-don (Japanese chicken and egg rice bowl)

1. *Cut* the chicken into bite-size pieces and *slice* the onions.
2. *Put* in a small pan the cut chicken, sliced onions, 2/3 cup of dashi (Japanese soup stock), 2 spoons soy sauce and sugar, and 1 spoon sake on medium heat.
3. *Simmer* for about 8 min. *Pour* the beaten egg evenly, and *turn off* the heat when the egg is half heated.
4. *Pour* the ingredients over the rice.

(2) Earthquake evacuation instructions for school staff

1. *Instruct* students to protect themselves from falling objects and other hazardous objects by keeping away from the windows, covering their heads, and staying under the desk.
2. *Secure* an exit (*open* the door) and *extinguish* any fire.
3. When the quake stops, *evacuate* students to the designated shelter area. [...]

(3) Method section

Participants *were recruited* in the author's writing classes. The participants were 20 first-year graduate students studying foreign language teaching. They *were* first *asked* to read the student text and rate it based on the distributed grading rubric. The participants then *received* the teacher training session for a 3-month period on writing and evaluation. After 3 months, the same participants *were asked* to read the same text again and rate it based on the same grading rubric. Their evaluation scores *were collected* and *analyzed* using a t-test. [...]

The above examples of (1) a recipe, (2) an evacuation manual for teachers, and (3) the method section show that the language features of the procedural genre include numerical unit lists and time sequences based on a conventional format with a set of procedural verbs (although the texts are simplified examples written for this chapter) that share broad rhetorical patterns. Verbs are often used in the present tense and the imperative form in the direct instruction text (examples [1] and [2]). The procedural verbs were italicized in the examples, and the sequence markers were underlined in example (3). The explanation for all three examples needs to be detailed but easy to follow for a person who wishes to replicate it. From these features, people can identify these texts as belonging to the procedural genre. Thus, these genres can be considered as consisting of a genre system based on interconnectivity of texts, although there are no obvious interactions between genres within the same discourse community. This genre system framework can be applied to other communicative functions, such as online restaurant reviews, book blurbs, and literature review sections, all of which include the language of evaluation. The language difficulty seems to increase, and the target audience becomes narrower when moving from the online restaurant review to the literature review, although the learning period for the respective genre is not necessarily time-sequenced according to difficulty.

The genre system based on interconnectivity in terms of the language function is closely related to the systemic functional linguistics perspective, which has been considered rather separately from the ESP perspective in most educational settings because ESP teaching and research are aimed at specific professions and often conducted independently by teachers and scholars with expertise in the target profession. Although the discourse community is the key to the ESP genre perspective, we can also see the genres across discourse communities centering on linguistic patterns because, in real life, a person can belong to multiple discourse communities at the same time or over time. Therefore, it is important to integrate these two perspectives in teaching to reflect the reality that the discourse communities and language features are interconnected.

We should keep in mind that learning is a continuous, sometimes linear process, but at other times, it is a nonlinear, cyclical process. To effectively and efficiently teach genres, it is important for us to utilize the language knowledge and skills learners already possess in different genres. For example, when teaching the method section of a research article, learners could recapture their previous learning experiences in other procedural genres. The integration of the two perspectives would help us not only to better understand the nature of genre and identify how to teach it effectively, by taking advantage of learners' prior knowledge of different genres, but also to provide learners with multiple ways to see the world of discourse and language use.

Genre and Soft Systems Approach

This chapter, so far, has argued that the concept of an ESP genre is a hard system which helps organize the complex language world. In this section, we describe how the genre perspective can be used as a tool to promote actions to improve a problematic situation in ESP classroom settings through a soft systems methodology proposed by Checkland and Scholes (1990). In the framework, the worldviews of the people concerned are important to transform the problematic situation. As described in the introduction, ESP has been recently introduced to tertiary education in Japan without many prepared instructors and with students not knowing what to expect. The first people concerned in this context are the teachers, the students, and the institution. They face many environmental constraints, such as the number of hours and resources available to the class, and differing worldviews among stakeholders

(Terauchi et al. 2010). For example, in a course on writing research papers, the students may wish to learn tips to efficiently write research papers, set rules and phrases that are suitable for any type of academic writing in their future career, or even quickly fix their writing errors and mistakes. The teachers could be English teachers or expert teachers from the students' target discipline. The former wish to focus on the academic paper's language features, and the latter wish to teach the students how to conduct research by guiding them to complete a research paper. The final actor is the institution, which wishes to produce internationally competent researchers who disseminate their research outcomes through their research papers.

The typical but various worldviews of the three main actors make it difficult to come up with an action that can satisfy all the expectations. In this case, we suggest employing the OCHA approach presented by Noguchi (2003). OCHA stands for observe, classify, hypothesize, and apply, representing activities to raise students' awareness of the genre and its linguistic features. The students make a corpus of their collected articles, including the journal's "Instructions to Authors" section, and analyze the texts' features in their various sections. Following the observe and classify activities, the students are asked to hypothesize about how they could apply the information to their writing and write the target section based on the hypothesis. In the activities, students can identify the purpose, audience, information, and language features (PAIL) to observe the genre text. PAIL was first introduced by Noguchi (1997) and is considered one of the most succinct descriptions of the essential elements of the ESP genre text.

Teaching based on PAIL guides students to identify these four elements, which are necessary to use English that is appropriate to the target genre. As illustrated by Noguchi et al. (2007), each student can see how the purpose, audience, and information materialize through the language in his or her field of research. If students want to write the materials and methods section of a science research article successfully, they need to understand that the section provides information for the confirmation of materials and methods used (Purpose) for researchers who, if necessary, repeat experiments (Audience). They need to give sufficient detail for repetition of experiments (Information), following the conventions for numerical units and format details specified by the journal (Language features). They learn, for example, that language features include using the past tense for the description of experimental procedures, while the present tense is sometimes used to emphasize new methods in theoretical research. Teaching also includes giving instructions on the type of rhetorical moves and the order in which the moves are used in this genre. Students identify moves in the corpus texts and examine why the authors employ these rhetorical structures.

The ESP approach in classrooms might be misunderstood as a top-down approach that focuses only on memorizing model language features given by the instructor; however, understanding why the language is used in that way needs to be incorporated into the teaching. The ESP genre-based approach has been empirically proved effective for graduate students learning how to write English research papers (e.g.,

Cheng 2008). This genre-centered approach applies to a problematic situation caused by stakeholders' various views and enables the students to acquire lexical, rhetorical, and technical features of the genre along with skills to analyze texts from other genres, leading them to become independent researchers, which should be encouraged to improve the problem in ESP classrooms.

Concluding Remarks

The ESP perspective and the concept of genre and the genre system allow us to be equipped to make sense of the English language in a time of great diversity, particularly in terms of the discourse community and the linguistic landscape. The concept captures the nature of the language used; the boundaries of situations are interconnected and not always clear-cut. In this chapter, we presented the genre model and systems of genres for ESP learners. The interconnectivity of genres can be interpreted mainly in two ways: one is based on the identity and continuity of the community members, whereas the other is based on the language function that can be commonly found in the SFG perspective. These two approaches, which are not mutually exclusive, both need to be employed in teaching. Understanding the elements and the evolving nature of the genre would not lead to an absolute interpretation of language use, but it would help us to make better sense of the language world, which is pedagogically meaningful.

The discourse community is constantly changing and emerging. For example, in the international academic and research community, whose working language is English, new research disciplines are born, and some existing research communities have become dominated by non-native speakers of English. Therefore, use of the English language in academic settings sometimes differs from the standard English taught in schools (Mauranen et al. 2010). The ESP framework, which focuses on professional discourse communities, helps to describe and identify the real and appropriate use, not the correct use, of the language. At the same time, the SFG viewpoint may bridge genres with very different discourse communities for lifelong learning.

The concept of genre in the ESP approach is becoming more important for English education in this rapidly changing world; it is a hard system that provides us with a more global perspective. The ESP genre approach equips learners with skills to analyze the genre text, even the genre they have not yet studied or that has not existed in the past. This chapter also presented how genre-based approaches can be used as a tool to improve a problematic situation in ESP classrooms through a soft systems methodology. When a problem situation is revealed based on a soft systems framework concerning how to understand the world of language, the ESP genre-based approach would offer helpful suggestions.

References

Bazerman, C. (1994). Systems of genres and the enactment of social intentions. In A. Freedman & P. Medway (Eds.), *Genre and the new rhetoric* (pp. 79–101). London: Taylor & Francis.

Bhatia, V. K. (2002). Applied genre analysis: A multi-perspective model. *Ibérica, 4*, 3–19.

Bhatia, V. K. (2004). *Worlds of written discourse*. London: Continuum.

Bloor, T., & Bloor, M. (2013). *The functional analysis of English* (3rd ed.). New York: Routledge.

Checkland, P., & Scholes, J. (1990). *Soft systems methodology in action*. Chichester: Wiley.

Cheng, A. (2008). Analyzing genre exemplars in preparation for writing: The case of an L2 graduate student in the ESP genre-based instructional framework of academic literacy. *Applied Linguistics, 29*(1), 50–71. https://doi.org/10.1093/applin/amm021.

Corder, S. P. (1973). *Introducing applied linguistics*. Harmondsworth: Penguin.

Dudley-Evans, T., & St. John, M. J. (1998). *Developments in English for specific purposes: A multi-disciplinary approach*. Cambridge: Cambridge University Press.

Hutchinson, T., & Waters, A. (1987). *English for specific purposes: A learning-centered approach*. Cambridge: Cambridge University Press.

Hyland, K. (2017). English in the disciplines: Arguments for specificity. *ESP Today, 5*(1), 5–23. https://doi.org/10.18485/esptoday.2017.5.1.1.

Iijima, Y., Watanabe, A., Maswana, S., Watari, H., Hori, S., Takahashi, S., Kanamaru, T., Tajino, A., & Terauchi, H. (2016). The current state and issues of academic English curricula in Japanese universities: Findings of a survey study. *Kyoto University Researches in Higher Education, 22*, 95–98.

Lado, R. (1964). *Language teaching: A scientific approach*. New York: McGraw-Hill.

Martin, J. R. (1999). Modelling context: A crooked path of progress in contextual linguistics. In M. Ghadessy (Ed.), *Text and context in functional linguistics* (pp. 25–61). Amsterdam: John Benjamins.

Martin, J. R. (2009). Genre and language learning: A social semiotic perspective. *Linguistics and Education, 20*(1), 10–21. https://doi.org/10.1016/j.linged.2009.01.003.

Mauranen, A., Hynninen, N., & Ranta, E. (2010). English as an academic lingua franca: The ELFA project. *English for Specific Purposes, 29*(3), 183–190. https://doi.org/10.1016/j.esp.2009.10.001.

Noguchi, J. (1997). Materials development for English for specific purposes: Applying genre analysis to EFL pedagogy. *English Teaching, 52*(3), 303–318.

Noguchi, J. (2003). Teaching ESP writing: OCHA in a CALL class. *Cybermedia Forum, 4*. Retrieved from http://www.cmc.osaka-u.ac.jp/publication/for-2003/40-45.html

Noguchi, J. (2009). The CALL classroom as a window to systemic literacy. *Cybermedia Forum, 10*, 17–21.

Noguchi, J. (2015). Secondary English education in Japan: An overview and a preview. In B. Spolsky & K. Sung (Eds.), *Secondary school English education in Asia* (pp. 33–46). Abingdon: Routledge.

Noguchi, J. (2017). Rikei ESP no ELF kyoyoudo syakudo no teian [A proposal of ELF tolerance scale for science ESP]. In Y. Nishina, N. Nakanishi, & M. Terui (Eds.), *Ouyou gengogaku no saizensen* [The frontline of applied linguistics] (pp. 1–10). Tokyo: Kinseido.

Noguchi, J., Miyama, A., & Okamoto, M. (2007). *Rikei eigo no raityingu* [English writing for science majors]. Tokyo: ALC Press.

Orlikowski, W., & Yates, J. (1994). Genre repertoire: The structuring of communicative practices in organizations. *Administrative Science Quarterly, 39*(4), 541–574. https://doi.org/10.2307/2393771.

Ozturk, I. (2007). The textual organisation of research article introductions in applied linguistics: Variability within a single discipline. *English for Specific Purposes, 26*(1), 25–38. https://doi.org/10.1016/j.esp.2005.12.003.

Swales, J. M. (1990). *Genre analysis: English in academic and research settings*. Cambridge: Cambridge University Press.

Swales, J. M. (2016). Reflections on the concept of discourse community. *ASp, 69*, 7–19. https://doi.org/10.4000/asp.4774.

Tajino, A., James, R., & Kijima, K. (2005). Beyond needs analysis: Soft systems methodology for meaningful collaboration in EAP course design. *Journal of English for Academic Purposes, 4*(1), 27–42. https://doi.org/10.1016/j.jeap.2004.01.001.

Tajino, A., & Suiko, M. (2005). Daigaku eigo kyouiku eno teigen: Karikyuramu kaihatsu eno shisutemu apuroochi [A proposal for university English language education: A systems approach to curriculum development]. In Y. Takefuta & M. Suiko (Eds.), *Korekara no daigaku eigo kyouiku* [The future of university English language education] (pp. 1–46). Tokyo: Iwanami shoten.

Tardy, C. M. (2003). A genre system view of the funding of academic research. *Written Communication, 20*(1), 7–36. https://doi.org/10.1177/0741088303253569.

Terauchi, H. (2001). *English for academic legal purposes in Japan*. Tokyo: Liber Press.

Terauchi, H., Fujita, R., & Naito, H. (Eds.). (2015). *Essential English for business meetings*. Tokyo: Asahi Press.

Terauchi, H., & Maswana, S. (2018). MAP Grammar and ESP: Beyond the classroom. In A. Tajino (Ed.), *A new approach to English pedagogical grammar: The order of meanings* (pp. 65–72). Abingdon: Routledge.

Terauchi, H., Yamauchi, H., Noguchi, J., & Sasajima, S. (Eds.). (2010). *ESP in the 21st century: ESP theory and application today*. Tokyo: Taishukan shoten.

Index

A. Tajino (ed.), *A Systems Approach to Language Pedagogy*, Translational Systems Sciences 17, https://doi.org/10.1007/978-981-13-6272-9

www.ingramcontent.com/pod-product-compliance
Ingram Content Group UK Ltd.
Pitfield, Milton Keynes, MK11 3LW, UK
UKHW021315130926
15127UKWH00002B/14
* 9 7 8 9 8 1 1 3 6 2 7 1 2 *